Praise for
The Dead Don't Dance

"An absorbing read for fans of faith-based fiction . . . [with] delightfully quirky characters . . . [who] are ingeniously imaginative creations."

—*Publishers Weekly*

"A strong and insightful first novel, written by a great new Christian voice in fiction. Brilliant."

—Davis Bunn, author of *The Great Divide* and *Elixir*

"*The Dead Don't Dance* combines writing that is full of emotion with a storyline that charts a haunting story of love and loss—and finding one's way back. Charles Martin quickly plunges readers into the story and takes them to a dark place. Then he draws them, like his protagonist Dylan, back to the surface, infusing them with renewed strength. Martin's writing is strong, honest, and memorable. He's an author to discover now—and then keep your eye on."

—Carol Fitzgerald, co-founder/president, Bookreporter.com

"*The Dead Don't Dance* affirms that even when the world drags us into its gloomy den, we can emerge battered but ever the victor holding life ecstatically by the tail. Charles Martin's wise and tender audacity lifts us out of our ordinary lives to help us see that the extraordinary is all around us, grander than our earliest visions, and filling our cups with the sweet nectar of life. You will fall in love with Martin's writing and believe in the goodness of humanity again. *The Dead Don't Dance* is the best book you will read this year! Bravo, Mr. Martin!"

—Patricia Hickman, award-winning author of *Fallen Angels* and *Nazareth's Song*

"*The Dead Don't Dance* is a poignant page-turner filled with loss, hope and redemption. With passages that shine as bright as the South Carolina moon, Charles Martin captures the heart of the land and its people. This novel is bound to linger with many readers and leave them wanting more."

—MICHAEL MORRIS, AUTHOR OF *A Place Called Wiregrass*

"This is the story of real person's *real* struggle with the uncertainties of faith, unadorned with miracles of the *deus ex machina* sort but full of the sort of miracles that attend every day life if you bother to notice. Charles Martin notices, and for that I commend him. He's unafraid of tackling the crucial questions—life, death, love, sacrifice."

—DUNCAN MURRELL, EDITOR AND WRITER

"Charles Martin writes with the passion and delicacy of a Louisiana sunrise—shades of shepherd's warning and a promise of thunderbolts before noon. Evoking a vivid picture of a young man's dance with dark and desperate moments of ordinary life, his story swirls like the river with drama, humour, and sense of hope. To many of us in England, the reality of America's deep south is as unknowable as the celestial kingdom of the orient in the days of sail, yet Charles has made it splendid and unforgettable. This is a lovely book that brims with heart and sensitivity, and most of all with a profound insight into what matters in our lives. I enjoyed it hugely."

—JOHN DYSON, WRITER, *Reader's Digest*

"*The Dead Don't Dance* is a gentle novel that reminds me of Robert Frost's famous poem, "For Once, Then, Something," in which "Water came to rebuke the too clear water": for Dylan Styles water means life, loss, and recovery. After a horrifying tragedy, he is adrift, searching for clarity, for an understanding of order that Frost's speaker never found. Charles Martin's debut novel is a moving, believable study of redemption pulled from the pieces of an all too-disordered world."

—BRIAN RAILSBACK, AUTHOR OF *The Darkest Clearing: A Novel* AND *Parallel Expeditions: Charles Darwin and the Art of John Steinbeck*

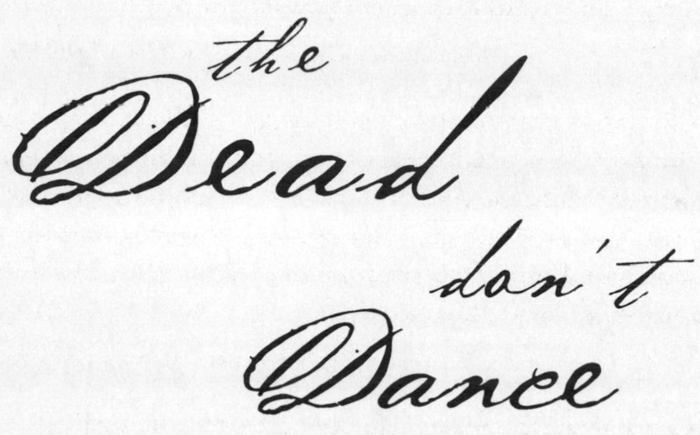

the Dead don't Dance

A Novel *of* Awakening

Charles Martin

Thomas Nelson
Since 1798

NASHVILLE DALLAS MEXICO CITY RIO DE JANEIRO BEIJING

For Christy

Thank you for throwing your blanket over me.
Without it, I would have grown cold.

Published in Nashville, Tennessee, by Thomas Nelson. Thomas Nelson is a trademark of Thomas Nelson, Inc.

Thomas Nelson, Inc., titles may be purchased in bulk for educational, business, fund-raising, or sales promotional use. For information, please e-mail SpecialMarkets@ThomasNelson.com.

Publisher's Note: This novel is a work of fiction. All characters, plot, and events are the product of the author's imagination. All characters are fictional, and any resemblance to persons living or dead is strictly coincidental.

Library of Congress Cataloging-in-Publication Data

Martin, Charles, 1969–
The dead don't dance: a novel of awakening / Charles Martin.
p. cm.
ISBN 978-0-7852-6181-0 (trade paper)
I. Title.
PS3613.A7778D43 2004
813'.6—dc22 2004000633

Printed in the United States of America
07 08 09 10 RRD 9 8 7 6 5

chapter one

LAST OCTOBER, AFTER THE SOYBEANS HAD PEAKED at four feet, the corn had spiraled to almost twice that, and the wisteria had shed its purple, a November breeze picked up, pushed out the summer heat, and woke Maggie. She rolled over, tapped me on the shoulder, and whispered, "Let's go swimming." It was two in the morning under a full moon, and I said, "Okay." The tap on the shoulder usually meant she knew something I didn't, and from the moment I'd met her, Maggie had known a lot that I didn't.

We rolled out, grabbed a couple of towels, and held hands down to the river, where Maggie took a swan dive into the South Carolina moonlight. I dropped the towels on the bank and waded in, letting the sandy bottom sift through my toes and the bream shoot between my knees. Leaning backward, I dunked my head, closed my eyes, then let the water roll down my neck as I stood in the waist-deep black river. Summer had run too long, as summers in Digger often do, and the breeze was a welcome comfort. We swam around in the dark water long enough to cool off, and Maggie spread a towel over the bleached white sand. Then she lay down and rested her head on my shoulder, and the moon fell behind the cypress canopy.

A while later, as we walked back to the house, her shoulder tucked under mine, Maggie knew that we had just made our son. I didn't know until four weeks later, when she came bouncing off the front porch and tackled me in the cornfield. Grinning, she shoved a little white stick in my face and pointed at the pink line.

Soon after, I started noticing the changes. They began in our second bedroom. Previously an office, it quickly became "the nursery." Maggie returned from the hardware store with two gallons of blue paint for the walls and one gallon of white for the trim and molding.

"What if she's a girl?" I asked.

"He's not," she said and handed me a paintbrush. So we spread some old sheets across the hardwood floors and started goofing off like Tom and Huck. By the end of the night, we were covered in blue paint and the walls were not, but at least we'd made a start.

The smell of paint drove us out of the house, so Maggie

and I shopped the Saturday morning garage sales. We found a used crib for sixty dollars, the top railing dented with teeth marks. Maggie ran her fingers along the dents like Helen Keller reading Braille. "It's perfect," she said.

We set up the crib in the corner of the nursery and made a Sunday afternoon drive to Charleston to the so-called "wholesale" baby outlet. I have never seen more baby stuff in one place in my entire life. And to be honest, before going there, I didn't know half of it existed. When we walked through the sliding glass doors, a recorded voice said, "Welcome to Baby World! If we don't have it, your baby doesn't need it!" The tone of voice gave me my first hint that I was in trouble.

Maggie grabbed two pushcarts, shoved one into my stomach, put on her game face, and said, "Come on!" Midway down the first aisle I was in way over my head. We bought diapers, wipes, pacifiers, a tether for the pacifiers, bottles, nipples for the bottles, liners for the bottles, bottles to hold the bottles and keep the bottles warm, cream for diaper rash, ointment for diaper rash, powder for diaper rash, a car seat, blankets, rattles, a changing table, little buckets to organize all the stuff we had just bought, a baby bag, extra ointment, cream, and powder just for the baby bag, booties, a little hat to keep his head warm, and little books. About halfway through the store I quit counting and just said, "Yes, ma'am."

To Maggie, every detail, no matter how small, had meaning. She must have said, "Oh, look at this," or "Isn't this cute?" a hundred times. When we reached the checkout counter, we were leaning on two ridiculously overflowing carts.

Some marketing genius had stacked the most expensive teddy bears right up in front. Only a blind man was without excuse. Maggie, wearing a baggy pair of denim overalls, batted her big brown eyes and tilted her head. In a deep, whispery, and all-too-seductive voice, she said, "Dylan, this bear's name is Huckleberry."

I just laughed. What else could I do?

I loaded up the truck and started to breathe easy, thinking the damage was over, but we didn't even make it out of the parking lot. Just next door to Baby World stood a maternity clothing store. Maggie, the possessed power shopper, stalked the racks and piled me high for over an hour. When I could no longer see above the heap of clothes in my arms, she led me to the changing room, where, for the first time in my life, a woman actually told me to come inside with her. Maggie shut the door, slid the latch, and pulled her hair up into a bouncy ponytail.

Over the next hour, my wife modeled each item of clothing while I marveled. The only light was a recessed forty-watt bulb above her head, but when she turned, lifted the ponytail off her neck, and whispered, "Unzip me," the light showered her five-eight frame like Tinkerbell's pixie dust. It fluttered off the blond, fuzzy hair on the back of her neck and the sweat on her top lip, over her square tan shoulders and down into the small of her back, along her thin hips and long runner's legs, and then finally swirled around the muscular shape of her calves.

God, I love my wife.

From shorts to shirts, pants, dresses, skirts, maternity bras, nursing bras, six-month underwear, nine-month underwear, jackets, and sweatshirts, the fashion show continued. As she tried on each item, Maggie stuffed the "eight-pound" pillow inside her waistband, put her hand on her hip, leaned forward on her toes, and looked at herself in the mirror. "Do you think this makes me look fat?"

"Maggs, no man in his right mind would ever answer that question."

"Dylan," she said, pointing her finger, "answer my question."

"You're beautiful."

"If you're lying to me," she said, raising her eyebrows and cocking her head, "you're on the couch."

"Yes, ma'am."

Leaving the dressing room, Maggie shone in full, glorious, pregnant-woman glow. Three hundred and twenty-seven dollars later, she was ready for any occasion.

Life had never been more vivid, more colorful, as if God had poured the other end of the rainbow all around us. Rows of cotton, corn, soybean, peanuts, and watermelon rose from the dirt and formed a quilted patchwork, sewing itself with kudzu along the sides of the old South Carolina highway. Ancient gnarled and sprawling oaks covered in moss and crawling with red bugs and history swayed in the breeze and stood like silent sentinels over the plowed rows. Naïve and unaware, we rumbled along the seams while Maggie placed my hand on her tummy and smiled.

At twelve weeks we went for the first ultrasound. Maggie was starting to get what she called a "pooch" and could not have been prouder. When the doctor walked in, Maggie was lying on the table with a fetal monitor Velcroed across her stomach, holding my hand. The doc switched on the ultrasound machine, squeezed some gel on her stomach, and started waving the wand over her tummy. When she heard the heartbeat for the first time, Maggie started crying. "Dylan," she whispered, "that's our son."

At sixteen weeks, the nurse confirmed Maggie's intuition. Maggie lay on the same table as the nurse searched her tummy with the ultrasound wand and then stopped when my son gave us a peek at his equipment. "Yep," the nurse said, "it's a boy. Right proud of himself too."

I hit my knees. At twenty-nine years old, I had looked inside my wife's tummy and seen our son. As big as life, with his heart beating, and wiggling around for all the world to see.

"Hey, Sport."

That started my conversations with Maggie's stomach. Every night from that day forward, I'd talk to my small and growing son. The three of us would lie in bed; I'd lift Maggie's shirt just over her tummy, press my lips next to the peach-fuzzy skin near her belly button, and we'd talk. Football, girls, school, farming, tractors, dogs, cornfields, friends, colors, anything I could think of. I just wanted my son to know the sound of my voice. After a few days, he started kicking my lips. Before I told him good night, I'd sing "Johnny Appleseed," "Daddy Loves His Sweet Little Boy," "The Itsy-Bitsy Spider," or "Jesus Loves Me."

Sometimes in the middle of the night, when the baby kicked or pushed his foot into the side of her stomach, Maggie would grab my hand and place it on her tummy. She never said a word, but I woke up feeling the warmth of my wife's stomach and the outline of my son's foot.

Toward the end of the first trimester, while rummaging through a yard sale, I found a rickety old rocking horse that needed a lot of glue, some elbow grease, and a few coats of white paint. I brought it home, set up my woodworking shop in the barn, and told Maggie to stay out. A week later, I brought it inside and set it next to the crib. Maggie looked at it, and the tears came forth in a flood. I think that was my first realization that new hormones had taken over my wife's body and mind.

Pretty soon the cravings hit. "Sweetheart." It was that whispery, seductive voice again. "I want some fresh, natural peanut butter and Häagen Dazs raspberry sorbet."

I never knew it would be so difficult to find freshly churned natural peanut butter at ten o'clock at night. When I got back to the house, Maggie was standing on the front porch, tapping her foot and wielding a spoon. As soon as I got the lids off, we plopped down in the middle of the den and started double dipping. When she'd polished off the sorbet, she said, "Now, how about a cheeseburger?"

At the end of her second trimester, she became pretty self-conscious. The least little thing really set her off. One morning, while studying her face in the mirror, she screamed, *"What is that? Dylan Styles, get in here!"*

Usually when Maggs calls me by both names, it means I've done something wrong. Left the toilet seat up or the toothpaste cap off, not taken the trash out, not killed every single roach and spider within two square miles of the house, or tried something sneaky and gotten caught. The tone in her voice told me I had just gotten caught.

I walked into the bathroom and found Maggs up on her toes, leaning over the sink and looking down at her chin, which was just a few inches from the mirror. Holding a magnifying glass, she said again, *"What is that?"*

I took the magnifying glass and smiled. Studying her chin, I saw a single black hair about a centimeter long protruding from it. "Well, Maggs, I'd say you're growing a beard." I know, I know, but I couldn't resist.

She shrieked and slapped me on the shoulder. "Get it off! Right now! Hurry!"

I reached into the drawer and pulled out a Swiss Army knife and slipped the little tweezers out of the side with my fingernail. "You know, Maggs, if this thing really takes off, we might be able to get you a job with the carnival."

"Dylan Styles," she said, pointing that crooked finger again, "if you want any loving for the rest of your life, you better quit right now." Maybe I was pushing it a little, but Maggs needed a perspective change. So I handed her the shaving cream and said, "Here, it's for sensitive skin."

Thirty seconds later, she had me balled up in the fetal position on the den floor, trying to pull out what few chest hairs I have. When she had adequately plucked me, she raised her fists like a boxer ready to start round two. "Dylan Styles, you better shut up and pull this evil thing off my chin."

Underneath the bathroom light, I pulled out the single rogue hair, placed it on her outstretched palm, and returned to the kitchen, laughing. Maggs spent the next hour poring over her face in the mirror.

Soon after, she lost sight of her toes. The baby was getting bigger and growing straight out like a basketball attached to a pole. Maggs stood helplessly in front of the mirror with an open nail polish bottle and wailed, "I'm fat! How can you love me when I look like this?" Then the tears came, so I did the only thing I could. I took her hand, sat her down on the couch, poured her a glass of ice water with a slice of orange, stretched out her legs, and painted her toenails.

When she was seven months along, I came in after dark one evening and heard her sloshing in the bathtub, talking to herself. I poked my head in and saw her holding a pink razor, trying to shave her legs. She had already cut her ankle. So I sat on the ledge, took the razor, held her heel, and shaved my wife's legs.

Somewhere around seven and a half months, I sat down to dinner—a dinner Maggie insisted on cooking—and found a package wrapped in brown paper. Untying the ribbon, I peeled open the paper to find a green T-shirt with *World's Greatest Dad* sewn on the front. I wore it every day for a week.

Getting heavier and feeling less mobile every day, Maggie nevertheless sewed the bumper for the crib and tied it in. The pattern featured stripes, baseballs, footballs, bats, and little freckle-faced boys. I bought a Pop Warner football and a Little League baseball glove and placed them inside the crib. On the floor beneath I clustered Matchbox cars, a miniature train set, and building blocks. When we were finished decorating, there was little room left for our son.

In the late afternoons of her last trimester, Maggie tired more easily, and I tried to convince her to take naps. Occasionally she'd give in. Two weeks before her due date, which was August 1, her legs, hands, and feet swelled, and her breasts became sore and tender. A week away, Braxton Hicks contractions set in, and the doctor told her to keep her feet up and get more rest.

"Try not to get too excited," he said. "This could take a while."

For some reason, and I'm not sure why, I had thought that as Maggie's tummy grew larger and she got more uncomfortable, she'd have less affection for me. I mean, physically. It only made sense. I had tried to prepare myself by blocking it out—*Don't even think about it*—but that time never came. Just three days before delivery, she tapped me on the shoulder. . . .

A week past her due date, the first real contraction hit. Maggie could tell the difference immediately. She was walking across the kitchen when she grabbed the countertop, bit her bottom lip, and closed her eyes. I grabbed The Bag and Huckleberry and met her at the truck. I was driving ninety miles an hour and honking at every car that got in my way when Maggs gently put her hand on my thigh and whispered, "Dylan, we have time."

I pulled into the maternity drop-off, and a nurse met us at

the car. When I found Maggie on the second floor, the doctor was checking her.

"Two centimeters," he said, taking off his latex gloves. "Go home; get some sleep, I'll see you tomorrow."

"See you tomorrow?" I said. "You can't send us home. My wife's having a baby."

The doctor smiled. "Yes, she is. But not today. Go get a nice dinner, then take her home. And"—he handed two pills to Maggie—"this will help take the edge off."

Helping Maggie into the truck, I said, "Your choice. Anywhere you want."

Maggie smiled, licked her lips, and pointed. A few minutes later we were sitting in the Burger King, where Maggie downed a Whopper with cheese, large fries, a cheeseburger, and a chocolate shake. I ate half a cheeseburger and two French fries.

That night Maggie slept in fits, and I slept not at all. I just lay there in the dark, watching her face and brushing her Audrey Hepburn hair out of her Bette Davis eyes.

At six o'clock Maggie bit her lip again, and I carried her to the truck.

"Four centimeters," the doctor said as he pulled the gown over Maggie's legs. "It's time to walk."

So we did. Every floor. Every hallway. Every sidewalk.

Walking through the orthopedic ward six hours later, Maggie grunted and grabbed the railing, and one of her knees buckled. I grabbed a wheelchair, punched the elevator button, and tapped my foot down to the second floor.

The doctor was on the phone at the nurses' station, but he hung up quickly when he saw her face. We stretched her out on the bed, strapped the fetal monitor over her stomach, and I cradled her head in my hands while the doctor listened.

"Okay, Maggie, get comfortable." Then he pulled out this long plastic thing and asked the nurse to cover it with gel. "I'm going to break your water and start you on Pitocin."

While I was thinking, *You're not sticking that thing in my wife,* Maggie sighed and gripped my hand so hard her knuckles turned white.

"That means two things: it will bring on your labor more quickly, and"—he paused as the fluid gushed out—"your contractions will hurt a bit more."

"That's okay," Maggie said, while the nurse swabbed her right arm with alcohol and inserted the IV needle.

Fifteen minutes later, the pain really started. I sat next to the bed, holding a wet towel on her forehead, and fought the growing knot in my stomach. By midnight Maggie was drenched in sweat and growing pale. I called the nurse and asked, "Can we do anything? Please!"

Within a few minutes the anesthesiologist came in and asked Maggie, "You about ready for some drugs?"

Without batting an eye, I said, "Yes, sir."

Maggie sat up and leaned as far forward as her stomach would let her. The doctor walked around behind her and inserted the epidural in the middle of her spine just as another contraction hit. Maggie moaned but didn't move an inch.

God, please take care of my wife.

Breathing heavily, Maggie lay back down and propped her knees up. After one more contraction, the epidural kicked in. Her shoulders relaxed, and she lost the feeling in her legs. At that moment, if I had had a million dollars, I would have given every penny to that man. I almost kissed him on the mouth.

The next two hours were better than the last two days together. We watched the monitor, the rise and fall of every contraction—"Oh, that was a good one," listened to the heartbeat, laughed, talked about names, and tried not to think about what was next. It was surreal to think our son would be there, in our arms, in a matter of moments. We held hands, I sang to her tummy, and we sat there in quiet most of the time.

About one-thirty, the lady next door had trouble with her delivery, and they had to wheel her off for an emergency C-section. I've never heard anybody scream like that in all my life. I didn't know what to think. I do know that it got to Maggie. She tried not to show it, but it did.

At two o'clock, the doctor checked her for the last time. "Ten centimeters, and 100 percent effaced. Okay, Maggie, you can start pushing. We'll have a birthday today."

Maggie was a champ. I was real proud of her. She pushed and I coached, "One-two-three . . . " I'd count and she'd crunch her chin to her stomach, eyes closed and with a death grip on my hand, and push.

That was two days and ten lifetimes ago.

chapter two

THE SMALL, PRIVATE ROOM THEY PUT US IN WAS dark, overlooked the parking lot, and sat at one end of a long, quiet hallway. The only lights in the room shone from the machines connected to Maggie, and the only noise was her heart-rate monitor and occasionally the janitor shuffling down the hall, rolling a bucket that smelled of Pine Sol over urine. Somebody had shoved Maggie's bed against the far wall, so I rolled her over next to the window, where she could feel the moonlight. By rolling the bed, I unplugged all the monitors, setting off several alarms at the nurses' station.

A pale-faced nurse slid through the doorway and into the room. She stopped short when she saw me sitting next to the bed, quietly holding Maggs's hand. She almost said something but changed her mind and went to work instead, repairing what I'd torn apart. Before she left, she grabbed a blanket from the closet, put it over my shoulders, and asked, "You want some coffee, honey?" I shook my head and she patted me on the shoulder.

Maggie has lain there "sleeping," unconscious, ever since the delivery. I wiped her arms and cheeks with a warm, damp rag and then felt her toes. They were cold, so I looked through our bag, found a pair of socks that I gently slid over her heels, and put another blanket over her feet. After pulling the sheets up around her shoulders, I sat down next to the bed and tucked her hair behind her ears, where I still felt some dried blood. For the third time, I ran a towel under some warm water and wiped her face, arms, and neck.

I don't remember my arms being sore afterwards, but I do remember it took the nurse three tries before she found my vein. Maggie needed a lot of blood pretty quick, so I gave one more pint than they normally would allow. The nurse knew Maggie needed it, so when I grabbed the needle and told her to keep going, she looked at me over the top of her glasses, opened another Coca-Cola for me, and kept drawing. I walked back to the delivery room with both pits of my elbows taped up, sat next to the bed, and watched my blood drip into my wife.

While I was sitting in the quiet beneath the moon, a wrinkle appeared on Maggie's forehead between her eyebrows—her trademark expression. A sure sign that she was determined to figure something out. I placed my palm on her forehead and held it there for a few seconds while the wrinkle melted away and her breathing slowed.

"Maggs?"

I slid my hand under hers and thought how her callused fingers seemed so out of place on someone so beautiful. Under the rhythm and short blips of the heart-rate monitor, I watched her heart beat, listened to her short, quick breaths, and waited for her big brown eyes to open and look at me.

They did not.

I stared out the window over the parking lot, but there wasn't much to look at. South Carolina is one of the more beautiful places on God's earth—especially where the wisteria crawls out of the weeds that can't choke it—but the parking lot of Digger Community Hospital is not. I turned back to Maggie and remembered the river, the way the light followed Maggie's eyes, her smile, her back, and how the water had dripped off her skin and puddled on her stomach. "Maggs," I said, "let's go swimming."

chapter three

THE DAYS TURNED INTO NIGHTS AND BACK INTO days, and I became afraid to blink, thinking I'd miss the opening of her eyes. During that time, I'm pretty sure other people came in and out of the room, but I never saw them. I think I remember Amos putting his hand on my shoulder and telling me, "Don't worry, I'll take care of the farm." And somewhere during one of the nights, I think I remember smelling the lingering aroma of Bryce's beer breath, but for seven days my entire world consisted of Maggie and me. Anything outside that picture never came into focus. The periphery of my life had blurred.

On the afternoon of the seventh day, the doctor took me

out into the hall and gave me his prognosis. Consternation was painted across his face, and it was clear this wasn't easy for him, no matter how much practice he must have had at delivering bad news. "Dylan, I'll give it to you straight," he said.

The seconds melted into days.

"Maggie's out of what we call the hopeful window. The longer she stays in this vegetative state, the more involuntary muscle responses she'll begin to have. Unfortunately, these muscle responses are from spinal activity, not brain activity. Within the next few weeks, she's got a 50 percent chance of waking up. The following month, it drops in half. Following that . . . " He shook his head. "Of course, this is all just statistics; miracles can happen. But they don't happen often."

Later that afternoon, the hospital executive responsible for accounts receivable stopped in for a visit. "Mr. Styles, I'm Mr. Thentwhistle. Jason Thentwhistle." He stepped into the room and extended his hand.

I immediately didn't like him.

"Yes, well, I think we should talk about your financial arrangements."

I turned my head slightly and narrowed my eyes.

"Coma patients often require long-term hospital care. . . ."

That was all I needed to hear. I hit him as hard as I could—maybe as hard as I've ever hit anybody. When I looked down, he was crumpled on the floor, his glasses were broken in three pieces, his nose was twisted sideways and smashed into his face, and blood was pouring out of his nostrils. I picked up his heels and dragged him out into the hallway because I didn't want him bleeding on Maggie's floor.

"D.S., YOU BEEN HERE SINCE YOU LEFT THE HOSPITAL?"

I opened my eyes, remembered Thentwhistle, and looked around. The head hovering over me was familiar.

"Dylan?" A big, meaty black hand gently slapped me twice in the face.

That was definitely familiar. "Amos?"

Slapping my cheek again, he said, "Hey, pal? You in there?"

I must have moaned, because Amos grabbed me by the shoulders and shook me.

"Yeah, yeah," I said, swatting at his hands, "I'm in here." My head was killing me, and the world was spinning way too fast. Amos's hands stopped the spinning but not the pain.

"D.S.?" Amos brought his face closer to mine. "Have you been here since you left the hospital?" He was still out of focus.

"I don't know. When did I leave the hospital?"

"Tuesday," he said, shading my face with his hat.

I swatted at it because it looked like a buzzard. "What day is today?" I asked, still swatting.

"Thursday." Amos crinkled his nose and waved his hand. "And it's a good thing it rained, too." Waving the air with his hat, Amos said, "D.S., you stink bad. Whatchoo been doing out here?"

I reached for the tractor, pulled at the tire rod, which my

grandfather had bent twenty-one years ago pulling stumps, and tried to pull myself up. I could not. I thought for a minute, but I couldn't remember. "Thursday?"

I pulled my knees up and scratched my neck and the four itchy bumps on my ankles under my jeans.

Amos looked doubtful.

I guessed again, "Tuesday?" The rush of blood to my head caused my head to bob, rock, and crash into the cornstalk that was growing up out of an anthill.

Amos caught my head. "Here, you better sit still. I think you been sitting in the sun a little too long. How long you been out here?"

Ordinarily Amos's English is pretty good. He only drops into the South Carolina farm-boy dialect when talking with me. After twenty-five years of friendship, we had developed our own language. People say marriage works the same way.

"I need to get to the hospital," I muttered.

"Hold on a minute, Mr. Cornfield. She's not going anywhere." Amos tapped the plastic cover on the tractor's fuel gauge. "And neither is this old tractor. We got to get you cleaned up. If it weren't for Blue, I'd still be driving around looking for you."

Blue is a blue heeler and the most intelligent dog I've ever known. He's seven years old and is better known as the "outdoor dog" that sleeps at the foot of our bed.

I rubbed my eyes and tried to focus. No improvement. Amos was about to brush my shirt off with his hand, but he took a second look and thought better of it.

"My truck's low on gas. Where's your car?" I said. "Can you take me there?"

Seeing me return to life, Blue hopped off the tractor, licked my face, and then sat between my legs and rested his head on my thigh.

"Yes, I can," Amos said, articulating every letter. "But no, I will not. I'm taking you to work."

Amos wasn't making a lot of sense.

"Work?" I looked around. "Amos, I was working until . . . well, until you showed up." I shoved Blue out of the way. When he gets excited, he drools a good bit. "Go on, Blue. Quit it."

Blue ignored me. Instead he rolled over like a dead bug, turned his head to one side, hung out his tongue, and propped his paws in the air.

"D.S." Amos ran his fingers around inside his deputy's belt. "Don't start with me. I ain't in the mood." He put his hat back on, hefted his holster a bit. Then he raised his voice. "I've been looking for you all morning in every corner of every pasture. All thirty-five hundred acres." Amos waved his hands as if he were on stage or telling a fish story. He could get animated when he wanted to. "Then a few minutes ago, I'm driving past this field, and I see this rusty old thing your grandfather called a tractor sitting driverless and parked out here at the intersection of Nowhere and No Place Else. Except one thing sticks out and grabs my attention."

Amos reached over and began scratching Blue between the ears. "Ol' Blue here is sitting at attention on top of your tractor like he's trying to be seen. So I turn the car around and think to myself, *That'd be just like that old fool to go through one week of hell and then walk out of the hospital, only to end up out here and act like he's farming.*

He reached over, picked up a handful of sand, and slung it into the corn. "Dylan Styles"—he looked down a long row of corn that was planted in more of an arc than a straight line—"you're an idiot. Even with all your education. You can just about strap an alphabet behind your name, but I'm your friend and I'll tell it to you straight: You're a sorry farmer and a danged idiot."

Amos is smart. Don't let the deputy's badge fool you. He took this job because he wanted it, not because he couldn't find anything else. Amos takes nothing from nobody—except me. He's big, articulate, black as black comes, and my oldest friend. He's a year older than I am and was a year ahead in school. In my junior year of high school, we were the two starting running backs. They called us Ebony and Ivory, for obvious reasons.

Amos was always faster, always stronger, and he never once let anybody pile on me. I've seen him take two linebackers and shove them back into the free safety on more than one occasion. The only reason I scored my first touchdown was because he carried me. I got the ball, grabbed his jersey, shut my eyes, and he dragged me eight yards to glory, where I saw the goal line pass under my feet. When I looked up and saw the crowd screaming, Amos was standing off to the side alone, letting me take the credit and soak it all in.

Later that year, the Gamecocks gave him a scholarship. He lettered four years and was an all-American three. From day one he studied criminal justice and learned everything about it that he could. Right after graduation, Amos applied with Colleton County and came home. He's worn that badge ever since. Last year they sewed sergeant's stripes to his shirtsleeves.

I rubbed my eyes and steadied my head between my hands. The world was spinning again, and the ants at my feet weren't helping my perspective any.

"Is there somebody else around here I can talk to?" My voice was pretty much gone, and all I could muster was a smoker's whisper. "Amos, have you had your coffee this morning? Because I'm tired and I don't quite remember how I got here, but I think you're riding me. And if you're riding me, that's a pretty good sign that you have not had your coffee."

Amos was really animated now. "I've been traipsing around this piece of dirt you two call home all morning. Thanks to you and your disappearing stunt, I ain't had the pleasure of my morning cup of coffee. What is it with you Styleses and this piece of dirt? If you're gonna choose someplace to catch up on a week with no sleep, you could have picked a better place than the middle of a cornfield. In the last hour I have ruined my pants, scuffed my boots, torn my shirt, and there is no telling how much pig crap I've got smeared on me right now. Why do you keep that old pig?"

"Who? Pinky?"

"Well, of course, Pinky. Who else makes all this stuff?" Amos pointed at his boots. "In all my life, I have never seen a pig crap the way she can. You ought to enter her in a contest. It's everywhere. What do you feed that thing?"

"Amos . . . A-Amos." I stuttered and shivered. "It's got to be close to ninety, and I feel like crap. I'm itching everywhere, and I've got a headache. All I want to do is see my wife. Please, just help get me back to my house."

Amos knew when to quit.

"Come on, D.S. Inside." He picked me up and hooked his shoulder under mine. "Ivory, did I already tell you that you need a shower?"

"Yeah, I heard you the first time."

We crashed through the corn and limped toward the house.

Pulling me along, Amos asked, "What's the last thing you remember?"

"Well," I said, aiming my toes toward the porch, "I was sitting with Maggs when this suit from the hospital poked his pointy head through the door and asked me how I intend to pay my bills. He started to say something about how expensive it was to keep Maggie there. So I did what any husband would have done. I turned around and clocked the pointy-headed son of a—"

Amos held up his hands. "I get the picture."

"I dragged him out in the hall, and Maggie's nurses started looking him over. But to be honest, they didn't seem real eager to start tending to him." I glanced at the cut on the knuckle of my right hand. It was still puffy and stiff, so I guessed I had hit him pretty hard. "I don't remember too much after that."

Amos carried me a few more steps to the house. Without looking at me, he said, "An executive from the hospital named Jason Thentwhistle, with two loose teeth, a broken nose, new pair of glasses, and one very black and swollen eye, came to the station to file a complaint against one Dylan Styles. Said he wanted to press charges."

Amos kept his eyes aimed on the back door, but a smile cracked his face. "I told him that I was really sorry to hear about his altercation, but without a witness we really couldn't do anything." He turned and held me up by my shoulders. "D.S., you can't go around hitting the very people who are taking care of your wife."

"But Amos, he wasn't taking care of my wife. He was being an—"

Amos held up his hand again. "You gonna let me finish?"

"I should have hit him harder. I was trying to break his jaw."

"I didn't hear that." Amos wrapped his arm tight about my waist, and we took a few more steps.

I stopped Amos and tried to look him in the eyes. "Amos, is Maggs okay?"

Amos shook his head side to side. "No real change. Physically, she seems to be healing. No more bleeding."

"I'd drive myself, but I might have to push my truck to the station, so can you please just take me there without a bunch of conversation?" I asked again.

Amos dug his shoulder further under mine, dragged me closer to the back porch, and said, "After your interview." He grunted and hoisted me up onto the steps.

"Interview?" I sat down on the back steps and scratched my head. "What interview?"

Catching his breath, Amos wiped his brow, straightened

his shirt, gave his gun belt another two-handed law enforcement lift, and said, "Mr. Winter. Digger Junior College. If you can survive the interview, you'll be teaching English 202: Research and Writing."

It took a minute, but the word *teaching* finally registered. "Amos, what are you talking about? Speak English."

"I am speaking English, Dr. Styles. And in about two hours, you'll be speaking it with Mr. Winter about the class you're going to teach." He smiled and took off his sunglasses.

Amos only calls me doctor on rare occasions. I finished my doctorate a few years back, but because I quit teaching after graduate school, few knew it, and fewer still called me by the title. Although I was proud of my accomplishment, I had little reason to make sure everybody knew about it. My corn didn't care what kind of education I'd had. It sure didn't help me drive that tractor any straighter.

"One thing at a time," I said, shaking my head. "Will you or will you not take me to see my wife?"

"D.S., have you been listening to me?" Amos raised his eyebrows and looked at me. "Dr. Dylan Styles Jr. is soon to be an adjunct professor at Digger Junior College, teaching English 202: Research and Writing. And"—Amos looked at his watch—"Mr. Winter is expecting you in his office in an hour and fifty-seven minutes."

He unfolded a slip of paper from his shirt pocket and handed it to me. "Don't fight me on this. They need a teacher, and for a lot of reasons, you need this."

"Name one," I said.

Amos wiped the sweat off his brow with a white handkerchief. "Taxes, to begin with. Followed by your loan payment. Both of which are coming due at the end of the month, and the chances of you actually producing anything but a loss on this piece of dirt are slim to none. Teaching is your insurance policy, and right now you need one."

"Amos, I've got a job." I waved my arms out in front of me. "Right here. Right out there. All of this is my job." I pointed to the fields surrounding the house. "And how do you know when my taxes and loan payments are due?"

Amos dropped his head and pointed to the soil. "D.S., you and I grew up right here, playing ball on this field. You busted my lip right over there, and"—he pointed to his house—"two hundred yards across that field and over that dirt road is my house and my dirt. So I know about dirt. I don't want to see you and Maggie lose it." He spat. "Heck, I don't want to lose it. So don't fight me. Put your education to work, listen to what I'm saying, and get in the shower while you can still afford to pay for hot water."

"How's Maggie?" I asked again.

"She'll live. She's stable. At least physically. Mentally . . . I don't know. That's His call." Amos's eyes shot skyward.

"Amos," I said, as the world came slowly into focus, "tell me about this whole teaching thing."

During graduate school in Virginia, I had taught seven classes as an adjunct at two different universities to help us pay the bills, and, I hoped, secure myself a job when I got out. But after I defended my dissertation and graduated, nobody would hire me. I got a feeling it wasn't my credentials as much as it was my background. A farm-boy-turned-teacher, at least this one anyway, was not something they wanted on their faculties.

Unable to get a job in the field that I had chosen, I hunkered down in the field that I owned. I was not my grandfather, Papa Styles, and nobody was knocking on my door, asking for advice, but for three years Maggie and I had been making ends meet out here in this dirt. Amos knew this. He also knew that having been snubbed once, I wasn't too eager to go crawling back in there—especially at a community college as an adjunct. I had moved on.

"Digs, room one, English 202. You've taught it before."

"But Amos, why? Between what's in the ground, what will be, the pine straw lease, and the two leased pastures, we'll make it. My place is with Maggie, not nurse-maiding a bunch of dropouts who couldn't get into a real school."

"D.S., don't make me look foolish. Not after I went to bat for you. And don't thumb your nose at those kids. They're not the only ones who couldn't get into a 'real school.'" Amos had a brutal way of being honest. He also had a real gentle way of making me eat my pride. "And this isn't my doing. It's Maggie's."

"Maggie's?"

"She saw an ad in the paper that Digs was hiring adjuncts. So she called Mr. Winter a month or so ago and inquired about it. She was going to talk with you after the baby was born."

"Yeah, well . . . " I felt numb. "She didn't get a chance."

"And as for your tax records and loan payment, Shireen at the station pulled your file and ran a credit check for me.

Which, by the way, is real good. I'm just trying to help you keep it that way."

I shook my head and suppressed a wave of nausea. "Amos, if I could throw you in general quarters with all your law-abiding buddies . . . "

"D.S, how long are you going to fight me on this? You know good and well that every one of my jailbird buddies deserves to be there. They know it too."

Amos was right. He pegged it pretty square on the head. Everybody knew he was fair, even the folks he arrested. Amos was who you wanted to catch you if you ever broke the law. You'd get what you deserved, but he'd be fair about it. Amos enforced the law. He didn't rub it in your face.

"Besides," he whispered, "it's Maggie's wish."

Somewhere in the last three days I had rolled in pig excrement. Now it was smeared on Amos's hands and shirt. He brushed himself off, making it worse, paused, and then looked right at me.

"D.S., here I am. My uniform is now covered in pig crap, and I've got a radio, loaded gun, big stick, and this badge. If I could trade places with you, I would. But since I can't, I'm here to ask you, please go inside, shower twice, shave, and get dressed. Because deep down, you know it's best for you." He scanned the cornfield. "It's best for your wife, and it's best for this place."

Sometimes I wished Amos weren't so honest.

"Who's staying with her?" I asked.

"I was until a little bit ago. The nurse is now. She's a sweet girl. Pastor's daughter. She'll take good care of her. D.S., there's nothing you can do for Maggie. That's God's deal. I don't understand it and I don't like it, but there is nothing you or I can do for her. Right now what we need to worry about is you and making sure that the mailbox out front goes right on saying 'Styles.'

"And for that to happen, you got to teach. This is what it comes down to. And don't give me any of that stuff about not teaching again." Amos pointed his finger at me and poked me in the chest. "You are a teacher. Why do you think God gave you Nanny to begin with? You think that was just some big cosmic mistake?" He spat again. "You think she just shared all that with you so you could keep it bottled up and to your lonesome?"

Amos put one foot up on the steps and rested his elbow on his knee. "Not likely. You may like farming, but you're no Papa, at least not yet. You can hide out here if you want to, but it'd be a sorry shame. Now are you gonna get cleaned up, or do I have to hose you down myself?"

I opened the screen door and stumbled into the house, mumbling, "Dang you, Amos . . . "

"Hey, I'm just honoring my promise to your wife. You married her. Not me. If you want to complain"—Amos pointed toward the hospital—"complain to her."

"I would if I could get there."

"After your little chat with Mr. Winter." Amos smiled, grumbled something else to himself, and then walked to the kitchen and began washing out the percolator.

chapter four

I SUPPOSE YOU COULD CALL ME A LATE-LIFE MIRACLE. At least I'm told my parents thought so, because my dad was forty-two and my mom forty when she gave birth to me. I have sweet memories, but not many because Dad died in a car accident pretty close to my fifth birthday and Mom suffered a stroke strolling down the cereal aisle of the grocery store six months later.

My grandparents took me in after their daughter's funeral and raised me until I turned eighteen and headed off to college. Despite the absence of my parents, love lived in our house. Papa and Nanny saw to that. They poured their love into three things: each other, me, and this house.

When my grandfather built our two-bedroom brick farmhouse more than sixty years ago, he pieced the floors out of twelve-inch-wide magnolia planks and dovetailed them together without using nails. They were strong, creaky, marred with an occasional deep groove, and in the den where my grandparents danced in their socks to the big band music of Lawrence Welk, polished to a mirror shine.

Papa covered the walls in eight-inch cypress plank, the ceilings in four-inch tongue-and-groove oak, and the roof in corrugated tin. I have no memory of the house ever being any other color but white with green trim and shutters. Why? Because that's the way Nanny liked it, and Papa never objected.

One summer, standing on a ladder and painting the underside of a soffit for the umpteenth time, he looked down and said with a smile, "Never argue with a woman about her house. Remember that. It's hers, not yours." He waved his paintbrush toward the kitchen and whispered, "I may have built it, but in truth, we're just lucky she lets us sleep here."

Whenever I think of Nanny's home, I remember it glistening white and green under a fresh coat of springtime paint, landscaped with whatever was blooming, and cool from the whispering breeze ushering through the front and back doors, which she propped open with two retired irons.

Papa had several eccentricities. The top three were overalls, pocketknives, and Rice Krispies. The first two fit most farmers, but the third did not. He'd pull a saucepan from the cupboard, fill it to the brim with cereal, cover it in peaches, douse it with half a pint of cream, and polish off an entire box in one sitting. Not surprisingly, the first few words I learned to read were *snap, crackle,* and *pop.*

Born poor country folk, Nanny and Papa didn't make it too far in school. Born before the Depression and raised when a dollar was worth one, they were too busy working to pursue higher education. But please don't think they were uneducated. Both were studious, just in a nonacademic way. Papa studied farming, and he was good at it. For the sixty years that he turned this earth, it stayed green more often than not. His reputation spread, and people drove for miles just to rub shoulders at the hardware store and ask his opinion in between the feed and seed.

While Papa plowed, Nanny cooked and sewed. And late at night, after she had untied her apron and hung it over the back screen door, she read. We owned a TV, but if given my choice, I preferred Nanny's voice. After Walter Cronkite told us everything was all right with the world, Papa clicked the television off and Nanny opened her book.

After school, I'd spot Papa on the tractor, run across the back pasture, climb into his lap, and listen to him talk about the need for terraced drainage, the sight of early-morning sunshine, the smell of an afternoon rain, the taste of sweet corn, and Nanny. When our necks were caked in dust and burnt red from a low-hanging sun, Papa and I would lift our noses and follow the smell of Nanny's cooking back to the house like two hounds on a scent.

One morning when I was about twelve, I was standing in the bathroom, getting ready for school, listening to a loud rock 'n' roll station hosted by an obnoxious DJ that all my friends listened to.

Papa walked in with a raised brow, turned down the volume, and said, "Son, I rarely tell you what to do, but today I am. You can listen to this"—he pointed to the radio, which, thanks to his tuning, was now spewing country music—"or this." He turned the dial, and hymns from the local gospel station filled the air.

It was one of the best things my grandfather ever did for me. Listen to Willie singing "My Heroes Have Always Been Cowboys," and you'll understand what I mean. About the same time I was flipping through the three channels we received on our dusty Zenith and came across a show called *The Dukes of Hazzard.* I heard the same voices from the radio singing their theme song and put two and two together.

Before long, I planned my week by what I was doing at eight o'clock on Friday nights. Nanny and Papa watched with me because *Dallas* followed, and they had to know who had shot J.R. But from eight to nine, the TV was mine. I fell in love with Bo and Luke Duke and amused myself by mimicking everything they did. With Papa's help I bought a guitar, learned to play "Mommas, Don't Let Your Babies Grow Up to Be Cowboys," and began wearing boots. All the time.

Papa worked hard six days a week, but like most Bible-Belters, never on Sundays. Sundays were reserved solely for the Lord, Nanny, and me. We'd spend the morning in church, then gorge ourselves on Nanny's fried chicken or pork chops. After a lazy afternoon nap we would walk down to the river, where we would feed hooked earthworms to the bream or listen to the wood ducks sing through the air just after dark.

Papa was never real vocal about his faith, but for some reason, he loved putting up church steeples. In the fifteen years I lived with Nanny and Papa, I saw him organize twelve steeple-raising parties for nearby churches. Pastors from all around would call and ask his help, and as far as I know he never told one no. The denomination of the church mattered little, but the height of the steeple did. The taller, the better. The closest stands a mile from our house, atop Pastor John Lovett's church—a rowdy AME where the sign out front reads, "Pentecost was not a onetime event."

After attending my fourth or fifth raising, I asked him, "Papa, why steeples?"

He smiled, pulled out his pocketknife, began scraping it under each fingernail, and looked out over the pasture. "Some people need pointing in the right direction," he said. "Myself included."

Nanny grew sick my junior year of college. When we knew it was serious, I broke every posted speed limit on the drive home. I bounded up the back steps just in time to hear Papa hit his knees and say, "Lord, I'm begging You. Please give me one more day with this woman."

After sixty-two years, the music stopped, the lights dimmed, and their dance atop the magnolia planks ended. The loneliness broke Papa, and he followed three weeks later. The doctor said his heart simply quit working, but there's no medical terminology for a broken heart. Papa just died. That's all.

Growing up, I had always wanted to travel out west. When Nanny and Papa died, I found my excuse, so I dropped out of school and drove toward the setting sun. I had grown up watching Westerns with Papa, so all that wide-open space held some attraction. Besides, that's where the Rockies were. I spent weeks driving through mountain after mountain. Saw the Grand Canyon; even sank my toes in the Pacific Ocean. I'm pretty low maintenance, so I ate a lot of peanut butter and slept in the back of the truck with Blue. We kept each other warm.

When I got to New Mexico, I came pretty close to running out of money, so we loaded up and came home. When I finally made it back to Digger, almost a year after Papa's death, the vines and weeds had almost covered the house, a few shutters had blown off, the paint had flaked, and a fence post or two had fallen, pulling the barbed wire with it. But the well water still tasted sweet, the house was dry, and Nanny's breeze blew cool even on stagnant August afternoons. Papa knew what he was doing when he built the place.

I spent six weeks cleaning, painting, sanding floors, repairing the plumbing, oiling doorknobs and hinges, and fixing fence posts and barbed wire. I also spent a lot of time on the tractor, just trying to get it working again. The sound reminded me of Papa, but it had sat up too long and a few of the hoses had rotted. I drained the fluids and changed the plugs, distributor, and hoses. After some careful cussing and a few phone calls to Amos, she cranked right up.

On a trip to the hardware store, I bumped into Maggie. We had known each other in high school but never dated. In hindsight, that was really dumb. But I was too busy hunting, fishing, or playing football. At any rate, I wasn't dating, or studying, for that matter. That came later.

Papa once told me that before he met Nanny, his heart always felt funny. Like a jigsaw puzzle with about two-thirds of the pieces missing. When I met Maggie, I realized what he was talking about. Most guys talk about their wives' figures, and yes, mine has one, but it was her Audrey Hepburn hair and Bette Davis eyes that stopped me.

After two or three more "accidental" hardware meetings, I got my nerve up and asked her out, and it didn't take long. If I had had any guts, I would have proposed after two weeks, but I needed six months to work up the courage. I bought a golden band, we married, and somewhere on the beach at Jekyll Island beneath the stars, she persuaded me to finish my degree.

I enrolled and started night school at the South Carolina satellite campus in Walterboro. If Nanny and Papa's deaths had taken the wind out of my sails, then Maggie helped me hoist anchor, raise the sails, and steady the rudder.

For most of my life, and thanks in large part to Nanny's prodding, the only thing I was any good at was writing. When I enrolled as a freshman at the University of South Carolina, I registered in the English program and started down the track toward a creative writing degree. It's what I was good at, or so I thought.

During my first three years of college, I wrote some stories and sent them off to all the magazines you're supposed to send stuff to if you're a writer. *The Saturday Evening Post. The New Yorker.* I've still got a folder of all my rejections. Once my folder got pretty full, I quit sending my stories.

But Maggie continued to believe in me. One day while I was finishing my senior year at the satellite, she printed a few of my pieces and sent them to Virginia along with an application for graduate school. For some reason, they accepted me into their master's program and even said they'd pay for my classes and books. I don't know if that's because I wrote well or because I couldn't afford it, but either way, they paid for it.

So Maggie and I charted a new course, and I returned to school. It was not long after, though, that my grand illusions of plumbing the deeper meanings in storytelling, fired by Nanny's love of reading, were shattered. Graduate school was no lighthouse. If it weren't for Victor Graves, a gnarly old professor who laughed like a rum-drunk sailor, I'd have never made it. Vic took me under his wing and helped me navigate.

After I wrote my thesis, Vic encouraged me to apply to the doctoral program. With little hope but no other direction, I did. Three weeks later I received my acceptance letter, which Maggie framed and hung above my desk. I couldn't believe it. *Me? A doctoral student? You've got to be kidding. I'm the guy who didn't study in high school.* But the letter said they wanted me, and once again they said they'd pay for it—which was nice, because without the financial backing, I wasn't going. They gave me a fellowship, and I got to work.

Thanks to Vic, lightbulbs began clicking on like a Fourth

of July celebration, and it was there that I really discovered just how smart Nanny really was.

It wasn't easy, but we made it. We lived in an upstairs, one-room apartment, and while Maggie waited tables, I worked the morning preload at UPS. I woke early and she worked late, so for about two years, we didn't see each other much.

Despite Vic's best encouragement, I quickly found that my grandmother had forgotten more stories than most experts would read in a lifetime. And not only did she understand them better, but she had a knack at helping others do the same. Just because you know something, or think you do, doesn't mean you can teach it.

Beneath the sly, academic façade, and hidden behind their glossy degrees, most of my teachers were just frustrated hacks who couldn't write a great story if their lives depended on it. Out of the void of their own missing talent, they found a sick joy in tearing others' apart. Maybe I could do better, I hoped. Maybe I could teach Nanny's wonder through Papa's pocket-knife practicality and shield the students from the poisonous cynicism around me.

I accepted an adjunct position at my university, teaching freshman and sophomore English. I enjoyed the classroom and the interaction with the students and even helped click on a few lightbulbs myself. All I wanted to do was introduce other people to the power and wonder of language. But all the covert backstabbing and infighting along the tortuous path to tenure drove me to the brink of drinking. If the pen is mightier than the sword, it's also a good bit bloodier.

Instead of finding Nanny's fireside wonder shared amid my colleagues, I found ivory-tower experts ripe with stoic discontent and bent on tearing down castles they could never rebuild, simply for the sake of saying something.

While I struggled to help kids look for universal truths and themes that great stories revealed in unforgettable ways—themes like love, humor, hope, and forgiveness—and maybe encourage them to transpose those through their fingers and onto paper, my colleagues stood on soapboxes with raised brows and asked, "Maybe, but what is *hidden?*" They reminded me of pharmacists who crushed their pills into powder and studied the contents under a microscope while never bothering to swallow the medicine.

Caught in a postmodern pinball machine, I became pretty well disillusioned. I never voiced it to Maggie, but she could read me. She knew. After graduation, she gave me a good talking to. So I swallowed my disgust and filled out twenty applications for schools scattered about the South. I licked the stamps, dropped them in the box, and hoped the grass grew greener in some other pasture. When the last "we're-sorry-to-inform-you-letter" arrived from my own hometown junior college, we quit our jobs, packed up my books, and came back here.

Virginia is pretty, but it can't hold a candle to South Carolina. We hadn't even walked in the front door when I realized that my love for farming had much deeper roots than the shallow shoots I'd put down in academia. As I looked out over those fields where I had passed many a happy day, I knew I'd miss the students, the lively exchange of ideas, and the sight of lightbulbs turning on, but little else. I was glad to be home.

The well water smelled like eggs, the faucets dripped like Chinese water torture, and both toilets ran constantly, but Maggie never complained. She loved the narrow, coal-burning fireplace, the front and back porches, and the two swinging screen doors that slammed too loudly and squeaked in spite of oil. But her two favorite pleasures were the tin roof beneath a gentle rain and Nanny's breeze.

I had never measured it, but including the porches, the house probably covered twelve hundred square feet. But it was ours, and for sixty-two years, love had lived here.

Like riding a bicycle after the training wheels had been removed, I hopped on the tractor, sniffed the air for any hint of rain, and cried like a baby all the way to the river. Papa had taught me well, and once away from the classroom cobwebs and textbook chains, I remembered how to farm. In our first year, I sold the pine straw from beneath our fifteen hundred acres of planted pines, leased two five-hundred-acre blocks to part-time farmers who lived in Walterboro, and drilled soybean seed into the remaining five hundred acres of our thirty-five-hundred-acre tract. By the end of that year, we had made money.

Maggie looked at Papa's picture on the mantel, stroked the skin around my eyes, and said, "You two have the same wrinkles." And that was okay with me. I liked watching things grow.

It was shortly thereafter that Maggie tapped me on the shoulder and said, "Let's go swimming." I remember lying on the riverbank, with my wife's head resting on my chest, looking at the water droplets fall down her pale skin and thinking that God must be pleased. At least I thought He was.

Then came the delivery.

THE FUNERAL PARLOR HAD PREPARED MY SON'S BODY. Amos and I drove by in my truck and picked up the cold metal coffin. I walked through the double swinging doors, bent down, picked it up, and walked back to the truck, where Amos lowered the tailgate. I gently slid it into the back. While Amos thanked the mortician for preparing things and giving us a few extra days, I climbed into the back and braced the coffin between my knees so it wouldn't slide around.

Shutting the tailgate, Amos climbed into the cab and drove us the twenty minutes back to the farm. Underneath a sprawling oak tree on the sloping riverside, next to my grandparents, I had dug a hole with the backhoe for the larger cement casket. Amos parked. I picked up the box that held my son, and we walked over to the hole.

After we stood there for some time, Amos cleared his throat, and I set my son down next to the hole. Then Amos handed me his Bible. It had been a while. Maybe last Christmas. Maggie always liked to read about the Nativity scene.

"What should I read?"

"Psalm 139."

I split the big book down the middle with my index finger. The thin pages crinkled and blew in the breeze, and I had a hard time finding the right page. When I found the psalm, I read what I could.

O Lord, You have searched me and known me.
You know my sitting down and my rising up;
You understand my thought afar off.
. . . Where can I go from Your Spirit?
Or where can I flee from Your presence? . . .
If I make my bed in hell, behold, You are there.

About midway through, I fell silent and Amos took over from memory.

. . . For you formed my inward parts,
You covered me in my mother's womb.
. . . My frame was not hidden from You,
When I was made in secret . . .
And in Your book they were all written,
The days fashioned for me.

When he finished, he stood with his head bowed and hands folded in front of him. The breeze picked up and blew against our backs. Then in a deep, low voice he began singing "Amazing Grace."

I did not.

While Amos sang, I knelt down next to my son and put my head on his casket. I thought about the things that were not going to happen. Baseball. The tractor. Finger painting.

"Dad, can I have the keys?" Buying his first pair of boots. Girls. The first step. Fishing. A runny nose. Tag. Swimming. Building a sandbox. Vacation. Big brother. All the stuff we had talked about. I faded out somewhere into a blank and empty space.

Amos's singing brought me back. With each of the six verses, he sang louder. When the song was over, Amos wasn't finished. "D.S., you mind if I sing one more?"

I shook my head, and Amos, looking out over the river, started up again.

When peace, like a river, attendeth my way,
when sorrows like sea billows roll . . .

Since college, Amos had spent two days a week singing in the church choir. He was a church history buff and especially liked the stories surrounding the writing of hymns. Years ago, floating on our raft down the river, he'd told me the story behind "It Is Well with My Soul," and I'd never forgotten it. I sat there, resting my head on the cold metal coffin of my baby son, a child I never knew, a child I never held, and thought about Horatio G. Spafford.

Spafford was a Chicago lawyer, traveling to Europe with his family for the summer. There he is, boarding a steamer with his family for an Atlantic cruise, but he gets called away for business. He sends his family ahead and plans to meet them in England. A storm comes up, sinks the ship, and all four of Spafford's children drown while holding hands on the bow.

A strong swimmer, his wife reaches land and sends him a telegram, saying simply, "Survived alone."

Broken, Spafford catches the next steamer. When the ship gets to the place where his children drowned, the captain brings him up to the bow.

"Here. This is where." He leaves Spafford to stand alone on the bow.

I want to know if he broke down. Fell to his knees. How strong was the urge to Peter Pan off the bow? Had it not been for his wife waiting on the other shore, would he have jumped? I think I would have. That dark water would have reached up and swallowed me whole—frozen man. But not Spafford. He stands up, wipes the tears, scans the water, and returns to his cabin, where he writes a poem.

What kind of a guy writes a poem at the place where his four kids went down? What kind of a guy writes anything when his children die? Well, the poem got off the boat in Spafford's pocket in Europe, somebody tied some notes to it, and there it was, coming out Amos's mouth.

The doctors say Maggie "probably" won't be alive long. Tell me yes or no, but don't tell me probably. Yet had it not been for probably, and the picture in my mind of Maggs lying there, limp and bleeding, I'd have lowered my son down on top of me and let Amos sing for both of us.

He finished his song, his face a mixture of sweat and tears, and I laid my son in the hole. Amos grabbed a shovel.

"Hold it," I said.

I walked back to the truck, picked Huckleberry off the

front seat, and tucked him under my arm. I brushed him off, straightened the red bow tie around his neck, and then knelt next to the hole and laid the bear on top of the casket.

The cement made a grinding sound as we slid the casket into place. I let the first shovelful spill slowly. Gently. Quietly.

The riverbank sloped to the water. The river was quiet and dark. Minutes passed. Amos wiped his face, put on his glasses, and walked to the truck. Sweat and cold trickled down my back in the ninety-eight-degree heat.

I looked at my hands. My eyes followed the intersections of wrinkle and callus and the veins that traveled out of my palm, over my wrist and up my forearm where, for the first time, I saw flecks of blood caked around the hair follicles. It was dark, had dried hard, and had blended with the sun freckles. Maggie's blood. I picked up a handful of dirt and gripped it tight, squeezing the edges out of my palm like an hourglass. It was damp, coarse, and smelled of earth.

I needed to tell Maggie about the funeral.

The tops of the cornstalks gently brushed my arms and legs, almost like mourners, as I walked back to the house. On the way, I rubbed the dirt from my son's grave into my arm, grinding it like a cleanser, until my forearm was raw and clean. The old blood gone and new blood come.

chapter five

THE DIGGER AMPHITHEATRE, BUILT ABOUT SIX YEARS ago, is one of South Carolina's best-kept secrets. It's ten miles from my house and a long way from nowhere. It rises up like a bugle out of pine trees and hardwoods, covering about three acres, most of which is parking lot. Whoever built it was far more interested in quality acoustics than quantity seating. During the construction, throughout the public hoopla surrounding the opening, and ever since, the donor has remained anonymous.

The amphitheatre is used about three times a year; the rest of the time it just sits there. It's hosted Garth Brooks, George Strait, Randy Travis. Vince Gill, James Taylor. Mostly country and bluegrass folks. The unplugged types. But we've had other names. Even George Winston. Bruce Springsteen came through once. Brought only his guitar. Maggie and I got to that one.

There are all kinds of myths about who built it. Some bigwig in Charleston with more money than sense. A divorcee from New York who was angry at her husband. An eccentric from California whose family homesteaded this area. Who built it depends on whom you talk to. One night a few years back, I learned the truth.

I was driving home at about two in the morning, and I swore I heard bagpipes. I stopped my truck and crept through the woods to the top of the hill. Sure enough. A broad-shouldered man stood center stage in the amphitheatre, wearing a kilt and playing the pipes. I sat and listened for about half an hour. Curiosity eventually got the best of me, and I found myself standing on the stage with a half-naked man. Once his eyes focused on me, he adjusted his skirt and shook my hand. We struck up a conversation, and somewhere in there the guy decided that he liked me. His full name, I learned, was Bryce Kai MacGregor, and when he plays the bagpipes, he wears a kilt. But after six or eight beers, the plaid skirt is optional. He has fiery red hair and freckles, and looks like a cross between a coal miner and a troll—just one big flexed muscle. Bryce is not ugly, although he could take better care of himself, and he has penetrating green eyes.

North of town, where things are more hilly, sits his home—a drive-in movie theater. Though the drive-in has been closed for more than fifteen years, Bryce is a Friday night regular who watches whatever strikes his fancy. The Silver Screen is actually more white than silver, and the largest of the three screens has a big hole in the left corner where a buzzard flew into it. Unfortunately for the buzzard, it got itself stuck and just hung there, flapping its wings in a panic. Bryce climbed up the back of the screen and shot the bird out with a twelve-gauge. A Greener, no less. He just stuck its head in the left barrel and pulled the trigger. "Buzzard removal," he called it, and opened another beer.

His usual sundown activity is to sit in the bed of his truck, drink beer, and watch the same old movies by himself. He owns hundreds of reel movies, of which his favorites are John Wayne Westerns. Normally at a drive-in, a moviegoer sits in the front seat of the car and hangs the speaker on the window. But Bryce's truck window is broken, and he can't fit his cooler in the front seat, so he backs his truck up front and center and spreads out on a lawn chair in the bed.

Most of the speakers in the parking lot are broken and dangling from frayed wires, so he starts the movie and then drives around until he finds one that works. When he finds a live one, he duct-tapes it onto the tailgate or the handle of the cooler. That often takes a while, because Bryce is usually so drunk that he can't remember where he last found one that worked. In his speaker search he has run into or over most of the speaker poles, which presents a bit of a problem to the exterior of his truck.

But that's not a concern to him, because he hardly ever goes into town, not even to buy groceries. He does most of that on-line now, which is odd if you think about it. As drunk as he stays, he can still find the computer when he needs it, and he can usually make it work. In about two days, a white delivery truck drops a half dozen boxes at his gate. An exception to the no-town rule is if he runs out of beer before the truck arrives.

Some folks think he's a rebel or some sort of burnt-out Vietnam kook. Bryce is no rebel. Different, yes, and in a world of his own, but he quit rebelling a long time ago. He has no one. No family. No wife. No kids. Look up "alone" in the dictionary and you see a picture of Bryce. As best I can gather, he dropped out of high school, lied about his age, and got shipped off to Vietnam for his senior trip.

They put him in a Special Forces unit, and from what I eventually gathered, they kept him busy. In the bottom of his closet is a fifty-caliber ammunition can where he keeps all his medals. All seventeen. He brought them out and showed them to me one night while we were watching *The Green Berets.* He was quick to tell me that five of them weren't his. They belonged to a buddy who didn't come back. That meant Bryce had been awarded twelve. Twelve medals. They were all colors, purple, bronze, silver. Mostly purple.

Like most boys, Bryce came home different, and he's been the same ever since—living alone with his beer and his bagpipes and his movies—and his trust fund.

So occasionally, ever since that first night in the amphitheatre, I check up on him. I'll sneak up the path to the parking area of the drive-in, and there stands Bryce. Front and center. Butt naked, except for his boots. Blowing 'til his face looks like a glow plug. Drunk as a skunk. Rattling off "Amazing Grace," "A Hundred Bottles of Beer on the Wall," or "Taps."

We usually end up watching movies together. We'll drink beer and sit in the silence, or if we can find a speaker that works, listen to the static spewing from the box between us. The poor audio doesn't seem to bother Bryce. He knows most every word of every film by heart.

SHORTLY AFTER THE DAY MAGGIE TACKLED ME OFF THE front porch and shoved the pink line under my nose, we climbed the hill and knocked on Bryce's trailer door, because we figured he'd want to know. Ever since I first introduced him to her, he'd shown a special affection for Maggie. I guess after so much killing, Bryce is attracted to things that are tender and full of life.

Hand in hand, we knocked and listened while Bryce cussed and tripped over the empty beer cans on his way to answer the door. He greeted us wearing nothing but his boots and a straw hat. When he saw Maggie, he slowly reached behind the door and grabbed a framed poster of John Wayne to cover himself from belly button to kneecap.

I nudged Maggs, and she leaned in on her tiptoes and whispered in Bryce's ear, "Dylan's gonna be a daddy."

It took a second to register, but when it did, Bryce's already dilated pupils grew as large as the end of a beer bottle. His eyes darted from side to side, he held up a finger and slowly shut the door. To call Bryce a friend, you have to be willing to live with a few eccentricities.

The noises behind the door told us that Bryce was tearing apart the inside of his trailer, looking for a pair of pants. A few minutes later he opened the door, wearing a yellowed and stretched-out T-shirt—as a pair of shorts. He had shoved his boots through the armholes, hiked it up around his waist, and buckled a belt over it to hold it around his hips. The neck hole hung down around his knees and flapped when he walked.

Bryce crept up to Maggie, knelt, and slowly placed his ear to her stomach like a safecracker. Then he wrapped his arms around her waist and pressed his ear farther into her stomach. Maggie is more ticklish than any human being alive, so the pressure of his forearms on her ribs and his ear pressed against her tummy started her to giggling. With Maggie laughing, Bryce could no longer hear whatever he was listening for, so he squeezed tighter. The crescendo grew, and thirty seconds later, Maggie was laughing so hard and wiggling around so much that Bryce just picked her up off the ground, tossing her over his shoulder like a duffel bag, and continued listening while Maggie flung her feet and laughed hysterically.

"Bryce Kai MacGregor!" she said, pounding him on the back.

Bryce set Maggs on her feet, nodded as if satisfied that there actually was a baby in her tummy, and held up his index finger again. He disappeared into the trailer, only to return half a minute later holding a beer and two dirty Styrofoam cups. After popping the tab, he poured half a sip in Maggs's cup, a full sip in mine, and kept the remainder for himself.

Beneath the shadow of the silver screen, Bryce raised his can, we clinked Styrofoam to aluminum, and the three of us drank to our son. We set down our cups and started walking toward the fence when Bryce shouted after us. "Maggie, what's your favorite movie?"

All true Southern girls have only one favorite movie, and they've all seen it ten thousand times. It's stitched into their persons like sinew and veins, and if you listen close enough, they'll whisper dialogue from entire scenes in their sleep. When it comes to their education, Scarlett O'Hara may have as much practical authority as the Bible. Maybe more.

Maggs curtsied beneath an imaginary dress and batted her eyelids. Dragging out her sweetest Southern drawl, she said, "Why, Rhett Butler!"

Bryce looked at me for interpretation, but I just shrugged. "You're on your own, pal."

Bryce scratched his head, and pretty soon the *Ohhh* look spread across his face as the lightbulb clicked on.

A couple weeks later, the UPS man delivered two oversized boxes to our front porch, saying they had been drop-shipped direct from the manufacturer—one that specialized in Southern plantation period furniture.

I looked at the box and wondered if Maggs had taken her nursery shopping on-line, but she read my face and said, "Don't look at me. I had nothing to do with it."

We cut away the cardboard and there, mummified by eight layers of bubble-wrap, sat a handmade and hand-oiled rocking chair with matching foot cradle. Finding no card, and wanting to make sure it was ours, we called the manufacturer and spoke with the owner. He told us that a man who was definitely not from south Georgia called and asked if his company could build nursery furniture for a Southern lady who already owned a crib but little else.

The owner responded, "Sir, we can build most anything if you can give us an idea of what you want." The next day they received an express package containing a videocassette.

Want to guess which one? Handwritten instructions scribbled on a yellow sticky note told them to "take notes and furnish the nursery, minus the crib." The buyer paid them double to speed manufacturing and delivery, so the guys in the shop spent their lunch breaks watching the movie clip and then arguing over the drawings for Maggs's chair and cradle.

Maggie wanted to thank Bryce without embarrassing him, so she cooked him a roast, smothered it in gravy, carrots, and potatoes, and bought him a key lime pie to satisfy his sweet tooth. She wrote a note, left the dinner at his front door, and spent the next two days swaying in that chair and nudging the cradle with her big toe.

On the third night I waited until she fell asleep, then picked her up and laid her down beside me. When I woke the next morning, she was still there, but somewhere during the night she had carried that chair and cradle in from the nursery and slid them over next to the bed.

chapter six

DESPITE THE HEAT, I ROLLED DOWN MY SLEEVES, walked into my second-story classroom, opened the windows, straightened the desks into rows, and cleaned the chalkboard. Soon kids shuffled in, eyed the available seats, and chose ones that suited them. The room was hot, and proximity to airflow was prime real estate.

The second bell rang, and I cleared my throat. "Good morning."

Faces looked back at me blankly. The silence was heavy, but the nonverbals were raucous. The silence said, "Look, man, we ain't no happier about being here than you are, so let's get this over with."

I let a few more minutes pass, thinking eager stragglers might rush in, but they didn't. Clearing my voice again, I picked up my roll book and eyed the first name. "Alan Scruggs?"

"Here."

In my first year of teaching, I established the habit of identifying students by their places in the classroom until I got to know their work and personalities. When Alan said "Here," my mental note sounded something like, *Second row from the window. Center of room. Reading a book.*

"Wait, you skipped me."

I looked up. "Who are you?"

"Marvin Johnson!" The speaker leaned back in his chair. "See, *J* come befo' *S.*"

It doesn't take the class clown long to identify himself.

"I don't usually start with the *A*'s."

"Oh, tha's cool." He looked around at the other students. "I's jus' lettin' you know. Thought you mighta forgot." My new friend smiled, showing a mouthful of white teeth.

I returned to the roll. "Russell Dixon Jr.?"

"Yeah."

A deep voice came from my left. *Against the window, front row. Big, broad shoulders. Sitting sideways. Looking out the window. Never looked at me.*

"Eugene Banks?"

"Uh-huh."

Left side next to the window. Two back from Deep Voice. Looking out the window. Also never looked at me.

"That was enthusiastic. Marvin Johnson?"

"Yo." It was my alphabetically conscientious friend. *Front-and-center and liking it. Smiling. Big ears. Sweatpants. Tall and athletic. Shoes in a tangle.*

The contrast between my non-air-conditioned room and his sweatpants room struck me. "You look like you just rolled out of bed. Aren't you hot?"

"Who, me? Naw." He waved his hand. "See, dis' what I wear." The kid was a walking attitude, an uncrackable nut—or so he hoped.

"Amanda Lovett?"

"Yes, sir. Both of us." A sweet, gentle voice rose from next to the window. *Front left, against the window, in between Uh-Huh and Deep Voice, and . . .*

"Both?"

She patted her stomach gently. "Joshua David."

I admit it, I'm not proud of my second reaction—the one that questioned her morals. I thought it before I had time to wish I hadn't thought it, but it didn't last very long.

"Joshua David?"

"Yes, sir," she said again, holding her hand on top of her stomach.

"Well," I said, recovering, "you make sure that young man makes it to class on time."

She broke into an even larger smile that poked two dimples into the sides of her cheeks. "Yes, sir."

Laughter rippled through the room. Somebody against the window said, "Yes, sir" in that mocking tone that kids are so good at. I looked up and waited for him to finish.

"Kaitlin Jones?"

"Koy," a voice from the right rear of the class said quietly.

I looked up at a young woman whose face was nearly covered by a combination of sunglasses and long hair.

"Koy?"

"K-o-y."

"I could see you better without those sunglasses."

She half smiled. "Probably." She didn't move a finger.

Uh-Huh, Deep Voice, and Front-and-Center laughed, but I didn't push it. The first day was not the time to draw lines. I finished the roll, noted the changes and preferred nicknames, and leaned back against the desk. There I was again, in the front of a classroom. Roped in by Maggs and Amos.

"My name is Dylan Styles."

Marvin interrupted. "Professuh, is you a doctuh?"

"I am."

"So, we should call you Doctuh?"

I checked my seating chart, although I already knew his name. "Marvin, my students have called me Mr. Styles, Professor Styles, Professor, or Dr. Styles. Do you have a preference?"

My question surprised him. When he saw that I was serious, he said matter-of-factly, "Professuh."

"Fair enough." I paused. "My wife . . ." Bad way to start. ". . . calls . . . me Dylan, but school administrators don't usually like students and teachers operating on a first-name basis. So the rest of you can pick from the list. This is English 202: Research and Writing. If you're not supposed to be here, you may leave now, or if you don't want to embarrass yourself, just don't come back after class is over. I suppose if you don't want to be here, you can leave too."

A voice from the back, next to the window, interrupted me. Its owner wore dreadlocks down to his shoulders, and when he had passed my desk on the way in, I was hit by a strong smell of cigarettes and something else. Maybe cloves. Whatever it was, he had been in a lot of it. His eyes were glassy and looked like roadmaps. "Professuh, ain't none us want to be here. Why don't we all leave?"

A wave of laughter spread across the room. Yo high-fived Uh-Huh and then slapped Deep Voice on the knee. I checked my seating chart and started again.

"B.B., I understand. But the fact is that 'not wanting to be here' is what landed each of you in this particular class a second time. Do you really want to make that mistake again?" Scanning the room, I said, "Anyone?"

Quiet replaced the laughter. Watching their faces straighten, I thought, *Maybe that was too much, too soon.* From the far right middle I heard somebody say, "Uh-umm. That's right too." I checked my seating chart. Charlene Grey.

From the middle of the room someone asked, "Professuh, was yo' granddaddy that farmer that everybody used to talk to in the hardware store? The one that raised all the steeples? I think they called him Papa Styles."

"Well, a lot of farmers fit that description, but yes, I called my grandfather Papa, he made a lot of friends in the feed and seed section, and he had a thing for steeples."

Marvin sat back in his chair, tossed his head up, and pointed in the air. "Yo, Dylan, answer me something. Why they send the grandson of a steeple-raising farmer to teach us how to write? I mean"—he looked over each shoulder, garnering support, and then pointed at me—"you don't look like much of a professor. What makes you think you can teach us anything?"

The class got real quiet, as though someone had pressed an invisible pause button. Three minutes in, and we had reached a silent impasse.

What struck me was not that he asked the question. Except for the gold-rim glasses I wear when I'm reading, I look more as though I should be riding or selling a tractor than teaching an English class—cropped blond hair, oxford shirt, Wranglers, and cowboy boots. No, it was a fair question. He could have phrased it differently, but it was fair. Actually, I had already asked it of myself. What surprised me was that Marvin had the guts to express it.

"I don't know. Availability, I suppose. Mr. Winter's probably got an answer." I was losing ground. "Okay, English 20—"

Marvin interrupted again. "But I don't want Mr. Winter's answer. I asked you, Professuh."

Sneers and quiet laughter spread through the room. Marvin sat low in his chair, in control, on stage and loving it.

I walked to the front of his desk and put my toes next to his. To be honest, I was too scattered to have said it the way I should. My body may have been in that classroom, but my heart was lying next to Maggie.

I took a deep breath. "Marvin, if you want the title of Class Clown, I really don't care." I waved my hand across the class.

"I don't think you'll get much of a challenge. What I do care about is whether or not you can pass my class. Your ability to make everybody laugh is secondary to your ability to think well and learn to write even better. Do we understand each other?" I leaned over, laid my hands on his desk, and put my eyes about two feet from his.

Marvin half nodded and looked away. I had called his bluff, and everybody knew it. I had also embarrassed him, which I wouldn't recommend. For the first time that hour, no papers were ruffling, nobody was trying to outtalk me, and nobody was looking out the window.

I let it go.

I backed up, walked to my desk, and leaned against it because I needed to. I then made a few procedural announcements and mentioned the syllabus. Everyone followed along. Point made. *That's probably enough for one day.*

My introduction had taken, at most, four minutes. Once finished, I said, "It's too hot to think in here." I gathered my papers and began packing up. "See you Tuesday. Check your syllabus, and read whatever is printed there. I have no idea because I didn't write it."

My class beelined for the door, shooting glances at one another and whispering as they left.

Funny. What had taken ten minutes before class now took less than thirty seconds. Maybe it was something I said.

The only student to stop at my desk was Amanda Lovett. She rested her hand on the top of her tummy. "Professor, are you the one who's been at the hospital the last week, sitting next to the coma patient on the third floor? The pretty woman, um . . . Miss Maggie?"

When I first learned to drive, I always wondered what it would be like to throw the gear shift into reverse while driving down the highway at seventy miles an hour.

"Yes, I am."

Amanda chose her words carefully. Her eyes never left mine. "I work the night shift at Community as a CNA. I . . . I was working the day you two—I mean three—came in." She fumbled with the zipper on her backpack. "I'm real sorry, Professor. I help to look after your wife. Change her bed linens, bathe her, stuff like that." Amanda paused. "I hope you don't mind, but when you're not there, I talk to her. I figure, I would want someone to talk to me, if . . . if I was lying there."

I now knew how the emperor felt with no clothes.

"Professor?" Amanda asked, looking up through her glasses, her face just two feet from mine. I noticed the skin right below her eyes. It was soft, not wrinkled, and covered with small droplets of sweat. It startled me. I saw beauty there. "I'm real sorry about your son . . . and your wife." She swung her backpack over her shoulder and left.

I stood there. Naked. The only comfort I found was that she didn't even realize she had done it. Her eyes had told me that.

Going out the door, she stopped, turned around, and said, "Professor, if you want, I won't talk to her any more. I should've asked. I just thought . . . "

"No," I interrupted, rummaging through my papers. "You talk to her . . . anytime. Please."

Amanda nodded. As she walked away, I noticed that the shirt she was wearing was one Maggie had tried on in the maternity store. I sat down at my desk, stared out the window, and felt absolutely nothing.

chapter seven

FEW FOLKS KNOW THIS, BUT BRYCE MACGREGOR IS probably the richest man in Digger. His dad invented a gadget, something to do with how railroad cars hook together, that made his whole family a bunch of money. I know that doesn't sound like a gold mine, but Bryce said that every train that's been produced in the last fifty years uses this contraption. I guess that would add up. Bryce gets a royalty check about once a week. Sometimes more than one.

Three years ago I was in his trailer and saw a bunch of envelopes scattered about. One of them had been opened, and its contents lay on the floor. It was a check for twenty-seven thousand dollars. Bryce saw me looking at it and said,

"Take it. You can have it. Most of 'em are like that. Some are more. Some less." A few minutes later, Bryce passed out. One beer too many.

I couldn't find a pillow, so I wadded up a couple sweatshirts and propped up Bryce's head. He was snoring pretty good and could have really used a bath, so I opened a few windows and didn't bother to shut the door behind me. Nobody ever went up there anyway. The breeze would do him more good than harm.

I don't think Bryce ever remembered that night, but I did. There was more than a quarter of a million dollars on the floor in checks made out to him. I left that check, and all the other checks, right there on the floor. I didn't want Bryce's money, and the secret of his trust fund was safe with me. But I didn't want him taken advantage of, either. And there are enough money-grubbers in Digger, small town or not, to rob Bryce blind.

So a few weeks after that, I got to thinking about Bryce while harrowing a section of pasture. What was a half-naked drunk, probably the richest man in South Carolina, doing, living in a trailer next to a drive-in movie theater that had been closed since the early seventies? I said to myself, "This is just not right. This could turn out real bad if someone doesn't start taking care of Bryce." So I went up to the Silver Screen and gathered up all those envelopes. Bryce showered once a week, and I made sure that once a week was that day. Once Bryce was smelling sociable, we loaded up my truck and the three of us—Bryce, Blue, and I—drove to Charleston to talk to the man who Bryce said handled his trust fund.

The man's name was John Caglestock. A skinny little man with rosy cheeks and round glasses that hung on the end of his bulbous nose. Legally, the man had no actual control over the fund, but he was careful to make it his daily priority. His firm made some good commissions from handling Bryce's affairs. But Bryce could be intimidating when he wanted to. Whatever Bryce said, Mr. Caglestock did.

After our meeting, due in large part to the way Bryce talked about me, Mr. Caglestock did whatever I said. Bryce called me his brother, and the man brought out some paperwork and had me sign it. I told him I wasn't anybody's brother and I wouldn't sign anything, but Bryce told me to do it. That way I wouldn't have to "drag his butt" down here again.

So I read it, got the gist of it, and signed it. From then on, the firm had to run every transaction by me before it did anything. Bryce's orders. In essence, I couldn't spend any of Bryce's money on personal matters, but I could look over the firm's shoulder and see where it wanted to invest it. And Bryce thought that was good.

About once a month Mr. Caglestock would call me, and we'd have a real polite conversation in which I approved or denied every transaction he wanted to make. The more time I spent with Bryce, the more I realized that behind the drunk façade, Bryce had moments of lucidity in which he really knew what he was doing. I guess he knew the day I took him to Charleston.

In the three years since I've been talking with Mr. Caglestock, Bryce has made a pile of money. He's more than doubled his fund. Looking back, I realize that has more to do with the market and Mr. Caglestock's research and advice than my input. Caglestock knows his stuff, and he taught me a lot.

One day Maggie asked me if Bryce had a will, and I said I didn't know. I started doing some digging and found out that he did not. And he had no one to leave anything to. That worried us, so I went up to his trailer one afternoon and asked him, "Bryce, if you were to die tomorrow, who would you want at your funeral?" Without batting an eye, he said, "The bugler."

That didn't give Maggie and me much to go on. Just whom do you leave forty or fifty million dollars to when the guy who owns it isn't saying? We decided that while we had no right to play God, we could do a better job than the state. So we had Mr. Caglestock draw up a will that left the whole kit and caboodle to the children of the men who had served with Bryce in his unit in Vietnam. Most of them never knew their fathers, but Bryce did. He kept their dog tags in his ammunition box. About fifteen in all.

So why did I do all this if I didn't want the money? I guess because Bryce couldn't, or at least didn't, and I didn't want him getting taken advantage of by a bunch of Charleston lawyers who found him incompetent to handle his own affairs. And since Bryce's fund has doubled, they can't accuse me of that. Besides, between Caglestock and me, they've made good money. I'm not sure even Bryce knows how directly I handle his fund. It's an odd thing. Caglestock will call me, we'll move two to three million dollars from one stock or fund to another, and yet personally, I'm scratching to pay the taxes on our property. Bryce makes more money off the interest in his investments in one week, or sometimes even a day, than I'll make all year.

A TORNADO BOUNCED OVER DIGGER LAST NIGHT. IT PICKED up a couple of houses, disassembled them piece by piece, and scattered the remains for miles. I didn't hear it, but those who did said it sounded like a really mad freight train. After a phone call reassured me that the hospital hadn't been in its path, I wanted to see the damage, so I loaded up and drove across town. It was an odd thing. On one side of the road, everything was exactly as it had been the night before. On the other side, it looked as though God had taken a two-mile razor to the earth's face. One man woke up to a neighbor phoning to say his tractor was sitting upside down in his tomato patch more than a mile from where the owner had parked it the night before. Others didn't wake up. There were three of those.

I finished my chores around the house, cleaned the yard and then myself, and drove out to Bryce's. By the time I crested the top of the hill by the Silver Screen, it was late in the afternoon. Bryce was standing in a kilt and wearing combat boots, holding bagpipes in one hand and a beer in the other. "Morning, Dylan," he said with a smile. His white barrel chest glistened in the afternoon sun. Bryce had quit wearing a watch long ago, and sometimes, if his nights ran long, so did his mornings.

"Morning." Blue ran up to smell and greet Bryce. "Thought I'd come see how the storm left you. Everything still here?"

"No problem," Bryce barked in his best Scottish brogue.

Looking around, I noticed that one of the screens he no longer used had been torn from top to bottom. The canvas that was once tacked to plywood now flapped in the wind, exposing the splintered plywood that was separated and ripped right down the middle.

"Looks like that one didn't fare too well," I said, pointing.

"Yup," Bryce said between gulps. "No big deal. Only need one." Bryce threw his now-empty can on the ground and walked toward his trailer. He came back carrying a blowtorch. To my amazement, he walked across the parking lot into the second lot and up to the wooden housing at the base of the torn screen. He sparked the blowtorch, adjusted the flame, and held it against the wooden housing. After a few seconds, flames appeared. After a few minutes, the wind caught it, fueling the fire, and it rose up to the screen. The screen and structure behind it caught fire and burned like film in a projector.

Bryce walked back to his trailer and returned to me without the blowtorch but with a beer in each hand. He handed me one, and we watched the screen burn to the ground. Bryce lifted his beer above his head and said, "To the Silver Screen."

IT WAS WELL PAST DARK WHEN I CRANKED MY TRUCK. I passed the amphitheatre, and all was quiet. I pulled off the shoulder, and Blue let out a big breath and lay down in the back. I cut the engine and sat in the quiet.

One night after a show, Maggie and I had lain in bed, ears ringing and too wired to sleep. Bathed in darkness and the sweat of a South Carolina summer night, she asked me why I was so quiet. And taking a chance, I told her what was on my mind.

"When I see those people on stage, sometimes I think about the little drummer boy. Standing there, offering his gift. All he had. Right there at the foot of the King. I wonder what that moment was like. Was it quiet all except for the sound of a drum? Were the animals shuffling about? Chewing hay? Where was Joseph? Was Jesus sleeping, up 'til He smiled? And the smile. What did He feel? I . . . I wish I could wring out my soul, like the drummer boy, and then stop midwring, and know, in that minute, that that—whatever *that* was—was the perfect expression of a gift."

I pointed out the window toward the amphitheatre. "Those people, when they stand before the world, just before the sound fades, they know that they're doing the very thing they were created to do. Their faces show it. Gift affirmed. They know life. That's it. That moment, when the fans come alive and the King smiles, is living. Sometimes, I just wonder what it'd be like to play my drum for the King. Did the drummer boy stand like Pavarotti, hang the notes off the balcony, stop midbeat, and listen to himself? Did he notice the moment, or did it pass by unmarked?"

I thought she'd laugh, maybe lecture me. Not Maggie. When I had finished, she ran her fingers through my hair, wrapped her arm and leg around me, and pressed her chest to mine. "Have you ever had that feeling? Ever?"

"I think so."

"Where?"

I looked up at the ceiling fan, hypnotized by the backward-spinning mirage caused by the forward spin of the blades. "Maybe a time or two in class. It's hard to say."

A few nights later, Maggie packed a brown-bag dinner, blindfolded me, put me in the truck, and started driving.

"Where're we going?" I asked.

She just kept driving, and after fifteen minutes of U-turns and "shortcuts," we got where we were going. She pulled over, grabbed my hands, and led me to a gate, where she fumbled with some keys and unlocked what sounded like a padlock. Loosing the chain, she pushed open a creaky fence and then led me a hundred or so yards to a series of steps. At the top of them, my feet told me that the surface had changed from concrete to something hollow, maybe wood. She led me a few feet farther, then placed her finger across my lips. It was quiet. Pin-drop quiet.

I heard her shuffle away from me and down the steps. Then, while I stood there wondering what in the world was going on, she started screaming at the top of her lungs.

"Whooooo! More! More! More! Whooooo!"

It scared me so bad I ripped off the bandanna, only to find myself on the stage of the amphitheatre and Maggie running up and down the rows of seats, holding a candle, waving her arms in the air and screaming like a wild woman. Throughout the rows she had placed cardboard people, maybe fifteen in all, and each held a burning candle. She whooped and hollered for ten minutes, dancing around as if she'd struck gold or come to hear the man at the mike. It took me ten minutes to get her to stop.

When I finally got her calmed down, we sat in the second row, propped our feet up on the first, ate turkey sandwiches, and watched a show that existed only in our minds. When I finished my sandwich and leaned over to kiss her, she had mustard dabbed in the corner of her mouth. I can still taste it.

Maggie could have made me feel foolish, even stupid for wondering outside myself. But she didn't. She took me down there, set me on the stage, and then acted like my own private audience no matter how foolish it made her feel.

Now I sat there in the moonlight and looked down at the amphitheatre through blurred vision. I opened the truck door, slid down the hill, and hopped the fence. I walked down the center aisle and climbed up on the stage. The moon reflected off the tops of the chairs like ten thousand candles, but I never opened my mouth. I knew no sound would come. Only tears. I lay down on the stage and hid from the demons that fed my doubts.

chapter eight

THE DIGS ENGLISH DEPARTMENT HAD TITLED MY class "Research and Writing," hoping that the students would do just that. This meant that from day one, they would need to be thinking about and working toward a term paper. It also meant that anyone waiting until the last minute would land him- or herself right back in the class a third time. I suppose most of my students knew this. The syllabus allowed for weekly, sometimes daily, quizzes, but the bulk of each student's grade would be determined by one single term paper.

With this in mind, I set aside the third day of class as optional. On the second day I told them, "The most important aspect of your paper is not your topic—there are thousands of interesting topics. The most important aspect is your question. You ask a vague question, you get a vague answer. Ask a specific question, and you tend to get a specific answer. I want specific questions and specific answers. If you have any doubt as to the effectiveness of your question, such as, 'Is it tight?' you'd better come see me on Thursday."

I was willing to answer questions, no kidding, but more than that, I just wanted to see who would show up if I gave them the option.

No one came.

That meant one of two things. Either they all had good questions, or they could not care less. The proof would be in the paper, and we'd find out toward Christmas.

BLUE AND I ARRIVED AT THE HOSPITAL AROUND FOUR IN the afternoon. We walked into Maggie's room, where her brushed hair told me that Amanda had been working. Around Maggie, the sun hung a peaceful light. The lack of tension in her facial muscles told me that she liked it. Aware but unaware, peaceful but not at peace, rested but tired, sleeping but not asleep.

I wanted to wake her up. To nudge her shoulder, watch her stretch and yawn, reach for a hug, sip coffee, and then head for the barn or slip along the river and watch the bass and bream break water or the wood ducks whistle overhead. I sat down next to Maggie, kissed her cheek, and she moved not at all.

The doctors say her brain registers "normal activity for a

person in this condition," whatever that means. They say, "All we can do is wait. Sometimes shock does the unexplainable to a person."

I'm having a hard time with this. If we can put a man on the moon, split an atom, move a heart from one man to another, cure polio, or build a hundred-story building, we ought to be able to wake up my wife. One minute she was awake and crying, reaching for our son. The next minute she was vomiting and then not awake. I can't explain that.

I sat with Maggie while the sun went down. Blue settled in on the blanket someone had folded in the corner. The same someone had filled a bowl of water next to it.

Just a couple days after the delivery, my friend Mr. Thentwhistle had sent a nurse to tell me that he was calling animal control to remove my "filthy canine."

"Ma'am," I said politely and pointing at Blue, "I've tried to tell him, but he won't listen to me. The dog goes with the girl."

She had left, reported to Mr. Administrator, and he called animal control. Animal control is a voluntary position in this county, and it happens to be held by Amos's dad, Mr. Carter. When Mr. Carter found out what kind of dog it was, he put two and two together and said, "No sir, that girl might need that dog. You best leave it alone."

I sipped coffee and held Maggie's hand in silence.

Maggie wasn't a real touchy-feely person, but she loved for me to rub her feet. In her bedside table she kept some moisturizing cream that she got at one of those sensory-overload stores in the mall. You know, the kind full of creams, candles, and all the fluffy crap that sits unused in your medicine cabinet. I didn't really like the smell, but she did. She said it smelled like honeysuckle. The label said "Body Butter."

For some reason, I don't smell too well. I mean, I can smell gardenias or bacon cooking or that perfume of Maggie's called Eternity, but on the whole, I don't walk around smelling life the way she does. Maggie can smell anything. We'll be walking in the mall, stop at the perfume counter, and she can close her eyes and differentiate between eight perfumes. To me, they all smell the same.

But a week ago, I brought that cream from the house and put it in her bedside table. I opened the drawer, pulled out the cream, slid my chair to the end of the bed, gently slipped off her socks, and rubbed. Starting with her heel, up through the length of her arch, between her toes, and finally up her calf.

Maggie has beautiful feet. Her toes are small, callused, trimmed. I used to kid her about having interchangeable toes, because they're all the same size. She has strong feet, a high arch, a slender heel, and a strong calf—working feet, I call them. She's a natural runner, with a much better gait than I have, and occasionally we jog along the river. But that's her second hobby. Her first love is her garden. She'd much rather dig in the dirt than run.

AT FIRST, MAGGIE AND I COULDN'T SEEM TO DEVELOP A routine at the hospital. At some times we were like two kids on a continual first date, and at others we were like Papa and

Nanny after fifty years. Sometimes I'd sit there and talk to her. Sometimes not. Sometimes the rubbing did all the talking. And sometimes, I just didn't know what else to say.

Sometimes when I walked into the room, Maggie's forehead was real tense. Today she had a wrinkle between her eyes, so I started rubbing her feet and the wrinkle disappeared. Who knows what coma patients are doing or thinking on the other side of their eyelids? Maggie's forehead made me think that they don't sleep all the time. I'm no expert, but sometimes when I walked into the room, I could tell Maggie was awake even though her eyes were closed and she looked asleep. Her face showed it. Sometimes it was her hands, but mostly it was her face. Then there were other times when she looked asleep, and I knew she was asleep. Her whole body looked relaxed. Sitting at the end of the bed, I rubbed a few more minutes, and Maggie slipped off to sleep. And no, I never told her about the funeral.

A wristwatch alarm on the arm of a nurse walking down the hall sounded at nine o'clock, and I woke up with my head slumped over next to Maggie's. I wiped off my drool and sat there a few minutes in the dark, letting her breath wash my face. The moon hung full, and a couple of clouds blocked the stars, but for the most part, it was clear and breezy. A sweet, South Carolina starlight serenade. If we were home right then, we'd be wrapped up in a blanket on the front porch. I tucked the covers up around Maggie's shoulders, checked her socks to make sure they covered her heels, set the cream next to the bed with the cap off, and pulled the door shut behind me.

Walking out Maggie's door, I noticed that Amanda had taped a note to the doorjamb. *Professor, come to church tonight. Daddy's preaching. 7:30. I'll save you a seat. Amanda.*

I pulled the note down, read it a second time, and thought to myself, *The life of a preacher's kid. Probably front and center every time the door is open.*

Blue and I slipped down the hallway, and a fat old nurse nodded at me as I left. She glanced over her reading glasses, looked me up and down, and continued reading. The silver chains hanging down both sides of her glasses outlined her square jaw and double chin like a cowbell. Blue and I walked down the stairs and out the ER, and I started my truck. We drove out the main entrance of the hospital, and I pitched Amanda's crumpled note out the window.

At 9:30 I rounded the last corner before home, and Pastor John's church came into view. The AME church was built in 1952. Since then, Sunday mornings had become a local spectacle. Almost a parade of sorts. Just prior to the ringing of the 10:30 A.M. bells, women in all shapes, sizes, and colors, escorted by their families, walked smack down the middle of the highway en route to their pew.

And hats? Hats galore. You've never seen so many hats. They say sometimes Pastor John stops midsermon to point out a new or good-looking hat. The women love it. They also love his preaching, which, according to his reputation, is pretty heavy on the fire and brimstone. People say he tells it like it is, and they like him for it.

The church is a good mixture of all races and sizes, and if

you drive by during the singing, it'll resonate through your windows. Even in winter when the front doors are shut. It's a good thing that steeple is tall and well built; otherwise they'd bring it down. Clapping, singing, even some dancing. You want good hymn singing? Go to Pastor John's church. You'll get it there.

Tonight, like every Wednesday night, was no exception. The place was packed. I slowed to an idle and found myself parked on the shoulder opposite Amos's Crown Vic. His radio was squawking voices and radio checks.

"Seven-twelve to HQ."

"HQ to 712. Go ahead, 712."

"Ah, I've got a . . . " An eighteen-wheeler carrying a load of pine trees whizzed by my window, causing me to miss the rest of the mumbo jumbo. After Amos had been appointed deputy, he told me, "D.S., if I don't learn my ABCs, they'll park my B-U-T-T in HQ and I'll be sorta-outta-luck." He spent weeks reading flashcards that he kept in his shirt pocket.

Law enforcement definitely has its own language. I guess it's a good thing. If I'm sitting there with a telephone pole lying over the top of my car and my feet resting on the engine block, I don't want a deputy with flowery language. I want somebody who can cut through the c-r-a-p and get my b-u-t-t to the h-o-s-p-i-t-a-l. Right n-o-w. Amos says that pretty much eliminates me from law enforcement. He's probably right. I'd be explaining to HQ what the situation looked like rather than what was needed. I see colors, not structure.

Based on the squawking, it was a dull night in Digger.

Apparently most of the population was in church, because every parking space was taken. Even the dirt spillover lot was full. I left my truck on the shoulder and slipped in the side door, where I was immediately met by an usher in a three-piece suit. An older, gray-haired gentleman, probably seventy-five. He smiled from earlobe to earlobe and held the door while I walked through it. You have never seen so many teeth. And straight? You could have drawn a line with them.

I stood there in jeans, scuffed boots, and a flannel shirt that I was rapidly trying to tuck in. I keep my hair pretty short, so that's never really a problem. Even when it's messed up, it can't look too messed up. The entrance to the church was warm and empty, except for Mr. Smiles and me. He asked me if I was a visitor, and I thought briefly about lying to him but figured the narthex of the church, beneath the apex of my grandfather's steeple, was not the place. I nodded without meeting his eyes.

Through the window of the door leading into the sanctuary, I could see Pastor John pacing slowly back and forth, wearing a purple robe and holding a well-worn book in his right hand. He'd aged, and his hair had grown white since I last saw him. The usher gently opened the door and stepped in. A sea of three hundred to four hundred people, pressed elbow to elbow, filled the upright pews, and lines of latecomers filled folding chairs all the way down the aisle and around the back of the pews. *This would never pass the fire marshal's inspection.*

The rounded sanctuary fanned out before me like a half circle. At the flat end stood the pulpit and Pastor John. Behind him stood an organ and forty or fifty folks in matching robes shouting "Amen" and "Umm-hmmm." The pews must have been fashioned by the Oompa Loompas because they were little; but judging from appearance, the size of the pew didn't seem to bother anybody. The pews did have padded seats, but I'd have given up the padding for a little shoulder room.

Before I realized what he was doing, the usher had walked smack-dab down the middle of the center aisle, intending to lead me to the front of the church where, wonder of wonders, Amanda sat next to an empty spot. I tried to stop him. I coughed and even thought about whistling, but Amanda turned, saw me, and started scooting over to make more room. I followed while the whispers grew out from me like aftershocks resonating from an epicenter.

When the usher got to the front row, he turned, opened his arm so the palm of his hand showed, and nodded his head. Still smiling. *Dang, that's a lot of teeth.* With my shirt starting to stick to my back, I slithered into the seat.

Amanda smiled, whispered, "Hi, Professor, I thought you might come," and folded her hands in front of her tummy.

I looked down and said nothing. Studying the carpet, I noticed that Amanda had slipped off her shoes, and it wasn't hard to see why. Her feet were pretty swollen. I looked up, and Pastor John stopped midsentence, waved his hands, and placed his right index finger against his lips.

After the congregation quieted and people stopped talking about me behind my back, he said, "For those of you who don't know him, Dr. Dylan Styles has just joined us. As you all know, we've been praying for his wife, Maggie, for several weeks now, and we will continue to do so."

Someone behind me said, "That's right." Across the room, someone muttered, "Ummm-hummm" and farther over to the left came, "Amen."

Walking to the other side of the stage, he said, "Please, make sure that all of you greet Professor Styles when I finish." Pastor John smiled and looked at me, then back at the congregation. "But not until I finish."

Looking back at me, sweat pouring off his face like a spigot, he said, "Welcome, son." It looked as though he wanted to say something else, but he didn't. Without skipping a beat, he picked up where he had left off and continued thumping that Bible across the pulpit. Based on his speaking and the audience's reaction, I had interrupted his sermon at the crescendo. After another ten minutes, once he had worked everybody into a pretty good frenzy, he finished and sat down in a big, wide, ornate wooden chair next to the choir.

An organ started, and my armpits were soaked. The place was like my classroom: real hot. Several women were methodically waving pieces of paper in tempo with the ceiling fans, which only served to circulate the warmth. My forehead was dripping, and I kept rubbing it with my shirtsleeve. Shortly, the music stopped, the sanctuary fell silent save the rustling of the choir's robes, and next thing I knew, the ushers were leading the choir to the railing. That only meant one thing.

Communion.

The choir made their way to the rail and knelt in unison.

Following Pastor John's prayer, the assistant pastor walked down the row of purple robes and placed white wafers in black hands. "The body of Christ. The bread of heaven."

After they had time to swallow, Pastor John followed with a great big silver cup. He moved methodically down the aisle. "Brother Michael, the blood of Christ. Sister Annie, the cup of salvation." When he had finished, the choir stood in unison and returned to their seats where, swaying in rhythm like the women's fans, they began to hum quietly. Like my cornfield, this place was constant movement.

Then out of nowhere, Mr. Smiles appeared next to me. He turned, extended his arm, showed his palm, and beckoned. I looked straight ahead and pretended not to notice him.

Amanda whispered, "It's okay, Professor. We ain't Catholic. You can go with us."

The row opposite me was filing out and up to the railing on the left. Mr. Smiles beckoned a second time, and my forehead wrinkled.

Pastor John broke in, waved at the organ, which went silent, and pointed his face toward the balcony. Looking at no one in particular but everyone in general, he said, "You all know how I feel about this." His hand swept across the railing. "Before you strut up here, remember what waits." His articulation was crisp and powerful, his wording careful and precise. He paused, moved the cup from one hand to another, pulled out his handkerchief, and wiped his forehead and cheeks.

"You all face a choice. You can rise from your seat, follow the person in front of you, stroll down this aisle, critique somebody else's Sunday best which they happened to wear on a Wednesday night, think about how hungry you are or where, when, and what you are going to eat when you leave here, and then kneel, nod, nip and sip, and return to your seat, having thought the bread stale and wine cheap." Pastor John wiped his brow again after unfolding and refolding the handkerchief.

"Or"—he moved the cup to the other hand—"you can slide from your seat, limp to this rail . . ." The humming grew louder. "Reach down, grab these splintery timbers, fall, rest your baggage against it"—Pastor John's voice rose above the humming—"extend your hands, take tenderly, place the body on your tongue, taste the grit, swallow, and feel the hunger build in your stomach. Then you can grasp this cup." Pastor John held the cup above his head with two hands, his powerful arms rippling through his robe. "Tremble, sip violently, feel the burn, taste the acrid smell, feel the splinters pierce your elbows, lean more heavily, and then look upon this cross." Pastor John pointed behind him without looking.

"You can reach up and place your trembling hands on callused, blood-soaked feet, let the red, slippery liquid run down your fingers, underneath your watchband, and come to rest in the crack of your elbow. You can lean your forehead against His shin, notice the crude and rusted nail, the shake and strain in His arms and legs, stick your hand in the hole in His side, notice the dried blood on His face, the thorns poking through the skin, smell the vinegar, feel the raw skin on His back, and hear the gurgle drowning out His breathing." Pastor John took a long, deep breath.

"Lastly, you can raise your head and feel the breath of God. And in that instant, if you so choose, you can see your own reflection. With all your zits, warts, blemishes, and scars. And there, amongst the scar tissue, are your demons. But having chewed, sipped, and swallowed, you can chase." The choir was humming louder. Pastor John's voice was calm, controlled, soothing, and resonating.

"People." He paused, knelt, leaned his arms on the railing, held the cup between both hands, and faced the congregation. "This is where you chase the demons that feed your doubts, your anger, your bitterness, and your lack of faith." Then in almost a whisper, he said, "Every last one." He stood and wiped his forehead. Except for the choir, you could hear a pin drop.

"Brothers and sisters, a demon's job is to kill you. To beat you to death. To rob you of anything that is not painful. This railing is where you give more than you take. Where you steal back. Where you kill what's killing you. Then, having chased and slain, you return"—Pastor John pointed to the pews and folding chairs—"bloody but unharmed, different but the same, changed but unchanged, moved but unmoved. A living battleground.

"People, we got hurting brothers and sisters here. Every one of us has a closet, and in that closet, we keep and feed our demons. Some's more full than others, but they're all busting at the seams. You all know most of mine. I've told you. What I haven't told you is in my criminal record. That's public. You're welcome to read it."

I shot a glance at Amanda. Peace bounced off the glisten on her face as she watched her father.

"People," Pastor John continued, "that space between your pew and this altar, between the red velvet cushion and these splintery timbers. Whether it's twenty feet or a million miles, it's not a question of distance. It's one of position." He calmly turned, walked to the end of the railing, and waited.

The humming continued. Mr. Smiles put his hand on my shoulder. The people next to Amanda were standing, waiting.

I rose.

I took three steps and knelt. Or rather, fell. If the railing had been much farther, I'm not sure I'd have made it. Amanda knelt next to me. I looked straight forward and followed Amanda's lead, holding out my hands, one clasped beneath the other. The assistant pastor gently placed a small white wafer in my white hand. I took it. If he said anything, I didn't hear it. Amanda did likewise and immediately placed it on her tongue and closed her mouth. I held mine out and looked at it, then placed it on my tongue. It was gritty, but I swallowed. I think my stomach growled, because out of the corner of my eye, I saw Amanda smile.

Silently Pastor John appeared with the cup that he held to my lips. "Dylan, this is Christ's blood, which was shed for you. Take it in remembrance of Him who died on the cross." He placed the cold silver cup to my lips.

I sipped.

My tongue and throat burned as I forced the liquid into my belly.

Then he moved to Amanda. "Baby, this is Jesus." He placed his hand on her forehead and prayed quietly.

When I opened my eyes, the railing was empty but for me. I don't know how long I had been there, but when I turned, everyone else was seated and about eight hundred eyes were turned directly at me. I quickly rose and plopped into my seat with an embarrassing thud.

Amanda sat with her eyes closed. Quiet. I hadn't seen Amos until now. Out of the corner of my left eye, I noticed that he was sitting at the end of the row opposite me with his attention focused on Pastor John. His uniform stood out, and his badge glistened in the lights. His belt, and Kimber, were noticeably absent.

At 10:47 P.M. Pastor John said a closing prayer, and as the choir sang, people filed out of their seats. A few headed for the door, but most headed for me. I was the center of several hundred people's attention and hands. After eight or ten minutes, Amos rescued me. He put his arm around me and led me toward the side door.

"Professuh," he said in his cornfield tone, "how 'bout a burger?"

"No." I paused. "I'm not hungry."

"Doc, that's horsepucky."

"What?" I said, looking at Amos.

"A few minutes ago, back over there, your stomach told me you were starving and needed a fat, juicy, greasy cheeseburger with bacon, extra pickles, and a little of Amos's secret sauce on the side."

"No . . . " I fumbled for my keys. "Thanks." I left Amos standing with three hundred people who had just heard him describe the cheeseburger. I started my truck, noticed a new exhaust leak, bumped the stick into drive, and drove home.

Pulling into the drive, I circled around back, parked on the grass, walked up the back porch, and pulled on the screen door, where the smell of Maggie's house tugged at my loneliness. Unable to face an empty house, I grabbed the blanket off the front porch, walked out into the cornfield, lay down with Blue, and named my demons.

chapter nine

When I woke up, the sun was just breaking the tree line. It was cold, I was shivering, and Pinky was rooting at my feet. Pinky appeared on our doorstep about two years ago. I looked at her and saw three months' worth of breakfast, but Maggs gave me the pointed finger and said, "Dylan Styles, if you shoot that pig, you're on the couch for a month."

So Pinky ended up in the barn with her own stall and two permanent slots in our daily calendar. Maggs even painted *Pinky* in bright-red letters above the gate. I feed her bulk dog food or kernel corn, sometimes a combination, but she'll eat anything that's not nailed down—and even some stuff that is. When she first appeared, she weighed maybe eighty pounds and needed a bath and a vet. Now she weighs a little over three hundred and expects to be hosed down weekly.

I'll never understand how someone so beautiful and so tender could love something so ugly. But make no mistake, that pig loves her back. Dang thing hates me, craps on my foot every chance she gets, but she just adores my wife. You've never heard such grunting and squealing as when Maggie rubs Pinky's ears and stomach. Pinky rolls and wallows and then rubs up against Maggie's overalls. Maggie doesn't care.

Maggie would squat down in the middle of the stall, and Pinky, holding her curlicue tail high in the air, would nose all the piglets out of the corner and up to Maggie, where she'd rub each one until it squealed with delight. Every now and then, Pinky would stick her nose under Maggs's hand, get a scratch between the ears, and then shove a piglet under Maggie's leg. Thirty minutes later, Maggie would walk out of the barn and smell like a pig all day. One morning last summer it was so bad, I had to hose *her* down. Maggie didn't care. She just laughed. Squealed just like Pinky.

Maggie loved the farm. Everything about it, from the creaking floors to the noisy screen door. The chipped paint, the front porch, Papa's swing, the smell of hay in the barn, the way the cotton bloomed in summer, the short walk through the oaks down to the river, the oak tree spreading across the barn that was bigger around than the hood of my truck, the artesian well and its sulfur water, the corn that waved in rows to the wind that sifted through it.

Maggie probably loved the corn best. Every night when the

breeze picked up off the river, she'd disappear to the front porch with hot herbal tea and stand there, watching the waves rise and fall atop the stalks. And on moonlit summer nights when she couldn't sleep or Blue woke her up barking at a deer, she'd grab a blanket, tiptoe to the porch, and sit on the steps as the moonlight streamed through the rows like a prism and lit the sandy soil beneath.

Daybreak would come, and I'd find her asleep against the column at the top step. I'd crack the screen door, Blue would pick his head up off her lap, and without saying a word, Maggie would lift her eyelids, smile, throw off the blanket, and then tear off the front steps with a giggle like a kid let out of church. We'd race through the cornrows all the way to the river, where she'd leap off the bluff and into the deep, black water below. Blue and I followed as if we were trapped in a Mountain Dew commercial.

One of Maggie's favorite foods was creamed corn. After our swim, she'd cut ten or fifteen ears, haul them into the kitchen, rub them over the creamer, and come out looking as though somebody had just shot her with corn puree.

When I was finishing my dissertation, she'd walk in late at night, silently offering a bowl of chocolate ice cream or coffee or whatever I needed to help me continue writing. If she sensed frustration and knew I was about ready to set a match to the whole blasted thing, she'd grab me by the hand, pull me to the porch, set me on the swing, and tell me to breathe deeply and watch the corn roll in waves. Thirty minutes later, she'd put her foot in my back and tell me to get back there and keep writing.

I miss that.

When I raised my head, Pinky stopped rooting, perked her ears, and snorted, showering me in pig snot. With her tail sticking straight up into the air, she ran back to the barn with her Charlie Chaplin gait. I have no idea how she got out in the first place, but I bet the answer will require new lumber.

I lifted myself off the sand and brushed off my face and clothes. They were cold and damp.

In the barn, Pinky huddled her little ones around her, although they weren't all that little anymore, and she made sure to keep me at a good distance. I threw some corn and tried to step closer, but she got her body in between me and them and then crapped on my foot. So I dumped the corn in a pile, hung up my bucket, locked the barn door, and headed for the porch. "Pigs!"

Back in the house, I made myself a pot of coffee and spent thirty minutes studying my classroom seating chart, trying to memorize appearance and characteristics with name. It would only work if the kids sat in the same place each class, but most kids do because people are creatures of habit. Take church, for example. Ever visited a new church and sat in somebody else's pew? Try it sometime. Whoever owns that pew will let you know.

I HAD BEEN IN MY CLASSROOM ONLY A FEW MINUTES WHEN Amanda walked in and smiled. Then she took one look at my forearm and raised an eyebrow. "Professor, what happened to your arm?"

I quickly pulled my pushed-up sleeve back down over the scabs and pus on my left forearm, cursing myself for letting it show. "Little run-in with a big pig," I lied.

She could tell I was covering up more than my arm. "You make sure you let me clean that for you at the hospital. You don't want it infected. I've seen that. And you don't want it."

Amanda sat down, and I stuffed my hand into my pocket. The midmorning sun was streaming through the magnolia and heating the classroom up pretty good. I had the fans set on "breeze," but the sun convinced me to crank them over to "hurricane" and really get the air flowing.

Marvin walked in, and I greeted him.

"Morning," he replied. Apparently not a good one. Under his breath, I heard him mutter, "It's hotter than a snake's butt in a wagon rut in here."

Russell followed, said "Mornin', Professuh," sat down, rubbed his eyes, wiped his forehead with a towel, and looked out the window.

Koy slipped in and sat silently in her chair near the back. So far, everyone was true to form.

I walked down the far-right aisle and stood next to an empty desk, just smiling. "Good morning, Sunglasses."

Koy half smiled, looked over the rim of her glasses, showed me the whites of her eyes, and said with a whisper, "Morning." Then she ducked her eyes, placed her hand on her forehead, and continued reading.

I counted heads, checked my chart, faced the class, and sat on the top of my desk with my legs dangling off the end.

Noticing this as an address posture, everyone quieted and looked at me with suspicion. "Would you please take out a piece of paper and—"

The class groaned.

"What are you moaning for? I told you there would be a quiz."

Russell turned to Amanda, who already had paper and pencil on her desk, and said, "Could I have a piece of papuh?" Marvin did likewise. Eugene and Alan had their own.

All my quizzes were ten questions. All of them together, which after a semester could total more than twenty, only counted for 10 percent of the grade, so fretting over one or two scores wasn't worth it. In addition, if a student was present for every quiz, I'd tack on 10 percent to the final grade anyway. None of my students ever knew this, but it worked. The process of knowing they were going to get a quiz, and not wanting to fail another one, had a way of causing people like Marvin to read and at least familiarize themselves with something they might not otherwise bother with.

"Question number one," I said, as my students leaned over their desks and placed pen to the paper. "What is your name?"

Everybody laughed, and Marvin said, "I always knew I liked you, Professuh."

"Question number two. Where are you from?"

Marvin smiled and licked his lips. Amanda quickly wrote her answer and looked back at me. Koy wrote without looking up or expression. Russell propped his feet up on the desk next to him.

"Question number three. What is your favorite color?"

Marvin, starting to take me seriously because he was looking at the possibility of acing my quiz, said, "You go, Professuh."

"Question number four. Why?"

"What?" Marvin's face was suddenly real tense. "Wha' you mean 'why?'"

Half the class wrote without comment. Marvin waited for my explanation, so I repeated the question. "Why is your favorite color, your favorite color?"

Marvin shook his head. "But there ain't no right answer. How you gonna grade it?"

Russell, Eugene, Alan, B.B., M & M, and Jimbo all waited for my answer. Everybody else wrote furiously.

"Take as long as you need," I said.

Marvin dropped his head and said beneath his breath, "How do I know why my color is my favorite color? It just is."

"Question number five."

Marvin's hand shot up. "Wait, I ain't finished."

"You can come back to it." Looking back at the class, I said. "What is your major?"

"Question number six. Why?"

Marvin dropped his pencil and looked at me with disgust. "Come on, Professuh."

"Question number seven. How many brothers and/or sisters do you have?" The room was really starting to heat up. The morning sun was turning into midday sun, and the fans were now blowing hot air. "Eight. How old are you?"

Marvin said, "You ain't allowed to ask that."

"Marvin," I said, smiling, "this is not a job interview. Just answer the question."

A few kids laughed. Marvin huffed.

"Nine and ten. Tell me your story. You have the rest of the period to do so."

Marvin raised his hand.

"Yes, Marvin?"

"What you mean, 'Tell you my story'? That could take a long time."

"Write what you can. Tell me what you would like me to know about you."

He raised his hand again.

"Marvin, get to writing."

"But Professuh," Marvin objected.

I looked at him. Tall. Trim. Fit looking. Probably pretty fast. I had heard he was a cornerback on the football team. "Marvin, how fast are you?"

"Wha' you mean?"

"I mean how fast do you run the forty?"

He tilted his head and rolled his eyes around as if he were trying to figure out whether or not this was a trick question. Then he said, "Fo-fo."

"Good," I said. "Then how about getting your mind and hand to work as fast as your feet?"

Marvin relaxed, smiled, and began to write.

chapter ten

I WAS STANDING IN THE SHOWER, BREATHING THE steam, when Amos climbed the porch steps. I had just finished cleaning in the barn and stank something fierce. I heard the creak of the springs, the slam of the screen door, and then, "D.S., you ready?"

"Ready?" I asked, poking my head around the corner.

"Ivory. Man, put a filter on that thing." Amos saw me walk past the door wearing my towel and put his sunglasses back on. "The UV is killing me. You need to get out more. A little tan here and there wouldn't hurt you."

My ancestors were Scottish. They came in through South Carolina, then through Tennessee, and ended up in Texas.

You'd think that hot Texas sun would have brought out some tan, but it didn't. Too many years in the highlands, I suppose. I've never had a tan, but I've been burnt a thousand times.

Amos covered his eyes, then made himself at home with my refrigerator, which was empty. "Don't you ever buy anything to eat? You're gonna wither away."

"There's PB & J and tuna in the pantry," I said from behind the door.

Amos poked around in the kitchen, rattled some plates and silverware, then yelled, "Boy, I'm tired of waiting on you. Would you get it in gear?"

I pulled a T-shirt over my head and said, "Amos, I don't know why you're here, but I've got a notion I'm not going to like it. And the last time you had that look, I ended up standing in front of a class of college kids, which I'm still trying to figure my way out of. Shouldn't you be working or something?"

"Ivory, Ivory, Ivory," Amos said, not looking up from the four pieces of bread on which he was spreading peanut butter. To Amos, a PB & J was not a snack, it was an experience. Too much peanut butter, and it was hard to swallow. Too much jelly, and it was too sweet. Too much of both, and it drowned out the bread. And Amos did not like wheat bread. White only. The kind you ordinarily feed to ducks or put on a hook.

Judging from his flair with the knife and the way he was putting the peanut butter on the bread, I could tell that he was in a good mood. I just wasn't sure why. Amos was a real prankster when we were younger, but when he got hired by the sheriff's department, he shelved a lot of that. Occupational hazard, I suppose. Show criminals you're a real human being with emotions and feelings, and they'll take you for a loop or leave you in a ditch somewhere, putting pressure on a real bad gunshot wound.

Nope, this was unusual. But it was the Amos I knew. It was also the Amos I needed to see. In the past, when he let his hair down this far, we usually got in trouble, but that was before the badge.

"Amos," I started, "when was the last time we got into trouble?"

"Tonight," he said, kind of dancing around the kitchen with a sandwich in one hand and another in his mouth. He was dressed in cut-off shorts, a worn and ragged John Deere cap, his beeper, a torn-up T-shirt that said "Protected by Kimber," and no shoes. This could only mean one thing.

The river.

WHEN AMOS AND I WERE TWELVE AND ELEVEN RESPECTIVELY, we built a raft. We had spent the previous month reading *Robinson Crusoe* and were in the middle of *Huckleberry Finn,* so we had a hankering. The raft took us most of a month, but we were a lot smarter about it than Crusoe. We cut cedars growing out of the water, so that when they fell, they fell into the water. We couldn't understand why old Rob didn't think about that before he cut that big tree so far from the ocean. We saw it coming the moment he cut it. I said, "He'll never get that thing in the water," and Amos said, "Yeah, how's he gonna drag it? It's not like he can move it." We were right. Rob never got it to the water.

We trimmed the top branches and bound together twelve cedar trees, about a foot in diameter each, and then floated the whole thing downstream to the main river, where we floated it into shallow water and tied it up. We did most of the work in the water, covering the base with about thirty smaller trees. We cut them in half and sanded the tops so that we actually had a flat floor that fit rather tightly into the subfloor beneath it. Made for a pretty good raft. At least Papa thought so.

On top of the flooring, which was twelve by twelve, we built a lean-to that could sleep both of us. We even put a wood-burning stove in it. We had planned to float to the Gulf, but then found out that our river didn't dump into the Gulf. Whoops.

The whole thing weighed a ton, and once it got good and waterlogged, probably more. Cedar trees are pretty heavy. It needed about eight inches of water to float. We'd travel down-river, however far we could get in a night, and then hook the raft to a barge going north to pick up soy, corn, or whatever the farmers were trying to get to the railroad in Brunswick.

In the span of a summer, we got to know most of the usual captains. We'd float a day or two, fish, eat whatever we caught, smoke a pipe like Rob and Huck, get dizzy, sleep, and then about Sunday afternoon, we'd throw a rope, hook a barge, and it'd pull us north. We could reverse in five hours what had taken us nearly two or three days.

That's not entirely fair. On our float down, we'd tie up and fish for a few hours, sometimes a day. It depended on if and where the fish were biting. Then we'd float until we felt like fishing again. On several occasions we thought about ditching the raft, but after all that work, we just couldn't do it. Too much invested. Besides, the barge captains were lonely and liked having somebody to talk to, and we liked not having to row that thing back up that river.

We tried that just once. Floated downriver about twelve miles, spent the night, then thought we'd paddle back up it. Not a chance. You'd think, as critical as we'd been of Crusoe, we'd have thought of that. Funny how you can think of some things and not others.

Then about fifteen years ago, I found an old forty-horse Evinrude that belonged to Papa. All the times I worked and played in that barn, and I never knew it was there. We took it to Bobby's small engine-repair shop in town, and Bobby spent a week tinkering with it, replacing this hose and that seal. Pretty soon he had it puttering like a champ.

Bobby helped us rig up a platform out of steel. We sank the bolts all the way through the timber and hooked the Evinrude to the back of the raft. That was the day that heaven came to Digger. A couple of five-gallon gas cans, and we could putter all the way back from a three-day float. It really changed the way we traveled. Sometimes we puttered upriver ten or so miles and then just floated back. The motor was a nice addition, but the floating was why we built the raft.

Floating the river is a delicate dance. Tenuous at best. If you've ever floated, you know what I mean. It's slow and silent progress, but you're not in control. Nobody controls the river.

To float the river you've got to trust something bigger than yourself, and you better not mind living halfway between Nowhere and No Place Else, because the river's not interested in the destination, only the process. Otherwise all rivers would be straight.

The river's got its own rhythm, and you either dance to it or you don't. Whether you're man or woman matters not because the river leads, and if you're stepping out of time, then it's your fault because the river changes its beat for no one. You want to go swimming? Go swimming. You want to sleep? Sleep. You want to fish? Fish. You want to go faster? Too bad. You want to slow down? Good luck. The river's got one speed, and it's not going to stop and wait on you. And unless it rains, it's not going to hurry you along either.

Amos and I made our pact with the river long ago. We built a raft, shoved off, and never complained. Rain, no rain, sun, no sun, wind, no wind, hot, cold, fast, slow, wet, dry. It really didn't matter to us. We were just boys, happy to go wherever the river carried us. And all the river cared about was that we were going in the same direction it was and that we could swim, because it didn't like us dying.

Rivers don't do death, that's why they flow. You may drown, sink to the bottom, and lie there a few days, swelling, getting all puffy. You might even get caught on a downed tree with bream and bass nibbling on your nose, but eventually the river's going to lift you up and beach you. Spit you out like Jonah. You're not going to make the trip. You can't go where the river goes. Rivers do life, and the dead don't dance.

On our maiden voyage, a three-day float, we read *Huckleberry Finn,* switching turns every chapter. Our favorite scene was Huck sitting on the raft, deciding whether or not to rescue Jim. "All right then, I'll go to hell" became our motto.

For us, the raft was a safe and easy place. While I read, Amos would lie flat, listen, and try to smoke a pipe. He coughed and sputtered a good bit, about like the Evinrude, but eventually he got it and seemed to enjoy it. I, on the other hand, tried Red Man. A mistake. Every time I put that stuff in my mouth, I'd end up chumming. Why in the world I continued to try still amazes me. Glutton for punishment, I suppose. I figured if Josey Wales and John Wayne could chew, then so could I. The only difference was that my life was not a movie. Mine was real life and showed all the unedited stuff, like me hanging my head overboard.

My dancing with the river was never poetic, but Amos got pretty close.

I JUMPED INTO SOME SHORTS AND GRABBED MY POCKET-knife, Papa's yellow-handled, two-bladed Case Trapper.

Amos started in again. "Come on, boy. I'm always waiting on you."

Amos and I lit out the front door and headed for the barn, where Pinky met us at the gate and tried to flip me with a stiff shoulder. She's got about 130 pounds on me.

Amos laughed, and I shooed her away. "Get out of here, you ol' biddy."

"That is one mean pig," Amos said as Pinky grunted and ran in circles around her offspring.

"You ain't seen nothing. That pig is the Antichrist," I said.

The Evinrude hung on a little rack I'd made years back. Even though we hadn't used it in a few years, I started it up every now and again just to hear the sound. We loaded it into the wheelbarrow—actually it was more of a manure cart, but we called it a wheelbarrow—and grabbed a couple of gas cans. Two cans were plenty for a one-night float.

It was getting dark, but the trail alongside the cornfield was light enough. The moon shimmered off the sand, and shadows followed us through the long, tall grass and even taller corn. Blue bounced along beside us.

"What happened to your arm?" Amos asked while pushing the wheelbarrow and nodding at my forearm. "That's a pretty good one."

"Oh, that's just, uh . . . I was moving some stuff in the barn, and Pinky tripped me up. Just came down on it wrong."

"You ought to send that thing to Smithfield. I'd tell you to make sausage out of her, but she's probably too dang tough."

"You got a point there," I agreed. A half mile later we rolled up to the riverbank and into the hollow where we hid the raft. The river was high, due to the moon, so floating it out would be easy. We pulled off all the branches that had either fallen on it or we had put on it, but there didn't seem to be as many as the last time we had done this.

"I think somebody's been on our boat," I said, pointing. "Less cover."

Amos nodded and looked at the raft. "Sometimes a man likes to be alone."

"When?" I asked.

"'Bout four weeks ago. I got tired of sitting there feeling useless and watching you hold Maggs's hand."

"Oh."

Amos mounted the motor and loaded the gas inside the lean-to. We had sealed it when we built it, so it was pretty good and dry. Matches even lit. Which would be nice once we got going. A fire helped keep the mosquitoes at bay, and this end of the Salkehatchie Swamp produced some big mosquitoes.

I grabbed the push pole, jumped on top of the poling platform, and backed out the raft.

We bumped into some old cedars, and Amos said, "D.S., you're getting rusty."

I gave a hard push and Amos, who was standing, lost his balance and almost went in the water.

"D.S., you get my Kimber wet and I'm gonna beat you like a drum right here on this raft in the middle of the river."

I laughed. "I ain't that rusty. And you might could whup me, but you're gonna have to catch me first, Mr. Donut."

Amos was actually pretty fit. He had gained a few pounds since high school—I'd say about ten—but it was mostly muscle. After high school his hair started thinning up top, so he just shaved it off. He said it was cooler and less hassle. Although I'd never tell him, Amos is a pretty handsome man, and he takes good care of himself. Spends about four days a week in the weight room. So between his head, his muscles, and the moon, he looked like a shorter, thicker, blacker version of Mr. Clean. I was glad we were on the same side.

"Listen here, half-pint, I'm within ten pounds of my playing weight. What are you? 'Bout a buck-seventy?" He eyed me up and down.

"One sixty-eight," I said.

"That's what I thought. You're almost thirty pounds *under* your playing weight."

"Yeah, but I can still outrun you," I said, laughing and looking downriver.

"But when I catch you," Amos said, flexing his right arm, "I'm gonna put you in the Carolina cruncher."

"Ebony," I said, smirking, "I think you're losing a bit. Your arms ain't what they used to be."

He took two steps, grabbed my legs, and tossed. The whole thing didn't take a second and a half. I went about fifteen feet in the air, then dived deep into the water. I swam back over to the raft and climbed up, something I'd done a hundred times. I wrung out my shirt and watched Amos stand atop the polling platform, smiling. It was good to be back on the raft.

We floated a few hours, not saying much. About three o'clock in the morning, Amos looked up from his pipe and broke the silence. "Have you been thinking what I think you're thinking?"

I knew what he was asking. This was why he had brought me to the river. Amos was checking my pulse, but it hurt too much just to come outright and say it. We needed the river and a few hours beneath the shadow of the moon to get him to the place where he could ask and me to the place where I could answer.

I looked up from my seat on the front of the raft. "If Maggs is already sitting in heaven, rocking our son, laughing with Nanny and Papa and our folks, and looking down on me, then she's never coming back, and I might live another sixty years." I shook my head. "I just don't know that I can make it through those years without her."

We floated along in the quiet, listening to the ripple and flap of water against the cedar timbers. An owl hooted, and on the air I smelled a charcoal fire thick with lighter fluid. Amos stood atop the poling platform on the back of the raft, his sweat glistening in the moonlight. Minutes passed, during which neither of us said a word.

My pulse must have been pretty weak, because Amos pressed me one more time. "What keeps you?"

I splashed water on my face and rubbed my eyes. "The thought of Maggie waking up. Her hand without mine. Her without me, staring at the same future that's bearing down on me."

Blue slept next to me, his ears pricking up every once in a while. We probably floated four or five miles while Amos wordlessly and methodically worked the pole. It was a warm night, so I dunked my head in the water and let it drip down and soak my neck and chest. Amos lit his pipe, and in the flash of the match I saw tears streaking his cheeks. At daybreak, we napped and fished. We caught a few bream, one or two bass, and ate lunch around noon. About dusk, we cranked the Evinrude and puttered back home, arriving around midnight.

I stepped onto the porch and pointed to the stringer. "Keep the fish. I'm not too hungry."

Amos nodded, looked as if he wanted to say something, and then stuck his right index finger in the air. He opened the trunk of his squad car, pulled out a cardboard box about two feet square, and set it on the porch. "Maggie found this at an antique shop in Walterboro. She was real excited. Stored it at my house so you wouldn't find it. I think she meant to give it to you on your first day of class. After the, uh . . . well, I didn't know what to do with it. So here it is." Amos looked out over the field toward the river. "I don't think she ever got around to writing a card."

Amos turned while tears slid off his square chin. He nodded and spoke quietly, as if his voice would amplify across the cornfield. "When you boil it down," he said, holding out his hand and counting with his fingers, "all we got left, all anybody's got, is faith . . . and hope . . . and love." He looked at his three fingers. "And we all gonna make it. All three of us."

I watched him cross the dirt road and head into his own driveway. I turned on all the lights, showered, wrapped myself in a towel, and stood in the den, staring at that box. An hour later, I sat on the floor and slit the brown wrapping tape. Inside, wrapped in dirty burlap, were a leather-strung drum and two hand-cut drumsticks.

I cried like a baby all the way to the hospital.

chapter eleven

I CONSIDER MYSELF A FAIR TEACHER. I DON'T ASK anything of my students that I wouldn't ask of myself. And one thing I would not ask of myself is to jump into a cold pool without sticking my toes in it first. Now, Amos, he's a different breed. It can be thirty degrees outside with a film of ice covering the surface of the water, and it's "Aw, just jump in. Get it over with. You'll warm up." Not me. Especially not when it comes to being cold.

I like to get comfortable with an idea before I take it on. Give me time to ruminate, and I can face most anything, but don't allow me an experience, and then with the sweat still rolling off my face, ask me to interpret it for you. I don't know what I think until I've had time to look in my rearview mirror.

The English department had structured my class around three papers, but it only cared about the third, the research paper. A passing paper was my student's ticket out of here. While the third paper had to meet certain length and style requirements, the first two were left up to the teacher's discretion, meaning I could tailor the assignment to need. Theirs and mine.

They needed to get their feet wet, get their engines running, get comfortable, and I needed to get to know them. I needed to place a face with a writing voice and so have a starting line against which I could compare their other two works. I needed to know who could and who could not. Who did and who did not. The first paper was the plumb line against which I compared the other two. It would also keep them honest.

The first assignment was an autobiographical essay. Easy enough. Everyone is an instant expert on the subject. No research needed. The only requirement is honesty, and sometimes a good sense of humor.

I spent most of Saturday reading essays to Maggie at the hospital. From prom night to car crashes to summer nights with bronzed, big-breasted women, they gave me real and honest stuff.

Marvin wrote about his last football game as a senior in high school. State champions. All-state player of the year. Marvin was no master of the English language, but he was able to get across his humor. He wrote the way he spoke, which to me is the sign of a good beginning. Good beginnings breed hope. And I had hope for Marvin.

Amanda wrote about growing up in Digger, about her dad and his past. She wrote about her desire to be a nurse for the critically ill. She wrote about being pregnant. She had an informative voice, similar to her speech. Her paper told the reader everything you'd want to know about Amanda in three pages. Except for one detail.

Alan wrote about his first car, a '69 Chevy Camaro. He bought it off a junk lot and set it on blocks for two years. He literally took it apart one piece at a time and put it back together again with new parts. Paint, interior, bodywork, engine, gears, transmission. It was all new, and he had built, rebuilt, or custom-ordered all of it. It sounded like a showpiece, and he provided me with proof. A certificate, "Best of Show," from the Walterboro Classic Car Roundup was stapled to the last page of his paper. Alan's voice was rough and his writing skills poor, yet he, too, got his point across. And judging by the erasure marks, he had put some real time and work into this. In some ways, it was clear Alan knew his writing skills needed taking apart and rebuilding, just like his first car. I had hope for Alan too.

Eugene wrote about his experiences in last year's Freak-Nik in Atlanta. He described four days of bars, the backseat of a big Oldsmobile, and bad indigestion. His paper was essentially his personal chronicle of four days of booze, women, and a dirty hotel, and he didn't spare any details. Even down to the little machine next to the bed that required four quarters for five minutes' worth of bad decisions. Eugene's paper confirmed what I had suspected: here was a ladies' man who was interested in one thing. His paper also confirmed something else I had suspected: here was an intelligent guy who had yet to put his mind to something other than the next girl or the next good time. Eugene was an entrepreneur, and without his knowing it, his paper illustrated that. He had a unique ability to handle details, to turn a bad situation into a better one, and to say the right word at the right time. I didn't need to hope for Eugene. He'd get out of there, which was all he wanted.

Koy, the silent one, hidden behind sunglasses and long hair in the back of the room, turned in a one-paragraph paper. I had specifically requested three pages. I don't understand why students do that. If the instructions say three pages, then at least make a go at it. If you want to run the race, then at least do it from the starting line. In Koy's one paragraph she attempted to hide herself the same way her sunglasses hid her eyes. Problem was, her ability to write was as effective a concealment as her glasses. Ironically, by her effectiveness in keeping the reader at bay, she revealed her remarkable writing ability. Her language skills surprised me. I wanted to hope for Koy, but I couldn't figure out what or why she was hiding.

The rest of the papers fell in line along the same ideas. Most were informational and dry; the students gave me what they thought I wanted, hoping, no doubt, that I in turn would give them what they wanted: an A.

The last paper in the pile was Russell's. I had little expectation for Russell because I have known and even played with a few Russells before. He was a gifted athlete, a walking Adonis, and he had no need for school because school was not his ticket. The NFL would be his ticket. Though he was only a sophomore, word was that scouts had been looking at him this year. For Russell's academic future that meant one thing only: he would transfer out of DJC, but he wasn't planning to graduate with a four-year degree. In his version of his prospects, Russell didn't need my class. At least not yet. If he blew out a knee, then he'd need it.

I refilled my coffee cup and propped my feet up on the end of Maggs's bed, slowly swaying in rhythm with the hum of her monitor. A cool breeze blew in through the window and swept the parking lot clean. The almanac predicted the coldest winter in twenty years. Maggs liked cold winters. One of the things she missed about Virginia was the snow. I liked to watch it fall but not stick, drift, or melt. Not Maggs. She loved being snowed in.

I picked up Russell's paper and began to read. To my surprise, it bled honesty. It seeped through the pores and bubbled over. And Russell didn't need to be honest. Why should he? Being honest showed that he could be vulnerable. And to show that he could be vulnerable showed that he could be touched, even beaten. Football players on their way up cannot afford to show what Russell's first paragraph showed me. Or so I thought. Two pages in, and I felt myself wanting to offer Russell an apology. I had misjudged him. He hid nothing.

Russell wrote about his folks and last year's homecoming game. His mom and dad drove from Roanoke, checked into their hotel, went to the game, and stood in the rain while their son played football. That night, Russell's dad caught a cold. The next day they all drove home to Roanoke for Thanksgiving. Russell wrote about his dad's lifelong work with the railroad. Several times, he flashed back from the action of the football game to times spent with his dad playing catch, fishing, saying "Yes sir," and just hanging out together.

I'm not sure Russell was aware of the extent to which it came across, but his paper made it evident that he and his dad had something most fathers and sons do not: a friendship. Without sounding clichéd, these two guys loved each other. Following Thanksgiving in Roanoke, Russell's dad developed pneumonia and died in the hospital two days later.

Two things struck me. One was that I couldn't possibly put a grade on it. It was one of those rare papers that existed outside of a grade. Two, it was apparent that Russell and his dad shared tenderness, intimacy, and trust. They probably hugged each other good night. Russell's description of his father's death was vivid and convincing: the sound of his cough, the color of the mucous, his dad's wrinkled face, the fear in his mom's eyes, the last time he kissed him.

I put down the essay, picked up my coffee cup, and watched the clouds roll past the window. Russell had put his heart on that page. All 280-plus pounds of it. Russell, whom I had wrongly put in the proverbial football player's box, with his big shoulders and deep voice and eyes always looking disinterestedly out the window, had done something no other student in my pile of papers had done. He had touched me.

chapter twelve

I WOKE UP IN A CHAIR NEXT TO MAGGIE, WHERE THE air smelled like magnolias. The Sunday morning sun was bouncing off her face, which had regained its color.

Amanda poked her head into the room and said, "Good morning, Professor. How about some orange juice?"

I nodded and wiped the sleep from my eyes. "Thanks."

She returned, placed it on the table, checked Maggie's IV and her blood pressure cuff, and then rubbed Blue between the ears on her way out. Around ten o'clock she returned, carrying some antiseptic and gauze pads. She motioned to my arm. "Professor, I'm cleaning that before it gets infected."

I looked at my arm and rolled my sleeve back down. "No thanks. It'll be fine."

"Professor, if I had a problem with my paper, I'd expect you to help me out. Same goes here, only it's reversed." She pointed to my arm. "Whatever was here is long since gone. You can quit now."

She pulled a chair up beside me and rolled up my shirtsleeve. Amanda worked quietly and quickly. She doused me with hydrogen peroxide, cleaned out all the dirt, and then poured some brown stuff all over it that stung so bad I almost cussed.

"Professor." Amanda studied my arm, dabbing it periodically with a Betadine-soaked cotton ball. "My daddy's having a baptism down at the river this afternoon. You're invited. Your deputy friend will be there. Daddy asked him to help the older folks down to the river."

"You think I need help getting into that river?"

"No, sir. I just thought you might want to come. It's a good time. Always lots of food." She smiled.

"How's the baby?" I said, nodding at her stomach.

"Healthy and growing," she said with a smile. "I'm eating everything that's not nailed down and some that is." She continued working on my arm.

"Do you talk to God at your daddy's church?" I asked bluntly.

Amanda didn't bat an eye. "I talk to God most everywhere and most all the time." She thought for a minute. "And yes, one of those places is my daddy's church." She fiddled with her hair, a little self-consciously. "Professor, do you ever talk to God?"

"No. Not since He quit listening."

She gathered her dirty pads and antiseptic and headed for the door. "At the river, down below my daddy's church, at two. You'll see the cars." She disappeared around the corner.

"Amanda?"

She poked her face back around the door. "Yes, sir?"

"You think I need to get in that water?"

"No, sir. I just thought you might like to come. Lots of people. And if you haven't had Mrs. Baxter's chicken, you haven't had fried chicken."

"You think I need to get cleaned up?"

She walked over to the head of the bed. "Professor, it's not just you. Everybody needs to get cleaned up sometime."

"What if there's not enough water?"

She tucked Maggie's hair behind her left ear. "It's not the water, Professor. And you don't have to get cleaned up to take a bath."

Amanda walked out of the room, and I placed my head next to Maggie's hand and slept.

chapter thirteen

I DRIVE AN OLD PICKUP BECAUSE I UNDERSTAND IT. It's simple. I don't understand a car that does not require a tune-up for a hundred thousand miles. What kind of car is that? Self-timing and loaded with computer chips. I understand a distributor cap, a carburetor, eight cylinders, a timing belt, and how to change the oil. When I first met Maggie, she owned a foreign car that we nursed through graduate school. Not long after graduation, it died, and we sold it to a parts supplier at a junkyard for three hundred dollars. But the first time I changed the oil, it took me the better part of a day just to find the filter. And even when I did, I had to be a contortionist to get to it. The human hand is not designed to do that. My truck is made so that regular people like me can change the oil every few thousand miles. Maggie's car was made so I had to pay a professional twenty-eight dollars to locate and unscrew the filter with a tool that cost him ninety-eight dollars.

My truck is a 1972 Chevy C-10, possibly the best truck Chevy ever made. It's got a long bed, which is partly rusted, a bench seat torn in several places, and it burns oil. It looks used because it is.

If it's knocking, I pull over, adjust the timing to fit the grade of gas, and keep going. Sometimes in the mornings, it needs a few minutes. I do too. What's wrong with that? I hit the starter, give it some gas; it coughs, spits, churns, and hacks itself to life, for one more morning, anyway.

When I get more than two hundred thousand miles on me, I'm quitting. There won't be any coughing, spitting, and churning. I'm just going to bump myself into neutral and coast.

I've thought about restoring it. Maybe new interior, new paint, an engine overhaul. Then I think, *No, I'm not going to do that. It's got more character the way it is.*

If Maggie had a choice, she would prefer not to ride in my truck. And that's putting it nicely. She laughs at me everytime I climb in. "I can't believe you actually own that thing, Dylan Styles. It's pitiful. You look like *Sanford and Son.* All you need is some furniture sticking out of the back, and you could have your own sitcom."

I tried to tell her that Red Foxx drove a Ford, but she wouldn't hear it. She just shook her head and said, "I married a man in love with a truck that's the same age as me. I guess I should be happy. At least it's not another woman."

A pickup truck just fits the way my brain works. I can throw stuff in the back and forget about it until I need it. I like the way the starter sounds when you crank it. I like the way the door sounds when you close it. I like the way the tailgate sounds when you lower it. I like the way the muffler sounds at idle. I like the play in the steering wheel. I like manual door locks. I like the horn because it's loud. I like the rattles my truck makes when I drive it. I like the way it trusts me to read the gauges and the way the gas cap screws completely off—no strings attached. And I like the way it drives.

Some folks like that "new car smell." I like that old truck smell. Sweat. Dirt. Oil. Preemissions-controlled exhaust. Hay. Pig feed. And whatever's blooming. Leave your windows down. Let it breathe. Wipe the dew off the seats in the morning. Automobiles take on the smell of their environment.

In May, when Maggie's gardenias bloom, I park it so close that the branches hang in the window and the blooms spill over the seats and dash. The next morning I get in, and it smells like Maggie. Who would want new car smell when you can have Maggie's gardenias?

AROUND TWO ON SUNDAY, I CLIMBED INTO THE TRUCK, feeling dangerously hungry. Blue and I cranked her up and idled out of the hospital parking lot. I rolled down the window, stuck my arm out into the hot breeze, and surfed my hand through the waves of air coming off the front fender. The new bandage was thick, bulky, and my arm throbbed inside it.

The cars stretched down the road about a mile before the church came into view. I rounded the corner before the final straightaway that intersected the dirt road that runs in front of my house and saw the river. I slowly passed the church and saw a line of people headed for the water. White robes for the women and shorts for the men. Probably two hundred people. I didn't see Amos, but I figured he was already down in the water. I could see Pastor John holding Amanda's hand as they stepped over the roots of an oak tree. Her other hand was cupped under the swelling her baby had made in her belly.

Pulling up under the oaks, I cut the engine and listened to the late-summer crickets; it's a lazy, psychedelic, summer sound that can send any man to the crazy house or into a deep summer nap. Blue whined and stuck his head from around the back of the cab and looked at me. I hesitated and sat sweating inside, still buckled in.

"All right, but just to look."

We slipped through the oaks and sat down on some moss on the south side of the folks in the river. Up on the bank, just downriver of the church, there were ten or fifteen picnic tables covered with checkered tablecloths and plates of fried chicken, potatoes, coleslaw, and what smelled like peach pie. I was hungry.

Up the river a bit, a father squatted next to his son, who stood with his pants at his ankles, spelling his name in the river. Probably thirty folks stood in a circle, waist deep in the river, around Pastor John. In his arms he held a screaming lady who had her hands raised. He dunked her three times, and each time she came out of the water screaming a garbled "Hallelujah!" After the third dunk, Pastor John led her over to Amos, who helped her up out of the water and gave her a towel.

She was shorter but bigger than Amos. She hugged him and kissed his cheek, tears pouring off her face, then went on to hug about thirty other people who must have been family and friends. These people really liked each other. Pastor John kept dunking people, and Amos stood by with a huge grin, ready to help. Some people Pastor John dunked once. Others twice. Some three times. And one man he dunked four times. I guess he really needed it. The fourth time, Pastor John held him underwater for close to thirty seconds, at which time the guy really started waving his arms. Pastor John brought him up, hugged him, and passed him to Amos, who gave him a towel and set him next to a woman who offered him a comforting shoulder.

Dunking those thirty people took a little over an hour, because Pastor John was good at this. I think he enjoyed it too. And he made it fun for everyone. Any time he took someone's hand, he'd relate chapters from his or her sordid past to the others in the group. He always ended it with an encouragement about how that person had climbed up from sordid to surrendered. When he finished talking, the congregation members would clap and throw their arms up, and he'd go to dunking.

This was no sprinkling. Pastor John splashed water everywhere, and everybody got wet. The last person to go was a child, maybe nine or ten. Pastor John took the little boy in his arms, held him close, and nuzzled his nose. When the boy said he was scared to go in the water by himself, Pastor John went under with him. He went under three times, and when he came out the last time he held the boy high in the air. The dad waded over and gently took his son from Pastor John as he let him back down in the water.

With the baptism over, Pastor John prayed. The group in the water held hands, and the group out of the water held hands or stretched their arms out over the ones in the river. Pastor John prayed for those he had baptized and for those who needed baptizing and then asked the blessing on the food.

Pastor John could pray. And it wasn't a posturing thing, as if he were trying to one-up those around him. Something about it was different. It was personal, powerful, and real, as though he were talking to somebody right there in the group.

When he finished, everyone climbed out of the river and made a mad dash for the tables. All at once, as if someone shot a gun, the women fell into place, pouring sweet tea, passing plates, and piling them high with chicken, rolls, and slaw. They had done this before.

Within five minutes, all two hundred people had food and drink and places to sit. Behind me I heard a stick crack.

"Professor, I brought you a plate." I was leaning against an oak tree, peering through the small stems of one of Maggie's favorite plants, resurrection fern. It's a funny little fern that grows out of the cracks of the bark, spends most of its days brown and crinkly only to soften up and turn green at the first sight of rain. I pulled my nose out of the fern, and Amanda offered the plate a second time.

"Hi, Amanda." I looked for Blue, who was licking Amanda's ankle. *Thanks, Blue.*

"You look like you could use some food."

"No, really, I'm not hungry."

From the other side of the picnic tables I heard, "Don't let him lie to you, Amanda. Give him the plate. He'll eat it. He's so hungry now, he don't know if he's got a stomachache or a backache." Amos waved a chicken leg at me and smiled a greasy "I'm-eating-a-chicken-leg-and-liking-it" smile.

Amanda offered me the plate, piled high with a sample from every bowl, and then handed me a Styrofoam cup overflowing with tea. "We've only got one flavor, and I hope you like it sweet."

The plate probably weighed five pounds, but I took it. Blue sidled up next to me and started sniffing the underside of the plate.

"I saw you when you pulled up," she said. "I thought you'd come."

"Oh." I didn't know what else to say. My first reaction was to drop the plate and disappear, but I was stuck. Amanda led me to a table near her father, and I started nibbling at some chicken, trying not to inhale it.

Pastor John wasted no time. "I understand you are my daughter's professor."

"Yes, I am."

He stuck out his hand. "Good to see you, son."

"I don't think I ever told you, but you did a nice job at my grandfather's funeral. Thank you."

"Your grandfather was as fine a man as I've known. Did more talking with his hands than his mouth. That's always made an impact on me." Pastor John looked back toward the steeple and waited for my reaction.

"Yes, he did on me too," I said, taking another bite of chicken.

"Now, about you being her professor." Pastor John's tone caught me all of a sudden. "Amanda seems to have a lot of homework here lately."

There was something behind his smile. The last thing I wanted was a temperamental and public conversation with the parent of a student. Not today.

"I hope so," I said, chewing.

Pastor John raised his eyebrows. "What, to give my child busywork?" He clasped his hands and rubbed them together. "To tell her what to think?"

Pastor John's eyes were penetrating. I should've run for the truck when I had the chance. I was in over my head, and I knew it. Mrs. Baxter's chicken wasn't tasting so good anymore.

"No, sir. That is not my intent."

His eyes, switching between his bifocals, his normal lenses, and the space above his glasses, wandered over my face. Then he leaned his face into mine and said, "Well then, son, what is your intent?"

Maybe it was hunger. Maybe it was fatigue. Maybe I just didn't care. Whatever it was, my answer was a silver bullet. I shot it into my target with the expectation that it would do damage. I put my plate down, wiped off my mouth, and fired.

"My intent, sir, is to help her learn how to think better. To help her question what she thinks by *how* she arrived there. To equip her with the tools to consider and process. If I can do that, her writing will take shape soon after." I sipped my tea, swallowed a mouthful of chicken, and said, "That is my intent."

I picked up my plate again and dug around for a chicken leg. Maybe it was because I needed to remind myself, but before he could ever open his mouth, I pointed at him with the chicken leg. "Sir." I paused. "Pastor John, to be honest, I'm not looking for an amount of work. I hate to grade papers, and I don't slap little silver stickers on passing quizzes. I'm looking for a process. I'm interested in *how* Amanda gets from here to there. And to be brutally honest, I don't really care where she starts or where she finishes. That's your job."

With my voice echoing off the river, I began to notice how quiet it had gotten, how everyone was listening to me, and how much I had said. Being tired and hungry does strange things to a person.

Pastor John sat back, took off his glasses, wiped them with his white handkerchief, and looked at me through his now-naked eyes. He smiled, nodded his head, and muttered, "Huh-huh," as if he was talking to somebody I couldn't see. Then he slapped me on the knee and said, "Son, welcome back. You let me know if you need anything." He stood up and put his hand on my shoulder. "And Professor, I miss your grandfather. Seeing you reminds me of him. And it's a good remembrance too. I think he'd like it very much."

Everybody had long since quit talking and was listening to

the two of us. I guess our voices carried a good bit under those oaks.

"Son, you give my child all the work you want to. If she doesn't give you what you want when you want it, you let me know." He patted me on the shoulder and started making the rounds to check on his flock.

Amos got up quickly, brought his plate, and sat down next to me. "Listen here, you little squirt. I didn't bring you out here to put that doctoring mumbo jumbo on my pastor." He smiled and pointed his own chicken leg in my face. "You got to learn to tone it down."

"What? I say something wrong?" My face was covered with chicken grease.

"It wasn't necessarily what you said as much as how you said it. And the fact that you said it at all. All that bit about 'process' and 'your job.' You should have heard yourself."

"Amos, you're half the reason I got this job. Now, are you going to let me do it, or do you want to do it for me?"

"Naw." Amos slipped into his southern drawl. "I think you got it covered there, Professuh."

"Good. You arrest people, and I'll teach them how to think so that you don't have to arrest them."

Amos got up and said, "I'm going back for more. You eat all you want. Talking all uppity like that probably worked you up a pretty good appetite." Amos wiped the smear off his lips and then turned and hollered, "Amanda, make sure that boy eats 'til he can't move."

Before thirty minutes passed, Amanda had handed me two

more topped-over plates. I felt like a tick and had to unbutton my jeans. I knew I gained eight pounds right there in that folding chair. Blue too.

The crowd thinned, and I helped Amos clean and clear tables. We carried them inside the church and stacked them against the wall in the narthex. As I was heading to my truck, Pastor John thanked me for my help, and Amanda gave me two more plates wrapped in cellophane and spilling over with food. I guess those folks were trying to tell me something.

On the top of the first plate she had written *Professor* and on the second *Blue*. Along with the plates, she handed me a milk jug of sweet tea. At this point, I had drunk so much tea and had to pee so badly that I nearly gave it back. Thinking better of it, I tucked it under my arm, and Blue and I headed for the truck. I drove until I was out of sight, then pulled over next to where the river bumps up next to the road. I got out, ran to the bank, yanked open my shorts, and peed for a minute and fifty-five seconds. A new personal record.

I drove in the drive and heard Pinky grunting, squealing and kicking the inside of her stall. When I had filled her trough, she grunted at me as if to say, "Took you long enough. Where you been?"

Nighttime and crickets found me rocking on the front porch, thinking about Maggie, my class, and how uncomfortable I had become in my own house. Home was quiet, and I didn't feel like walking inside. I was unable to put my finger on it, and my skin began crawling as if it were covered with poison ivy. Then it hit me. A stranger, silent and invisible, had moved into my home, taken Maggs's place, and begun to rearrange everything that was sacred to the both of us. Everywhere I turned, Memory had already been there.

I raced inside and searched the house but never got closer than the tail-end of her shadow. When I finally cornered her in the bathroom, I slammed the door and screamed from the hallway, "Pack your bags and get out! I don't want you here. Not today. Not ever!"

I had never lived with, much less slept with, any other woman, and I wasn't about to start now. "Maggie's coming home! You hear me? I said she's coming home."

I slammed the screen door, and Blue and I walked through the cornfield to the river.

chapter fourteen

JUNK MAIL WAS SPILLED AROUND THE BASE OF THE mailbox when I got around to opening it the following afternoon. I dug it out and stuffed it in my arms like firewood. Buried in the back of the heap was a conspicuous envelope. The VISA bill.

I hated that thing and moaned every time I saw it. I'd been paying it down since I took Maggs on that little surprise trip eighteen months ago. She had always wanted to do two things: fly to New York City and see *Riverdance.* It so happened that *Riverdance* was premiering in New York at that time, so late one night, after Maggs had gone to bed, I did some searching on the Internet and ended up booking flights, room reservations, and tickets.

I was busting at the seams to tell her, but managed to keep it a secret for two weeks. When the alarm went off that Friday morning, I poked her in the ribs and said, "Honey, pack your bag. Plane leaves in three hours."

Maggie lay there and pulled the covers back over her head while I showered. When I came back, I grabbed the covers at the foot of the bed and yanked.

She jerked up and said, "Dylan Styles, you know this is my only morning to sleep in. Now go away and leave me alone." Her hair was going everywhere, and she had a big sleep mark imprinted in her left cheek. She slammed the pillow over her head and motioned to the light switch.

So I pulled the *Riverdance* tickets out of my pocket along with the plane tickets and slipped them under her pillow. That got her out of bed.

We spent the weekend in New York City and saw the show from the third row, front and center. I had as much fun watching Maggie's face as I did the show. The next day we walked the streets like Dumb and Dumber, strolled through Central Park, toured Ellis Island, stood at the foot of the Empire State Building, and rode the elevators to the top and waved at the Statue of Liberty. Maggie loved every minute of it. Fourteen hundred and sixty-nine dollars later, we came home.

I opened the envelope, and the number at the bottom of the page said I had paid for the first twenty-four hours. Now I needed to pay for the second. I tossed the bill on the floorboard and bumped the stick into drive.

I drove past Pastor John's church, onto the hard road, and

up the hill at Johnson's pasture, where I crossed the railroad tracks midway. I made it into town just as Frank, the owner of Frank's Hardware, taped a "Back in Ten Minutes" sign to the front door.

Ten minutes is about the time it takes to drink a cup of coffee, so I headed across the square, bought a paper, and sat down in the corner of Ira's Cafe. Just as I slid into the booth, Amos saw my truck and parked his squad car. He pointed his toothpick at me and walked through the front door.

"Morning, Ira," he said to the lady cooking eggs behind the counter.

"Mornin', sugar. You sit down there with Mr. Quiet, and I'll be there in a minute."

Amos slid into the booth across from me. "Hey, buddy, what's up?"

I pointed across the square to the hardware store. "I'm waiting on Frank so I can buy bolts for the harrow."

Amos looked over his right shoulder. "Frank left another 'ten minute' sign?"

"Yup." I rummaged through the money section of the paper.

"How's our girl?" Amos asked.

"Same. I'm going there now. Soon as Mr. Back-in-Ten-Minutes finishes helping Ms. White with her latest emergency."

"That's the trouble with this town. Everybody knows your secrets."

"Tell me about it."

Ira walked up to the end of the table and kissed Amos on the cheek. "What you gonna have, sugar?"

Amos looked at me. "I just love the way she calls me 'sugar.'" Then he looked up at Ira. "Give me three over medium. No, four. I'm hungry today. A couple of biscuits and some of that good honey that George steals from his neighbor."

A guy wearing a white T-shirt and flipping pancakes hollered over his shoulder, "They're my hives."

Amos turned and hollered back. "Yeah, but the bees are eating from his flowers."

George hollered again. "At least that's what he told the judge. I can't control where my bees go. It's not like I can train them."

Amos laughed.

Ira turned to me. She was a fixture in this town and had worked at this cafe for as long as I can remember. Consequently, she knows everybody and everything about everybody too. If you tell Ira something, you might as well announce it on CNN, because the world of Digger will soon know about it. She was also the most colorful person in town, and everything she wore always matched. Shirt, skirt, shoes—all the same color. She looked like a walking color swatch. Today she was lime green.

"Good morning, Ira," I said.

"Good morning, honey. How you doing, Dylan?" She leaned down and gave me a big wet kiss across my forehead.

"I'm fine. Thank you," I said, wiping my forehead.

"You don't look fine. You look like somebody peed in your cornflakes." Did I mention that Ira was brutally blunt and had spent ten years married to a sailor?

"Thanks, Ira. I'll just have a biscuit, please."

"Okay, honey. Y'all give me a few minutes. I got to make some more biscuits."

Amos and I small-talked for ten or fifteen minutes, until Ira showed up with a plate of ten or twelve eggs and another plate of about a dozen hot, steaming biscuits. She slammed down both plates, poured two more cups of hot coffee, and did not leave a check on the table. She looked at me.

"Dylan, don't you get your butt out of my booth until you and Mr. Cue-ball here eat everything that I've put on those plates. You understand me, mister?"

"Yes, ma'am," I said. There was enough food on our table for five people.

Amos smiled, picked up a fork, and split a biscuit. "Well," he said, stuffing a buttered, honey-dripping biscuit into his mouth, "I think I made *America's Scariest Police Chases* last night."

"What happened?" I piled eggs on a biscuit.

"Well, I pulled this guy over for speeding about ten o'clock, and he decided he didn't want to be pulled over. He was driving a big, four-door Lexus. Before I knew it, we were going about 120 down I-95. Then he hops the median and starts racing down the back roads at the same speed. Mac at the motor pool said this morning that I just about burnt up the engine and definitely ruined a good set of tires. Anyway, this guy bangs his Lexus around a good bit and then parks it in the middle of Old Man Packer's duck pond. You should have seen that thing fly through the air after he hit that hay bale."

Amos stuffed some more eggs into his mouth. "The driver managed to swim out and spent last night in jail, but his car is totaled. Some people amaze me. There I was, just giving the guy a hundred-dollar speeding ticket, and he hauls off and wastes an eighty-thousand-dollar car and a night in jail. Not to mention what Judge Hand will do to him when I give my report. This is a crazy world we live in, Dylan."

"What'd he say when you pulled him out of the pond?"

"Nothing. He just stood there looking at eighty thousand dollars' worth of splash and bubbles. Never even loosened his tie. Looked like a respectable fellow too. I handcuffed him and placed him in the back of my car. When I asked him why he ran, he gave me some lip about how the police were always picking on him. I asked him if he thought seventy-two was too fast in a fifty-five zone. And you know what the guy said?"

"No. What'd he say?"

"He said, 'It depends on the person.' I said, 'Sir, the law is no respecter of persons. It is what it is.' He didn't like that. Got real quiet. Then he started talking about his lawyer, and anyway, he's in jail, and I'm here eating breakfast. How come you're not saying much?"

"'Cause I'm eating my fifth biscuit."

Amos smiled with honey dripping off his chin. "They're good, aren't they?" He pointed his butter knife toward the kitchen. "She's sweet as pie and can cook like nobody's business, but that woman can cuss like nothing I've ever heard. I guess thirty-odd years waiting tables in this place with that guy will do it to you."

"Tell me about it."

After forty-five minutes, Frank reappeared in his window, fixed his hair in the reflection, peeled the sign off his door, and unlocked the bolt.

I nodded my head. "Frank's back."

"All right. I got to go. Judge Hand is expecting me. I'll pay Ira. You hug Maggie for me."

"I'll do that."

And it was at that moment that the guilt set in. Guilt caused by the fact that for almost forty-five minutes I had not thought about Maggie, or the death of my son, or the fact that my wife was a vegetable in the hospital, eating from a tube and urinating into a bag.

The guilt landed on my stomach like lead. I walked out the front door, turned right down the alley next to Ira's Cafe, and vomited five biscuits, six eggs, and a pot of coffee. I wiped my mouth on my shirtsleeve and steadied myself against the brick wall. A second wave coursed through me, further emptying my stomach. I wiped the messy tops of my boots against my jeans, drove to the hospital and forgot why I needed to see Frank.

I slipped quietly into Maggs's room, and Blue jumped up on the bed, nestling his nose in at her feet.

"Hey, Maggs," I whispered in her ear. I would have given the farm to hear her voice.

"Hello, Professor," Amanda whispered as she walked into the room and interrupted the silence.

"Hi."

"I won't be but a minute." She checked Maggs's feeding tube and then began to tiptoe out. Just as she was about to disappear behind the doorframe, she turned around and whispered, "Professor, I won't be in class tomorrow. Doctor's appointment. I left you a voice mail at home, thinking I might miss you here. See you tomorrow afternoon, maybe."

"Okay. Thanks for letting me know."

Amanda left, and the silence crowded in again. Blue whimpered, as if to say, *Look, man, say something. She needs to hear your voice.*

I took hold of her hand. "Maggs, I miss the sound of your voice." That's when it hit me.

Voice mail.

I picked up the phone, dialed as fast as the rotary phone would let me, waited four rings, and then she picked up.

"Hi, this is Dylan and Maggie. Sorry we missed your call, but leave us a message and we'll call you back. Talk to you soon. Take care."

I quickly dialed back, wedging the phone between my shoulder and ear, dialing with one hand and holding Maggie's with the other. Blue crawled across the bed, put his front paws in my lap and licked the phone, whimpering. After the eighth time, I set the phone in the receiver, rubbed my face, and stared out the window.

chapter fifteen

I DISMISSED CLASS, GRADED QUIZZES FOR ALMOST an hour, then packed my bag and slipped out. Crossing the yard to my truck, I got curious, so I wandered over toward the fence. The football team was practicing on the far eastern side of the field. I threw my bag in the back and walked through the gate toward the scrimmage. I didn't necessarily want to see it as much as I wanted to smell and hear it.

As I was walking, I heard a voice behind me.

"You singing, Professuh?"

I turned around to see Russell towering over me like Goliath.

"Who, me? No, I'm just, uh . . . " Okay, I lied.

Russell smiled. "You was singing, Professuh." His eyes widened, and a grassy, sweaty smile cracked his face.

"Not really," I dodged. "Who do y'all play this week?"

"Professuh, that singing sounded good." Russell raised his eyebrows and tried not to smile. "Sing some more."

"Russell, I can't sing my way out of a wet paper bag."

"My daddy loved to sing. He liked blues and old hymns. Sang both so much he got 'em mixed up all the time. One minute he'd be singing 'bout a girl he once knew, the next it was the coming glory." Russell's smile came back, and he raised his eyebrows once again. "And you still ain't answered my question, Professuh. Was you singing?"

"Russell, it's '*Were* you singing.'"

"Okay, Mr. Professuh, sir." Russell had little quit in him. "*Were* you singing?"

"Yes, I was," I admitted, my eyes scanning the practice field.

"I thought so. Now, what was you singing?"

The last thing I wanted was a casual conversation with Russell. In class is one thing. Out of class, that's another. Students can't differentiate. Pretty soon, they start wanting to have out-of-class discussions in class. At that point, the idea of you as teacher, and them as students, hops on a ghost train and flies south. Never to return.

"Russell." I gathered myself. "I was singing a song my wife, Maggie, used to sing to our son before he was born."

"How's it go?"

"Russell, aren't you supposed to be out there somewhere, hurting somebody?" I pointed to the field.

"Professuh, you ain't answering my question." He put his hand on my shoulder.

Russell has a contagious smile. About like Pastor John's. It absolutely destroys any walls you throw in its place. You could rebuild Jericho, and Russell's smile would bring it crumbling down.

"Russell, let me put it to you this way," I said, looking at his hand on my shoulder. "There ain't no way in God's green earth I'm singing you a lullaby." I stepped up toward the fence, crossed my arms, and kept my eyes on the scrimmage, appearing intent on the action on the field.

"Professor," he said in his best English, "'Ain't' is not a word."

I laughed. I walked back toward him, stepping over pieces of wall as I went.

"Professuh, you don't laugh much, but when you do, it's a good laugh. You oughta try it some more."

What is it with these kids? I'm walking around here half-naked tripping over wall rubble.

Russell continued, "So how's that lullaby go?"

"No."

"Now, Professuh." Russell started talking with his hands. "They's no need to start getting huffy. We jus' having a friendly conversation, and you was about to sing me a song."

"Russell, go away. Go hit somebody. I'll see you in class."

"I ain't gonna do dat, Professuh. Been hitting people all day. That's how come I'm standing here. 'Cause I'm good at it, and all those boys over there ain't. Now come on, I heard it when I walked up here."

"How's your term paper coming?" I asked.

"Professuh, don't change the subject. We ain't in school. This is football, you see." Russell used his hands to paint along with his words. "In case you ain't never seen one, that's a field. That's a ball. This is grass. These are pads, and this is sweat. School is over there, and this is here. Let's keep 'em separate." His smile grew bigger. "Now are you gonna sing, or am I gonna bring this up in class? I am bigger than you, and . . ."

"Yes?" I said. "And what? I can flunk you in two shakes."

"I'm waiting." He tapped his size-fourteen cleats on the grass.

Every time I stood in Russell's presence, I noticed how big he was. He stood maybe seven inches taller than me, weighed at least 290 pounds, and had very little fat. Maybe 8 percent. With shoulder pads, he was huge. I was glad I didn't have to tackle him.

"If you ain't in there," the coach hollered, tobacco juice oozing out the corner of his mouth, "or standing on the sideline, I want you on a knee."

I sat down on a nearby bench, and Russell took a knee. He faced the scrimmage, one ear trained on the coach and one on me. He knew how to look as though he were paying attention. Sweat was pouring out of every pore, and Russell was in his element. Heat, pads, pain. Paradise.

I gave in and sang.

I sang Maggie's sweet lullaby, and maybe I wanted to hear it too. At first I murmured, barely above my breath, but Russell would have none of that.

"Professuh," he said, keeping his eyes pointed toward the

field, "that don't count. I can't hear you." He cupped his hand to his ear.

So I sang it for real, as if I were singing to Maggie's tummy. I finished my song, blinked away the glisten, and looked down at Russell, expecting chiding.

"Professuh," Russell said, strapping on his helmet, "you awright." He buttoned his chinstrap and didn't look at me. "You awright."

I don't know if he looked away because he didn't want to see the water in my eyes or didn't want me to see the water in his.

"See you in class, Russell."

"In class," Russell said with his back toward me.

I heard the second snap of his chinstrap, and Russell jogged off. Man, he was big. Powerful too. Whatever his folks fed him, it worked. There's no telling how much it cost to feed that kid when he was coming up.

I walked off the practice field, pulled the door of my truck closed, cranked her up, and headed for the hospital. As I was driving over the old tracks, I glanced back across the field and spotted Russell. He had rejoined the scrimmage, tackled the running back, and was now holding both the ball and the running back's helmet. The running back lay on his back, dazed, shaking his head, surrounded by three trainers.

Minutes later, I caught myself humming.

chapter sixteen

I DISMISSED CLASS AMID A PUDDLE OF AFTERNOON sweat. It was now almost October, but the lazy summer haze was hanging around, winning the battle against the cooler breezes that made a strong charge in the evening, but beat a retreat during the day. With every class, I kept threatening to buy a window unit and blow some a/c into this place. If I did, I'd bet my truck that the introduction of that window unit would change the seating chart. All my kids would be crowding around that thing—even Koy.

On her way out the door, Amanda glanced at my arm, looked down her nose, and shook her head. "You better let me clean that again." She left without another word.

I rolled down my sleeve, stuffed my hand in my pocket, and began packing my bag. As I was leaving, I almost stumbled over Koy, who was still seated. She had her hands folded in front of her mouth and looked as though she wanted to say something. I decided to help her out.

"You were quiet in class today."

"I'm quiet every day."

"True." I smiled and waited for her to say something else. I wasn't going to drag it out of her.

"Professuh." She lifted her book bag into her lap. "I write a lot, and, uh, I was wondering if maybe you'd look at this for me. Tell me whether you think it's any good."

I walked over and leaned against the desk next to hers. "Sure, I'll look at it, but don't take me as the sole measure for whether or not it's any good. I may say it's great when others think not. And I may say it stinks when it doesn't. I'm just one opinion, and unfortunately, I like what I like. Know what I mean?"

"Yeah, me too." Koy reached into her bag and pulled out a well-worn journal. This book had seen some time. She handed me the journal reluctantly and walked out of the room.

The pages were worn, tattered, and on them she had written thousands of words. I slid it into my backpack and turned to leave. When I did, I noticed Koy standing back in the doorway.

She turned slowly, pointing at the journal, and said, "Professuh, that's . . . that's me in there." She looked away, then turned and faced me. Her right hand came slowly up to her face and removed her glasses. Beautiful green eyes stared out at me. An emerald surprise.

Why would someone try so hard to hide something so beautiful?

She stepped forward, took a deep breath, and said, "Can we keep me between you and me?"

"Koy." I reached into my backpack and pulled out the journal. "If you're asking me whether or not I will keep what I read in this journal inside me and between us, the answer is yes. Absolutely. But trust? Trust is another matter. It's a choice. It's earned. It's something I don't do with everybody. Am I trustworthy? You have to decide that. Not me. It's your call. And if you ask me to read this journal, you're trusting me."

She stood motionless a minute, looked at the floor, glanced down the hall, put her glasses back on, tugged at her handbag, then walked over to me, grabbed the journal out of my hand, and left without a word.

Maybe I was too hard. Maybe not. Who knows? I do know this: most people, myself included, are at their most vulnerable in a journal. They pour it all out. Sometimes a journal is the only ear that will listen, or at least the only one that you want to talk to. So we talk until our hand can write no more and then, spent, we fall off to sleep or go to class or get back to work or whatever it was that we were escaping from in the first place.

I went home, piddled around the house, and then decided I'd drive to the hospital after the late shift had settled down. I was surprised when I found myself instead curled up on my front-porch swing, watching the sunrise light the corn tassels. Last thing I remembered was watching the wind make waves out of the corn rows.

Squinting in the morning sun, I saw that on the floor below me lay Koy's journal with a note on top of it.

Professor, I didn't want to wake you. Sorry about yesterday. Please read. Koy.

I percolated some Maxwell House, returned to the swing with a steaming cup, resisted a tug to get to the hospital, and started on page one.

By noon I had read the whole thing. Mostly poetry and short vignettes. Scenes of her life. No beginning. No ending. Snapshots absent a context.

When I finished, I had one question: why in the world was this girl in my class? Koy was good. I'm not talking about "she has good style" or even "control of the English language." Koy had a gift. The real deal.

Sitting there on my porch, holding that girl's mind and heart in my hand, I could only think of two real possibilities. Either she was a gifted genius unchallenged by school, sort of a Bill Gates with a pen, or something had happened to her. Something violent and sudden had taken away the tenderness and replaced it with the ice-queen demeanor and sunglasses.

What I held in my hand reminded me of a feeling that I had had several times in grammar school and rarely since. It was that awe mixed with incredulity that I got in Ms. Edward's music class while studying Mozart. Now I had it with Koy. How could someone so young produce something so fine and grown-up?

I put the journal down and sipped my coffee, which had long since grown cold. It was horrible. Maggie loved cold coffee. She used to pour a cup in the morning, let it sit a few hours, and then pick it up just before lunch. Sort of a midday caffeine hit. I never did figure that out. Why would anyone purposefully drink cold coffee when she could have it hot? I sniffed the top again, realized it had sat dormant for more than three hours, brought it to my lips, and sipped again curiously. The cold dregs swirled around my tongue and fell down my throat. I noticed a different taste and once again felt the cold hammer of loneliness slam me against the porch.

THE THERMOMETER OUTSIDE READ NINETY-EIGHT DEGREES, and not a single cloud dotted the clear blue sky. I walked through the hospital doors wearing a long-sleeved black T-shirt, Blue at my heels. All was quiet. Maggie lay in her room, a solemn sleeping beauty. Someone had recently brushed her hair and painted her fingernails. I checked her feet to see if they were cold and noticed that the same person had painted her toenails as well.

Maggie always slept wearing socks. She hated cold feet. Without them she put her feet on my back or stomach, depending on which side I happened to be sleeping at the moment. Blue licked her feet, rubbed his cold nose against her fingers, sniffed her hair, and lay down at the foot of her bed.

Maggie looked as though she were sleeping. Her expression didn't mirror the doctor's dooming comments about "permanent damage." About "never waking." We were now through the 50 percent range and well into the 25 percent chance of recovery. A few days ago, he shook his head and said, "Dylan, I'm just being honest. Prepare yourself."

But she didn't look like what her chart said she was. She looked like my wife on Saturday morning. She looked like she was about to wake up and float with me downriver. I walked into the room, picked up her chart out of the sleeve on the end of her bed, read the doctor's illegible comments, opened the window, pitched it as far as I could, and watched it flail into the reflection pond three floors below. They don't bar the windows on the rooms of vegetables. Not much danger of their jumping out.

I kissed her forehead. She was warm. She smelled like Maggie. I whispered, "Hey, Maggs, it's me," and sat down. She didn't move. I didn't expect her to. It's just that every time in our life that I whispered, "Hey, Maggs," kissed her forehead, and put her coffee on the table next to the bed, she woke up, turned on her side, put her head in my lap, took a deep breath, and said, "What do you want to do today?"

Maggie was a pretty intense sleeper. Sometimes I'd get up in the middle of the night, and her hand would be sitting upright on her forehead as though she were thinking or had forgotten something. Whatever she was thinking about, whatever she had forgotten, it had wrinkled the skin between her eyes above her nose. I'd lean over, pull her hand down to her side, kiss her gently, and place my hand on her forehead. She'd relax. The skin would ease, go soft, and the wrinkle would disappear. When I didn't wake up, and she spent most of the night in that tense wrinkle, she'd wake and her neck would be screaming with pain. I knew it was only evidence of her depth. Maggie is a simple complexity. A paradox. Meaning between extremes.

I put my head down next to Maggie's and breathed. It was the first time in our married life that she let me share the same pillow. I wanted to smell her. Hear her breathe. Listen to her feet shuffle under the sheets. I wanted to be with my wife.

I'm not talking about the sexual thing. God knows I could. I'm a man. This is my wife. I love her. But after the delivery, the hemorrhage, the blood, and what the doctors had to do, even if she woke right this minute, it would be months before that was physically an option. And then there's the emotional aspect. Maggie's strong, but not that strong.

No, I'm talking about that sweet thing that happens when you open your eyes and realize in the dim daybreak of dawn that your wife has nudged her head next to yours and that you're now breathing air she breathed. That sweet thing that happens when you realize this and then close your eyes and feel that soft rush of her breath tickle your eyelashes. The sweet thing that happens when, after feeling that soft rush, you doze, each breathing parts of the other's air.

About dark, long after my stomach started growling, Amanda walked in the door, pulling a cart.

Blue looked up from the floor and perked his ears.

"Hello, Professor. Hello, Miss Maggie. Hello, Blue." She stopped next to me, grabbed my left arm, and started pulling back the sleeve of my T-shirt. I winced and jerked it back, but Amanda would have none of that. "Professor, if you don't give me that arm, I'm calling in the doctor, a couple of really big nurses, and your deputy friend. So we can either do this the easy way, or we can do it your way."

I extended my arm.

My T-shirt was stuck to my flesh. Small circles of pus and serum seeped through the fibers of my shirt. Amanda took my wrist in her hand and started methodically cutting and peeling the shirt away. After about the third pull, I realized how much it hurt. My arm was raw meat.

While I winced, Amanda spoke to Maggie. "Now, Miss Maggie, don't worry. I'm taking good care of this arm until you get to where you can. At least when he's in this hospital. I can't speak for him outside of here, but in this hospital, I'll take good care of him. We need to get his arm healed up. From what I can tell, he's not real good at taking care of himself." Amanda looked at me. "He keeps picking at this thing like he's trying to get rid of something." She turned to Maggie again. "So it would help us all out if you'd just go ahead and wake up before this arm gets to where he can't use it anymore."

She finished bandaging my arm, held out her hand, and said, "Swallow this."

Shortly thereafter, I dozed off. About two in the morning, Amos tapped me on the shoulder and said, "D.S., let's go get some coffee."

Blue licked my ankle as I wiped my eyes and cleared the drool from my chin. I was groggy, but whatever Amanda had given me had worked. I kissed Maggs and put my hand on her forehead.

"See you tomorrow. Thanks for letting me share your pillow. I promise, if you wake up, you'll never have to do it again."

Amos and I walked out of the hospital and crossed the street to the all-night diner. It used to be a Waffle House that had long since gone out of business. Now the sign above the door read "Al's Diner, Open 24 Hours." I've never been there when Al wasn't working the grill. When that guy slept, I'll never know.

Amos and I sat down and ordered coffee, and I placed three orders for scrambled eggs.

"How is she?"

"Same."

"What's this business with your arm?"

"Huh?"

"I said, why do you keep doing whatever you're doing to your arm?"

"Oh. I just goofed it up working in the pasture."

"That's not what your nurse said."

"Yeah? What does she know? She wasn't there."

"She says that every time she sees you it's worse, and now you're trying to cover it up. That's why she's bandaged it like that. So you can't make it any worse."

"Amos, it's three in the morning. Can we talk about something else?"

"How's class?" he said without a break.

I looked up. "Shouldn't you be home sleeping or working or something?"

"I am working."

"My tax dollars are paying you for this time?"

"How's class?"

"You don't quit, do you?"

"Not when it comes to you." Amos smiled, his white teeth shining in the dim light of the diner.

I rubbed my eyes. "It's probably a good thing too."

"Have you figured it out yet?"

"Figured out what?"

"Amanda."

"Amos, would you quit talking in code? It's about three hours past my ability to translate."

"Have you figured out Amanda Lovett?"

"What's there to figure? I've got an attractive, kind, pregnant preacher's daughter sitting in the front row of my class, and she also happens to be my wife's nurse. Yes, I've got that figured pretty well."

"Yeah, but have you figured how that attractive, kind, sweet, unmarried daughter-of-a-preacher got pregnant in the first place?"

"No. I haven't spent much time on that."

"You probably thought she was just another statistic."

I rubbed my eyes and stared out the diner window. "Amos, please come to a point. Just about any point will do."

"Six months ago, Amanda Lovett was kidnapped, driven seven miles from town, and tied to a tree deep in the Salkehatchie.

She was then raped by at least two men, maybe more. Six days later, they dumped her on her daddy's lawn. You need me to draw you a picture?"

That was picture enough. "No, I got it."

"That girl, the same girl that bandages your arm, brushes your wife's hair, leaves a towel for Blue, and brings you orange juice in the morning, was beat up and left for dead. She was also impregnated." Amos sat back. "This is a small town, and word travels fast, but you Styleses have a tendency to keep to yourselves. Always have. Now . . . " Amos pointed his toothpick at me. "You want the answer to your next question?"

"Yes."

"Well." He tongued the toothpick to the other side of his mouth. "I could tell you, but you need to hear it from her. Ask her sometime. "

"Amos, did you bring me to this one-tooth establishment to tell me this?"

"Yup."

"Why?"

"'Cause you need to hear that there are folks in this world who got lives just as bad as yours. Life ain't fair, and welcome to earth."

"Thanks. I feel much better just knowing that."

I paid for the coffee and eggs, and Blue and I left Amos talking with Al. When I cranked my truck, Garth was singing a duet with Martina, but I turned it off and rode home in silence, except for the rhythmic sound of a nail in my tire hitting the blacktop.

chapter seventeen

FRIDAY NIGHT WAS THE BIGGEST GAME OF THE year, according to Marvin. This was "The Rivalry." Every school has a nemesis, and Digs's was South Carolina Junior College.

Blue and I walked up to the fence next to the track and stood parallel with the goal line. The bleachers were filled with kids, and because dogs make some folks nervous, I put a leash on Blue. He looked at me as if I had lost my mind.

"Sorry, pal. It's just for an hour or so."

I leaned against the fence and looked up at the clock. It was the third quarter, and Digs was beating SCJC by a touchdown, 27-20. From what I had heard in the classroom, Digs had speed and a decent quarterback, SCJC had a running back named Thumper, and both teams had defense.

The Digger defense was on the field, and Russell was lined up on the far side as defensive tackle. SCJC snapped the ball, and the quarterback rolled left—to Russell's side of the field. Russell ran over the offensive tackle and sacked the quarterback for what would have been a twelve-yard loss had the quarterback not fumbled the ball.

Players scrambled everywhere trying to pick up the pigskin. The stands erupted again in a wave of arms and a roar of penny-filled milk jugs. Out of the heap, Marvin came up with the ball and began running down my side of the field. His arms and feet were a blur. When he passed me, his face was a picture of gums, teeth, and unadulterated joy. He crossed the goal line twelve yards ahead of the nearest player, spiked the ball, and did some dance I had never before seen. Then Russell picked him up and they, and the rest of the defense, paraded to the bench. Score: 33-20.

I was saying something to myself about fast feet when I heard, "Hey there, Professor."

I didn't need to look. The seductive voice gave her away. I turned and said, "What? No sunglasses tonight?"

Koy reached up and pulled her sunglasses down from their perch atop her head. "How's that?" she said.

"Much better. I almost didn't recognize you."

Digs kicked off and tackled SCJC on about the twenty-two.

"So, what are you doing here?" Koy asked.

"Watching a football game," I said, pointing to the field.

"Don't most people do that from the stands?"

"Yeah, but I thought it might be too much for Blue. You know—all the noise."

"Oh," she said with a skeptical expression. She knelt down and rubbed Blue's head. "What's your story, Professor?"

"What do you mean, what's my story?" I asked.

"I mean, what's your story? Why's a good-looking, upstanding guy like you teaching a loser class like ours?"

"You think you guys are losers?"

"Come on, Professor. We're all adults here."

"Well, I used to teach some, had a break in my farming, and this class came along. I saw it, applied, and they accepted me."

"That ain't the way I heard it."

"It ain't?"

"No, it is not," she said in her best imitation of me. "Way I heard it was that you was found 'bout half dead in a cornfield by your buddy, the deputy, who I saw somewhere here tonight." She tilted her head, looking out over the field, and put her finger to her lips. "You know, he carries a big gun, and he ain't too bad-looking. Anyway, your wife knew you could teach, and he knew you can't farm. So the two of them signed you up and stuck you in this class with the rest of us losers."

I nodded. "All right, now that you know most of my story, what's yours?"

Koy picked her glasses off her nose and tucked them back on top of her head. "Professor, I'm just playing with you. You look like a sore thumb out here. You're about the only white person in this smelly armpit." She waved her hands across the crowd. "I thought maybe you could use some friendly conversation."

"Is that what this is?" I said, smiling.

"Oh, you ought to hear me when I'm unfriendly." Her right hand played with her earring.

"I'll pass. I like the friendly."

"Good." She moved up, rubbing shoulders with me, and rested her chin on her hands over the fence. "So what's the deal? Why are you here?"

"I like football. I wanted to see if Russell and Marvin are really as good as Marvin keeps telling me they are."

"Believe me, they're better. Up there, in that box"—she pointed to the press box above the stands—"are about sixteen scouts. The guys on the roof above them are the reporters who call the game. They kicked them out of the press box to make room for all the scouts."

I scanned the rooftops and wondered about Russell and Marvin's futures. Three years from now their lives, and lifestyles, would be very different. I turned back to Koy. "My story is simple, Koy. My wife and I moved back here after graduate school. I couldn't get hired as a teacher, so I leaned on what I knew—farming. But, as you so aptly stated, I'm not much of a farmer. Not yet, anyway. So, for a lot of reasons, my wife, with a little help from my friend Amos, signed me up to teach this class. And here I am."

"Professor, tell me something I don't know."

"All right."

It was fourth and seven. SCJC had the ball on Digs's forty-yard line. They handed the ball to Thumper, who lowered his head and shoulder and rambled for eleven yards. First-and-ten on the twenty-nine. At the snap, Marvin rushed in from his corner position to support, but like a lot of corners with good feet and little desire to butt heads, he tried to arm-tackle and strip the ball. He probably learned that from Dion, who could actually do it. After Thumper ran through Marvin and gained seven more yards, Marvin got up, buckled his chinstrap, and headed for the sideline. Guess he needed a breather. Russell, not needing a breather, stood in the huddle, waiting on the next call.

"Koy." I looked down. "You're goofing off, and your work shows it. What's in your journal is far better than what you produce in class. Why the difference?"

She blinked and batted her eyelashes. "Because school-work don't mean nothing."

I nodded. "You're right, but you've got a gift. And you're wasting it.

"Yeah, but . . . "

"But what?" I asked.

She put her head on the top rail of the fence and gazed out across the field. "Professor, I swear, sometimes you don't seem too bright when it comes to people. Can't you see? Look around you. This is Digger, South Carolina. I'm never getting out of here. I'm stuck in this cesspool, and you know it. Why you think they call this place Digger?"

"They call it Digger because you can dig yourself into or out of a hole." I paused. "And getting out of here is your choice. But it's not going to happen if you keep giving me half-completed work and a half-committed attitude. You don't do that in your journal."

Koy looked away and put her sunglasses back down over her eyes. "Yeah, well . . . I'm digging, all right." She stepped away from the fence. "I'll see you, Professor." She walked off the way she came: alone and at a distance from the stands.

Two minutes remained in the game. Thumper had rushed for over two hundred yards, but I don't think many of those yards were gained against Russell's side of the field. Digs was still up by ten points and looking pretty good. But a lot can happen in two minutes.

SCJC snapped the ball. The quarterback took a seven-step drop and threw deep down the far sideline. Marvin was in man-coverage and timed his jump well. He intercepted the ball on the ten, took a few lateral steps, and headed back up the sideline, where the free safety made a couple of good blocks and freed things up. Thumper took an angle and was just about to blindside Marvin when Russell decapitated him. Marvin took three more steps and was gone. Ninety yards.

He started dancing at about the ten. Danced all the way into the end zone and threw the ball through the goalposts. The referee threw the flag for excessive celebration, but Marvin didn't care. He danced all the way to the sideline, where every player and coach high-fived his hand or slapped his helmet. He went over to the bench, jumped up, raised his arms to the crowd, and started the wave. People were jumping and pennies were spilling all over the place. Come Monday, I knew he'd be a handful.

chapter eighteen

My screen door slammed, and Amos bounded into the living room, where I sat in the dark listening for an echo of Maggie's voice. It was mid-November, Canadian winds had blown in an arctic front, and the temperature had slipped to twenty-three degrees. I don't understand weather patterns all that well, but arctic front or not, it was butt-cold. The weatherman said it would drop another three or four degrees before the night was out.

Next to me were a pair of old Carhart overalls, hip waders, and my headlamp. Amos didn't say a word. Just popped his head around the corner, saw me, nodded, and turned back toward the door. I grabbed my stuff and threw it into the back of his truck. While I waved my hands across the heater vent inside the truck, one thought occurred to me. Winter had come, and Maggie would like that.

I turned to Blue and held up my hand like a stop sign. He laid down on the couch, let out a deep breath, and wouldn't look at me. The silent treatment. "Not tonight," I said. "Don't want you getting hurt." He whined and dug his wet nose beneath the sofa cushion.

Willard's parking lot was full by the time we arrived, crammed tight with trucks, dog boxes, blaze-orange vests, baseball caps advertising farm equipment, hip waders, chewing tobacco, Carhart overalls, and coffee cups now used as spit cups. Mr. Willard's thermometer, hanging on the gas pump, read twenty-two degrees, but that probably accounted for a little bit of wind chill.

A few weeks ago, Amos said he bought his dad some new insulated hip waders for this year's season. Amos parked his Expedition next to his dad's old Ford. His father walked over to him, running his fingers up the elastic suspenders. "Moose, I love 'em. Best I've ever owned."

"Glad you like them."

Mr. Carter put his hand on Amos's shoulder, and the two walked ahead of me toward Mr. Willard's store. Mr. Willard saw us coming and opened the door with a smile. Then he hung the "Closed" sign over the suction hook in the middle of the window.

His coffeepot was almost empty after Amos and I filled our mugs and a beat-up green thermos that looked as if it had rolled one too many times around the back of somebody's pickup. Back outside, Mr. Carter banged on the side of an empty Maxwell House coffee can for attention, then climbed atop the dog box wedged in the bed of his truck. He zipped up his coveralls, pulled up his collar, shoved his hands in his pockets, and began.

"Howdy. Now y'all come in close. That's better." His voice was blowing smoke, it was so cold. "It's too cold to yell. And Jim, don't stand too close to my exhaust. I don't want you passing out again. I don't want to hear any excuses from you when we get in the Salk."

Mr. Carter smiled, Jim shuffled his feet, and everybody laughed.

Jim Biggins, who is just what his name implies, owns a junkyard, but come winter, he supplies most of Digger and even some of Charleston with firewood. In seven years he's never run out of wood, and neither have the folks in Digger. He sells it cheap, and Jim has kept a lot of people warm long after their gas has been cut off.

A few years back, he had just come off working a double because the Weather Channel said South Carolina would experience a hard freeze. Once he got home, he pulled on his coveralls and came coon hunting. We got inside the swamp, and Jim just couldn't hold off the sleep any longer. No amount of coffee would change that. Just about the time the dogs treed a coon, Jim slumped over and fell asleep at the base of an old cypress, curled up like a baby.

Jim is about six foot six, dresses out at three hundred

pounds, and is the strongest human being I have ever known. There was no way we could tote him out of the swamp. So Mr. Carter and the rest of the boys continued hunting while Amos and I hung out in the swamp for a few hours, letting Jim nap. We made a fire and sipped coffee, and when Jim woke, he stood up, shook his head, and apologized. We walked out of the Salk about an hour before daylight. Since then, he's never let me pay for firewood, and I've never run out. Somehow every year it just shows up.

Towering over everyone from his perch in the back of the pickup, Mr. Carter addressed the crowd like the chairman of the board at the annual stockholders meeting. "I'd like to welcome everybody to the first coon hunt of this year." He eyed the full moon and cloudless sky. "Looks like we got us a good night."

Coon hunting in Digger is a religion, something passed down from father to son. Amos's dad has had the best coon dogs in the state for years. He's been winner or runner-up of the Greater Salkehatchie Coon Gathering for twelve of the last fifteen years, and he breathes coon hunting. It could be blowing forty miles an hour outside, treetops blowing right off the trees, but come first freeze of the year, Mr. Carter would load five or six of his best hounds and head to Mr. Willard's store.

Participation here is by invitation only, and Mr. Carter is selective. If you get invited, you better be able to keep up, and you better not have a problem walking ten or fifteen miles.

Mr. Carter prides himself on dogs that can hunt all night

and on into the next day. His dog kennel is a real operation. Twelve kennels raised four feet off the ground. Every dog has its own box, automatic waterer, and food bowl. Once a month Mr. Carter drives to the Wal-Mart distribution center and loads up his pickup with about eight or ten seventy-five-pound bags of Alpo. Twelve dogs can eat a lot of food, and they can get rid of it too. Every morning Mr. Carter cranks up his pressure washer and hoses down the concrete into a holding area, where he shovels the muck into a five-gallon bucket and dumps it into a hole that he dug with his front-end loader. In fifteen years, he's pretty well dug up his whole pasture, but he's got the greenest grass of any farm in Digger.

In almost twenty years, he's lost only one dog to snakebite, because he trains them to stay away from snakes. In springtime he waits for the weather to warm up and catches a rattler or moccasin crossing a road or slithering along some bank somewhere. He tapes its mouth shut and then puts both the snake and the dog into a closed space and buckles a shock collar on the dog. I'm not talking about a pet-supermarket bark collar that sort of tickles the dog into thinking that it ought not to sniff the snake. His collars do what they advertise. They shock. They aren't inhumane, but they're strong enough to straighten all four legs and bring a dog off its feet. He calls it electroshock therapy. Mr. Carter used to threaten to put one on Amos and me when we were kids, if he thought it was needed. As a result, we didn't let him know about all the trouble we got into.

With the dog and the snake in the same space, he would

let the dog do what it naturally did. Sniff. But every time the dog got close to or sniffed the snake, Mr. Carter lit him up with that collar. "Watch this," Mr. Carter would say. The dog would pace back and forth, looking at the snake out of the corner of its eye. The snake would coil up and silently watch the dog, wishing that its mouth weren't taped shut. The dog, not knowing that the ropy looking thing in the corner of his kennel wanted to kill it, walked over, sniffed, and attempted to place the snake between its teeth. Just about the time the dog's teeth touched the snake's skin, Mr. Carter mashed the big red button in the middle of the 2D-cell radio control in his hand. The dog yelped, jumped three feet off the ground, straightened all four legs, and returned to the opposite corner of the kennel, whining, never to sniff a snake again. Curiosity cured.

One year a fellow in Charleston called Mr. Carter and gave him a real stubborn dog named Gus. Gus was, and still is, cross-eyed as a goat and dumb as a brick. By Mr. Carter's account, the previous owner was tired of messing with him. To cure his stupidity, Mr. Carter caught a six-foot diamondback and put him in the kennel with Gus. Dumb Gus immediately went to sniffing, and Mr. Carter shocked—three times. Finally Gus got the picture. That collar just about killed him, but Gus is still alive and has never been snakebit.

Mr. Carter kicked the dog box to quiet one of his hounds and turned again to face the crowd at his feet. "Glad y'all could make it. John Stotton said he could not be here tonight 'cause Emma is feeling a little under the weather, but he promised to make it this weekend. Pastor John had a wedding over in Charleston. And"—he looked at Amos—"son, who am I forgetting?"

"Sam," Amos whispered.

"Oh yeah, Sam Revel said he's got some business in Columbia. All send their apologies. Butch Walker and his boys said a few of their milking cows got loose, but if they can join us, they'll be along shortly."

Every year we all compete to see who can come up with the best lighting apparatus. There's a science to it. You have to consider three things: weight, longevity, and candlepower. John Billingsly won last year's pat on the back with a one million candlepower Q-beam mounted to his chest, powered with a backpack full of four lithium ion batteries converted from an Apple laptop. John works in computer sales, and rumor has it that he's threatened to increase this year's output to two million candlepower. John doesn't understand overkill. He's the guy in town who trades his own computer in every three months whether he needs to or not, and the back of his toilet is full of magazines that tell you all about the latest computer technology. John even writes for some of them. A lot of school kids in Digger have benefited from his "used" models. Anyway, when he stepped out of his truck for coon hunting, he looked like a walking lighthouse.

Mr. Carter moved to the front of his dog box, eyed the crowd, and pointed to John Billingsly. "I think we can pretty well agree that John here is this year's hands-down winner in the light category. John, you outdid yourself again."

John smiled earlobe to earlobe, and four or five guys patted him on the back.

"Anybody with bad eyesight, stay close to John. But be careful; he looks like a walking runway light, so be wary of planes looking for a landing strip on the outside of the Salk."

After the laughter quieted, Mr. Carter continued. "Gentlemen, we haven't hunted the south end of the Salk in almost three years, so tonight I thought we'd drive that direction. Any objections?"

Mr. Carter's authority is never questioned. This is his show, and everybody knows it. Nobody spoke.

"Good. Now, Jimmy," he said to a man in faded green Carharts. "You still got that mangy female, Sally?"

"Yes, sir," Jimmy answered.

"Well, good. She seems to work real well with Badger, so we'll let the two of them out first. Now, y'all know that the first catch of the year is a training coon. It's not a keeper. So any of you that might be a little weak in the stomach ought to hang back once we get to the tree. Everybody agree?" Mr. Carter folded his hands and lowered his head as though checking off a mental list. "The CB's on channel seven, and if the reception is bad there, we'll go to fourteen. Everybody got a partner?"

One fellow in the back raised his hand. "No, sir."

"All right, Frank, me either. You're with me. Anybody else?" Nobody spoke. At that, Mr. Carter bounced off his dog box onto the tailgate and hit the ground at a trot. Sixteen truck engines started at one time amid a cloud of white exhaust and the pang and smack of glass-packs. Mr. Carter's old Ford slowly led the procession out of the parking lot.

That scene would make a great commercial. Represented there were about fifteen models and years of Ford and Chevy's best work trucks, all in varying degrees of worn out. All we'd need is a Bob Seger, Alan Jackson, or George Strait song, and we'd fit right in with Monday night football.

The commercial proceeded down Highway 42 until we got to McSweeney's Fork, turned right down South Salk Road, and drove four miles to Gunter's Hole, where we eased under the huge live oak limbs bordering the edge of the swamp.

Around Digger, the Salkehatchie is mythical. Everybody knows the stories. Confederate gold. Lost lovers. Indians. World War II German spies. Vietnamese foot soldiers. Eighteen-foot alligators. You name it, it's buried there. Somewhere beneath the slow-moving black water, the hundred-foot cypress trees, the hanging moss, and the swamp stench, there's a story to go along with most every idea you could have about a swamp. If you can think it, it's probably already been mythified.

Every coon hunter in the Salk is required to have two things: a radio and a partner, the idea being that if you get lost, at least you'll be able to talk to folks on the outside, and you won't be lonely. It happens about once a year. Rarely does anybody spend the night in the swamp, but several times they've walked out some ten or fifteen miles from where they walked in. The swamp itself is forty square miles of the exact same thing. Landmarks are difficult to make. Nobody "knows" the swamp, not even Mr. Carter. He's pretty good around the edges, most of us are, but we know our limits. Amos and I are as good as anyone. We've dug for a lot of Confederate gold in our days, even built a few *Swiss Family Robinson* forts in the cedars, but even we know where our experience stops and the swamp takes over.

And one more thing. When the sun goes down in the Salk, "dark" takes on a whole new meaning. It may be clear and starlight bright outside, but you step one foot inside that swamp, underneath the canopy, and it's a different story. No matter how familiar you might be with a particular area of the swamp, when dark comes, you turn around, try and find your way out, and things look real different. No matter how well you've marked it, orange surveyor's tape, breadcrumbs, or what, the darkness will make you doubt.

At Gunter's Hole, Mr. Carter unlatched the box doors, letting Badger and Sally catapult off the tailgate. The two bounded off into the darkness. We stood outside in the cold, engines idling, feet shuffling, listening to single barks like submarine pings as they faded a half mile, then a mile, then a little more. Talking was over. If you needed to communicate, you used hand signals, or worst case, you whispered.

Mr. Carter does not tolerate talking while he's listening to Badger. Varying tones are more difficult to pick up the farther he gets from the edge of the swamp. After a few minutes I could tell no audible difference in Badger's bark, yet a smile began to crease Mr. Carter's face. I had learned long ago that Mr. Carter's face could tell me far more than Badger's bark.

One second after Mr. Carter's crease reached a full smile,

Badger broke into an all-out hound wail—a totally different bark. It sounded like a cross between death and ecstasy, telling Mr. Carter that its nose had found what it'd been sniffing for. Mr. Carter had his hand on the dog box, so when Badger broke, he unleashed the second latch, and five dogs disappeared like four-legged ghosts into the swamp. The only trace of the dogs was the deafening chase bark. All the hunters cut their engines and hit their hunting lights.

Mr. Carter looked at me and said, "D.S., grab my Winchester."

I did. As kids, Amos and I had shot a dozen or so raccoons, more than a hundred squirrels, and a thousand aluminum cans with Mr. Carter's Model 61 Winchester. I knew this rifle.

A coon-dog fight is a brutal thing, and the coon usually wins if you aren't careful. That's where Mr. Carter comes in. He's seen many a blind dog following a coon fight, and he hates to see his dogs hurt. Even Gus. Grabbing a handful of dog leashes, Mr. Carter immediately sloshed into the swamp, following the dogs.

The mossy grass was frozen and crunchy, and a thin layer of ice covered the floor. Amos and I filed behind him, as did everyone else, and we slipped into the swamp with seven dogs, at least one raccoon, and about seven million candlepower of artificial light, thanks in large part to John Billingsly and the rest of the coal miner convention. We lit up the underside of the canopy like a runway. Wherever we looked was bright as day. Wherever we didn't look was an abyss.

One more thing about the Salk: you don't want to step where you haven't first looked. We followed Mr. Carter, who, despite his seventy-four years of age, moved pretty well. As the barking got louder, his pace quickened. After twenty-two minutes, we neared the tree, and Mr. Carter was almost running. Ice and black water were splashing everywhere.

Reaching the tree, he immediately tied up Badger and handed Sally to Jimmy, because if he didn't tie up Badger, the other dogs would never fight that coon. Gus, maybe, but the young dogs didn't have a chance. Badger is vicious when it comes to coons, and he never shares a fight with another dog. If he finds the coon, it's his to fight with. Go find your own coon.

Having tied up Badger, we backed up and started our laser light show in the trees above us while Gus and the four younger dogs stood against the base of the tree, barking. You'd think spotting a coon in a tree would be no big deal. Just shine and light up two orangish-yellow eyes. But old coons didn't get to be old coons in the Salkehatchie by being stupid. After a few minutes, Amos spotted a hole in the canopy where the moon was shining through. A rare sight. Rarer still was the fact that it was shining through silver-gray hair. The coon was sixty to eighty feet up, perched atop a short cedar limb, looking somewhere between scared and comfortable.

Amos turned to me, looked as if he was about to ask me a question, and then held out his hand, into which I placed his dad's Model 61. At Mr. Carter's command, all the hunters cut their lights, save one. His. He shined, and Amos shot. An effective tandem. Amos hit the coon exactly where he intended—square in the left rear hindquarter—and it started falling.

You'd think that a wounded coon that just fell forty to eighty feet, with the air knocked out of it, probably suffering a couple of broken ribs, maybe even a concussion, wild-eyed-scared, and facing six or eight bluetick hounds, would roll over and give up or just lie there and die.

Not hardly. The coon hits the ground, bounces three to four feet, swings at the first three dogs he sees, and takes five eyes with him. Young dogs usually get hurt because they stick their noses too close to the coon's reach.

We can meet, shake hands, pat backs, sip coffee, pull on hip waders, hang an assortment of lights around our necks, reach the swamp, release all the dogs, trek to the foot of a two-hundred-year-old cypress, and the thing on the back of everyone's mind is not the lights, the dogs, the chase, or even getting lost in the swamp, but the coon—and what he will do when he hits the ground.

No matter which way you slice it, if the dogs tree the coon, chances are that the coon is going to get the worse end of the deal. But for every one time we catch a coon, he makes nine escapes. I'm amazed at that thing that happens between a coon that's escaping and a hound whose job it is not to let him escape. Nature versus nature. A bluetick hound has the best nose on the planet, but a coon is one of the only animals that washes its food, and it can climb trees taller than Jack's beanstalk. I have walked away from the base of many a cypress tree, knowing full well there was a perfectly good raccoon at the top of it. We simply couldn't see it. The fit have a tendency to survive.

This coon bounced off five or six limbs on its way down and

landed with a thud. When it hit, it bounced, hissed, bared its teeth, swiped, landed again, and launched into Gus, whose crossed eyes straightened for a split second. He dodged the swipe, hunkered, sprang, and locked onto the coon's head, taking a good cut in the neck.

Fight over.

Two of the younger dogs each grabbed a hind leg and began chewing. The other two went for the body. The coon, half-dead from its descent, a quarter more from Amos's shot, and an eighth more from Gus's locked jaw, used its last eighth and took one final swipe at the dogs closest to him. Both took a good cut across the nose, and Jake was cut pretty deep around his right eye. Mr. Carter watched in quiet but ready judgment, taking notes and considering his training.

Gus sank down in the mud and laid both his front paws over what was left of the coon, which had long since stopped breathing. His locked jaw had not moved from where he first sank it. Mr. Carter told Gus to "release," which he did, and the coon lay motionless amid a circle of dogs, men, and blood-smeared sheets of ice floating in the water. Mr. Carter gently poked the coon in the eye with his rifle barrel to see if it blinked. If it did, he'd pull the trigger.

The air smelled of peat moss, coon, and dog. In more than twenty years of coon hunting, I had never looked away. But tonight the sight of blood, flesh, and a corpse was too much. Some blood had hit me in the face and dribbled down my cheek. I wiped it off and studied my fingers. The blood was red, warm, and sticky. The cold air quickly caked it, causing it to stiffen on my face like paint. It seeped into the cracks of my palm and the wrinkles in my wrist. When I wiped my face a second time, I caught a whiff of it.

"You coming, pal?" Amos asked.

"Yeah, just a second."

Amos took a handkerchief from his back pocket, dipped it in the swamp, and said, "Here, this'll help."

The water was cold, clean, and smelled of cypress roots. I scrubbed my face with Amos's handkerchief, then knelt to dip it in the Salk and rinse it out.

"Keep it," he said, nodding his head.

I dipped and rinsed it twice more. The water dripped off my face and made small ripples that raced around my legs as I squatted in the water. I closed my eyes and shivered as the cold took its place. I dipped my hands into the water and splashed my face. The water ran off my cheeks and down my neck. Some of it dripped back into the Salk and rippled about me. I stood up, exhaled a big white cloud of cold air, and wiped my face with my sleeve.

When I looked around, Mr. Carter and the procession were almost out of sight, and John Billingsly was bringing up the rear. Amos stood a few feet off, studying me quietly. Wrapped in the Salk, with the smell of swamp water sweetened with coon blood and dog sweat rising up around us, Amos said, "Hey, pal, you okay?"

The moon was high and bright now, glistening off the water like a spotlight. I looked down, saw my dark and distorted reflection, and spoke.

"The doctor told Maggs she could start pushing. She pushed, and I counted. Around three, the baby's head showed. Not all the way out, just where I could see the top of it. Then the doctor's face turned white. His eyes looked like half-dollars, and he ordered a nurse to go get some machine.

"Maggie looked at me with tired eyes. I tried to comfort her, but I had no idea what was going on. The doctor told Maggie to keep pushing while he put this suction thing on my son's head. A minute or two later, my son's head popped out. It was all smashed and blue.

"Maggie couldn't see it, but she could see my face. I don't know what my face said, but whatever it was, it probably wasn't what Maggie needed. At that point, two nurses pushed me aside and started pushing down on her stomach, trying to force the baby out. I held Maggie's head in my arms. She was tired. Real tired. The nurses kept pushing, and the doctor was barking orders everywhere. People were running all over the place. I heard a big gush and splash, and the doctor handed my son to a nurse.

"The doctor was tugging on the cord that was still inside Maggie. Blood was pouring out. Maggie's eyes closed, and she went limp."

One of the dogs barked somewhere, quickly answered by another farther north.

"On a table next to the wall, the nurse and doctors kept working on our baby. Pumping his chest, putting this mask over his mouth. He was blue and limp. Maggie's eyes opened again, she saw him, how blue he was, and . . . started crying.

Then her face went white and her eyes rolled back in her head and she threw up all over. That was the last time I saw her eyes open."

Amos shifted uneasily, and his lip quivered as his feet sank further into the muck below.

"A doctor came flying into the room, tying one of those masks around his face, and pushed me out of the way. I crumpled in the corner, lying in Maggie's blood. One doctor injected something into her arm. Another one tried to stop the bleeding. I felt numb. Maggie's blood pressure plummeted. Then I heard the paddles of the resuscitator and the doctors yelling, 'Clear!' My son's arms flew straight up in the air. His body bucked and then fell still and limp. The delivery doctor was sewing like crazy. After a few minutes, the doctors pulled their masks off and looked at the clock. They wrapped him in a blanket. Nobody even bothered to wipe off all the white stuff. I never held him. They didn't offer, and I didn't think to ask.

"Maggie stabilized a little bit. I stood up and noticed my hands. They were stiff and sticky, and so was my face. I leaned over Maggie. She had vomit in her hair. I grabbed a towel and wiped her face and cheeks and around her ears. I propped her head up on a pillow and tucked her hair behind her ears. The doctor just kept watching her monitor."

The tail end of the light parade had completely disappeared, allowing the darkness to return and silently surround us. I strained my eyes for any glimmer of light but saw none. The night grew thick, the canopy pressed in, and I felt alone.

"Somewhere about midnight on the second night, I fell

down. I woke up in a bed next to Maggie. The nurse said some big, bald-headed deputy sheriff, who had been in the hall for two days, picked me up and put me in bed next to Maggie. The doctors said that Maggie lost about half her blood. My son's head was fourteen centimeters in diameter and his stomach was eighteen. He weighed eleven pounds four ounces. I guess you know the rest."

We stood there for some time. I don't know how long, but it was long enough to get really cold.

Finally, Amos held up his hand and stuck three fingers in the air. Chin high, lip quivering, he whispered, "These three remain."

I nodded, and we walked out of the Salk.

Amos and I drove home with his heater on "scorch." The digital thermometer on his rearview mirror read eighteen degrees, and the coffee in my thermos was lukewarm and tasted like aluminum.

Pulling into the drive, Amos asked, "Do I need to worry about you?"

I shook my head.

"You sure?"

I nodded again.

"Hey." Amos put his hand on my shoulder. "Hug her for me."

I pushed the door closed, walked up the steps, and listened as Amos's tires crunched the frost on my gravel drive.

chapter nineteen

"PROFESSOR?"

I raised my head, and the sunshine blinded me. An odor of urine, Pine Sol, and Maggie hit my nose pretty quickly, reminding me what my life smelled like. Through fuzzy, dry eyes, I recognized Amanda, who sat next to me unwrapping the bandage on my arm.

"Good morning," she whispered. "Sorry to wake you, but class starts in an hour, research papers are due today, and I thought you might want to eat something." She pointed to the table behind me. Eggs, sausage, and toast sat steaming. "But not until I put a new wrapping on this."

"Thanks. It feels better."

Amanda pulled off the gauze and studied my arm. "Looks better, too, but"—she eyed me with suspicion—"I think we'll keep it wrapped another week. Just in case."

I nodded.

Amanda pointed her finger as if she was about to say something; her brow wrinkled as though she was thinking real hard. Then she pointed back to the food. "Blue already ate his. It's cafeteria food, so it's not great. But it's hot, and that's worth something."

"Thanks," I said, turning away and wishing for a toothbrush.

"Professor." She patted my arm. "This might scar—for life. You did a real number on it. I told the doctor about it, and he said you either need to leave it alone or get used to wearing long sleeves in public."

"What else did the doctor say?" I said looking at the bandage and letting my nose filter the air of Betadine fumes.

Amanda hesitated. "He said that you need to quit trying to rub the skin off your arm, and for me to tell him if you don't."

I nodded and looked back at Maggie. Without looking at Amanda, I said, "Amos told me about you getting kidnapped." I paused. "I didn't know." I looked up at her. "I'm sorry."

Without batting an eye, she said, "Me too." Then she laughed. "I'm sorry 'most every day."

"Why?" I asked. "Because of the baby?"

"No! Heavens, no." She tilted her head and patted her tummy, and her eyebrows drew close together. "It's not his fault, Professor. He didn't have anything to do with it. Two wrongs don't make one right." She tilted her head further, as though she couldn't understand the look on my face. "I'm sorry for those guys, whoever and wherever they are. They may not ever have to face me, or my dad, or even Big Amos, although I hope he catches them, but one way or another, this life or the next, their time will come. God knows. And to answer your next question, no, I don't hate them. And I certainly don't hate this little boy here."

"But . . . " I didn't know how to ask it.

"But what?" She smiled. "Yes, Professor, if you need to hear me say it. Remember, I'm training to be a nurse. They did what they could to make sure that I would not get pregnant, but my body didn't know I wasn't supposed to get pregnant. By the time they got me to the hospital, my body had already done what it was made to do."

I wanted to ask the next question, but I didn't have to.

"No, Professor. That was never an option. Not because of my dad, or his church, or anything like that. There was no pressure there. I made up my own mind. And no, I don't have some crazy wish to be one of the single mothers that I read about in the paper. I have no desire to become a statistic. At least, that one. I had hoped to do this the traditional way." She smiled again. "You know: a wedding, white gown, handsome man, and then the child thing. But . . . " She shrugged her shoulders. "I'll have to wait on that. He's out there. He's just got to find us."

She walked up next to the bed and patted Maggie's feet.

"Can I ask one more question?" I asked.

"Sure. I've been doing all the talking."

"You don't seem mad."

"Professor, that's a statement, not a question."

I smiled. "Okay, why then? Why aren't you standing out there on the front lawn, shaking your hand at the sky?"

Amanda shook her head. "Professor, God knows how I feel. I tell Him all the time." She raised her eyebrows and smiled. "How do you think I made it this far?" She looked out the window.

"I spent a few weeks pretty mad. We argued. I screamed a lot. But what good is it going to do? Yelling won't make me unpregnant, won't catch those two guys, and won't give me back what I lost. Maybe it's my daddy in me, but I think that if we could give God a choice, He'd prefer that we scream and argue rather than say nothing at all. And believe me, Professor, I've done my screaming." Amanda stood and put her hand on her hip. "Now, it's time to do my living. Although—" She batted her eyes and smiled slyly. "I keep the lines open."

She was quiet for a moment, then stuck her point-making finger in the air. "Professor, you didn't ask, but I'm going to tell you . . . at least this is what I'm banking on. If God is who He says He is, then He's big enough to handle my ranting and raving." She paused again. "And all my questions."

I held Maggie's hand and kept my mouth shut.

Amanda patted Maggs's foot again, turned, and walked to the door. "Professor?" she said.

"Yes?" I looked up at her.

"I probably talk more than I should, but you asked." She smiled again, placing one hand on the door and resting one leg, bending it at the knee. "What I really want to say is this: I'm just talking about me. I know other people have had tough times, too, but you asked, and I told you."

I heard a shuffle, and when I looked up, she was gone. Blue licked my knee, and the plate of steaming eggs, sausage, and toast began to smell real good. Maggie's feeding bag was half-empty, so we ate in silence.

At a few minutes before nine, I kissed her forehead, checked to make sure her socks were pulled up, folded Blue's blanket, and left for school. Walking down the hall, I realized how thickly Amanda had wrapped my arm. It looked like a billy club. Judging by the size and thickness of the bandage, it'd take thirty minutes just to cut it off.

chapter twenty

THANKSGIVING WEEKEND I WAS ALONE, PARKED ON the front porch and sniffing the air for the smell of turkey. There was none, only a lone fireplace somewhere south of my rocker. In my lap sat my students' research papers, which they had placed in my box by 5:00 P.M. the day before. My hope was to grade them over the four-day break and return them the next week, allowing the students the remaining three weeks of the semester to rewrite and make corrections.

In teaching my previous seven classes, I had developed a method for reading papers. I thought it helped bring fairness to the whole process. When starting a paper, I didn't look at the name until after I'd given it a grade. Also, I read each one twice. The process helped keep me honest. Sometimes, if I'm familiar with a student's topic, then I know whose I'm reading, but most times I have no idea.

Rocking with the rhythm of the corn, my eyes were focused on four particular research papers. They stuck out not because of their poor quality, but because they were good, real good. Even excellent.

After the second read, I was still impressed, but I had some suspicions. Then I looked at the names. No way. Not this year, not these guys, not anytime soon. I finished reading the rest of the papers a second time and spent Sunday and Monday thinking it over.

The answer was simple, but that was just the problem. *Do I question four students about their papers, accuse them of plagiarism, and hope I get a confession? I'm the teacher, that's my job. I think they're guilty. No, I know they're guilty. It's a nonissue. They're gone. It's out of my hands. School policy.*

It's not that easy.

Some students think that the teacher is paid by their tuition and consequently owes them something—as if showing up to class is admirable and completing assignments is optional. They're not all like that. I do have real students, the kind you hope you discover. Because that's what teachers do. We discover, or uncover, kids.

I spent the weekend thinking about my fibbing four. They weren't even discreet about it. A voice inside my head told me that it is not uncommon for a student to sue a teacher for such an accusation. It happens.

To be honest, there were two voices inside of me. One said, *Just give 'em back. Forget it. You really don't care. They're only cheating themselves. It's their future. You've got enough on your plate.* The other said, *Wait a minute, what are you doing?*

That second voice was the tough one. I fought it. *Hey, I'm just an adjunct. These kids will never see me again. All they want is a grade, and all I want is to get out of there and pay my bills.* But I knew that wasn't really true.

I sat on the porch, rocking, reading, and making absolutely certain. It wasn't too hard. In sum, I had four papers and four lives handed to me on a silver platter.

My students filed into class, and I handed out the papers, all except the four. I looked at those students and said, "Your papers were really good. Actually, they were great. You four hang out after class. I'd like to talk to you."

That was enough to quiet them for the remainder of class. Not one uttered a single peep. Marvin chewed on his lip, Russell looked out the window, and Eugene and Alan shifted their minds into high gear.

Class ended, the rest filed out, and my fib-four sat mumbling and tongue-tied in front and around me. They tried to pass over the uneasiness.

I said, "Guys, your papers were great, which is why you're sitting here. I want you to tell me about them."

Marvin spoke up. "Well, ain't you gonna give 'em back?"

"No, not yet. I want to ask you some questions first." I had the papers in my hand and was nervously but slowly shuffling them like a deck of cards.

"We'll get to that," I said. "Eugene, let's start with you."

Eugene was intelligent. He had a good sense of humor but was also curious and usually made a good contribution to my class. I liked him. It was evident that people respected him, because they listened to what he had to say.

Eugene tossed his head, slipped down in his chair, and gave me his best attitude-look, which said, *All right, but I ain't done nothing wrong.*

"Eugene, tell me about your paper. I'm impressed. It's really good. Just tell me about it."

"It's been a long time since I wrote it. I don' remembuh much. Whatchoo wanna know?"

He threw the slang in to get over his uneasiness, I knew, because he could pretend to speak like a Rhodes scholar when the urge hit him.

"Well, just tell me where you got the idea."

"I don't remember, but I asked you a few weeks ago if I could write about these two poems, and you said I could."

"I remember. All right, how about this: explain your thesis."

Silence.

"Well . . . explain your conclusions?"

"I don't know. It's been a long time since I wrote it." Whenever Eugene's mouth moved, his hands followed. His hands were starting to come alive as I asked him more questions.

The others began to get uncomfortable as they wrestled with how they might answer these same questions.

"Well . . . tell me what poems you used. What are the titles?"

"I can't remember, but one is about a ship and the other is about. . . ."

"Who is the author?"

"Dickinson, um . . . Emily."

"Good. Now, why these poems?"

Silence.

"Okay, you hold on to that. I'll come back to you."

Eugene breathed, but it was not an easy breath. His head was turning, and I could see that entrepreneurial side kick in. He was thinking about how he could make a deal.

I turned to Marvin. "Marvin . . . "

I had learned a few things about Marvin. He was the most highly recruited freshman Digs had ever signed. He'd probably enter the draft at the end of his sophomore year. If he stayed healthy, he could go all the way. Aside from football, he had a great sense of humor, always made me laugh, and I enjoyed having him in class.

About six weeks ago, I was in midlecture, and Marvin was gabbing away with anybody who would listen. I stopped in the middle of a sentence, looked him square in the face, and said in a tone he had not heard before, "Marvin, what's the one thing all great cornerbacks have to have to play in the NFL?"

Real quick, it got pin-drop quiet. Marvin laughed, cocked his head back, and said, "Quick feet, they all gotta have quick feet." He looked around the class, proud and looking for support for what he knew was the right answer. Eugene gave him a high-five. He leaned back in his chair.

I said, "No, there are a lot of guys who can run a 4.3 but aren't in the NFL. It's not quick feet."

Marvin sat up.

I turned back to the class and said, "Can anybody help Marvin? What is the one thing that all great defensive backs have to have in order to play in the NFL?"

It was quiet in my classroom. Then slowly students chipped in, "Good hands," "Size," "Like to hit," "Good eyes."

"Nope," I said, "that's not the one thing." I looked back at Marvin.

He looked up, slouched a little, and said kind of quietly, "They gotta listen."

"That's right, Marvin. Dion Sanders was one of the greatest to play the game not because he ran a 4.2, but because he knew how to listen. Marvin, I want you to learn to listen in my classroom. You with me?"

Since then, Marvin has listened more than he has talked. He's even asked a few questions. Now I looked at him, but he never gave me the chance to ask the question.

He pointed at his paper. "Professuh Styles, I wrote my papuh."

"Okay, then tell me about it. What's your thesis?"

"I don' remembuh, but I wro' my papuh." Like Eugene, he was using slang to cover up what he couldn't hide.

"Okay, here, on page one." I opened his paper and pointed to the first paragraph. "You talk about necromantic lust. What is necromantic lust?"

"Necromani' whut?"

"Ne-cro-man-tic lust. You use it right here in this sentence, which, I think, is your thesis."

Marvin squirmed, kind of flung his head, half-grunted, and slouched.

"Okay, here." I pointed again. "You talk about Aristotelian philosophy. That's a pretty broad topic, so let's just talk about his metaphysics."

"His meta-what?" Marvin's voice got high-pitched.

"His me-ta-phy-sics."

Silence. The other three were motionless. The heaters in the room were really working. On top of that, I noticed that my heart was pounding at a pretty good pace. Any louder and they'd be able to hear it. Somebody's foot shuffled on the dusty floor.

"Professuh Styles, I wro' my papuh, I jus' can' remembuh ri' now. But I wro' dit."

"Okay, then let's start over. What's your thesis?"

Silence.

"What's your conclusion?"

Silence.

"What's your title?"

Deathly silence.

"Okay, you think, and I'll go on to Alan."

Alan was always early to class. Always did his homework. Never caused a problem. Asked some pretty good questions and never talked out of turn. Even raised his hand. He braided his hair into about ten braids and wanted to go to work with his brother when he got out of school. I liked him.

He looked like he came up tough but also looked like he came up honest.

Alan's paper was the only one of the four that struck me as slightly different. There was no way he had written it—the language was too clean—but I did believe that he had typed it.

"Alan, tell me about your paper."

He launched into some of the specifics of his paper, relaying to me the highlights. Three minutes later, he finished speaking and rested his hands on the tabletop. His eyes told me he wasn't guilty, but they didn't necessarily say he was innocent either.

"Okay, what does this word mean?" It was a scientific term, and I can't begin to remember how to spell it. I had no idea what it meant. Neither did he.

"Okay, how did you organize your ideas?"

Silence.

"Okay, where did you get this information?"

"In a book."

"Well, you don't cite it, so how am I to know where it comes from? It's obvious that you've done some good research here. Your language is clean, but I just don't know where you got your ideas."

Alan must have had a poor grammar-school experience, because his written use of the English language was horrendous. Judging by his prior two essays, I know there was no way on God's green earth that he had written a single word of this, other than his name.

When I first read his paper, I saw quickly that he had given me what he thought I wanted. What he didn't realize, what none of them realized, was that I would work with each person from his starting point, not mine. They didn't know that. And they sure didn't want to believe it. Maybe that was my fault. Maybe that was the reason the five of us weren't down in the department chair's office right then.

"Okay, what does this sentence mean?" I read the sentence and then looked at him.

"Well, it mean dat de thing dey talkin' 'bout der is only foun' in space, and when it mix wit d'other elemen's, then it have dis effect." Alan was no dummy. He had a good head on his shoulders, and he knew his topic. He understood what was said; he just could never say it the way it was written.

"Then why not tell me like that rather than the way it is written here?"

Alan's eyes got real big, and he pointed at the paper. "Dat souns bettuh. And you'da graded me lowuh lik' you dun on de utter papuhs."

"Well, if that's the case, then who said it? I don't know, because you don't give anyone credit for saying it."

"I say it."

"Well, the way you just explained it and the way you wrote it here are two very different things."

Alan was quiet, and his forehead wrinkled.

"Okay, you hold on to that, and I'll go on to Russell."

At this point in the year, Russell had become my favorite. I know I'm not supposed to have favorites, or at least I shouldn't admit it. But Russell was a leader. Had it written all over his body. He was soft-spoken, kind, funny, curious, he cared about my class, and until now, I think he liked me.

"Russell, tell me about your essay." By this time, Russell knew the drill.

"Well, it's 'bout television and its impac' on kids."

"Great, tell me more."

Russell thought, and then he said, "Well, my sistuh helped me do som' research."

"That's fine. I told you to get help if you needed it. Now tell me more about your paper."

Silence. Eugene and Marvin had had just about enough of this, and their attitudes were feeding off each other. Eugene piped in, "I wrote my paper a long time ago, but I wrote it."

"Okay, while Russell is thinking, we'll start over. Eugene, tell me about your paper." I went through the whole thing again. And yes, I was more worried and more scared. I was losing, or at least getting nowhere, which was losing. I was also getting somewhat mad.

Finally I put the papers down. "Guys, does anyone in this room have anything he wants to tell me? Anything at all?"

The silence was thick. I started over.

"Eugene. Tell me about these two poems. What kind of analysis do you perform?"

Silence. But their nonverbal communication spoke volumes, and a consensus was beginning to develop. I could tell they had realized that if they all ganged up on me, they'd have a better chance of getting out of this than if they just covered themselves.

Eugene sneered at me. "Professuh Styles, it's been a while, so I can't remember it right now, but I wrote my paper." He pointed his finger in my face. "I wrote my paper." He laughed uncomfortably, sat back, and slouched as if he had had the last word.

I turned again to Marvin. "Marvin, let's talk about your paper. Where'd you get your ideas?"

Marvin slumped, threw his head in a show of disgust, grunted again, and looked out the window.

"Alan, can you give me a good reason why the language and organization in this paper are so different from your first two papers?"

Silence.

"Russell?"

I put the papers down on my desk, and their eyes followed. I looked out the window, then at them, and I asked one more time, "Does anyone in this room have anything at all he wants to tell me?"

They knew. I knew that they knew. And they knew that I knew that they knew.

Stalemate.

I looked at each one, not knowing what to say. Finally I picked up the papers and said, "Guys, you know what I call this." No one allowed his eyes to meet mine.

"You know what the university calls this."

Still quiet.

"Eugene, what do you call this?"

Eugene sat up. "Professuh Styles, I don't know, but I wro' my paper. I need this class to graduate. And I know I wro' my paper." Eugene was reaching. He wanted to deal.

I looked at Marvin. "Marvin, what do you call this?"

"I wro' my papuh."

"Alan, how about you?"

"I . . . I typed my paper."

Then I turned to Russell. "Russell, what do you call this?"

No movement. No talking. No breathing. They had consensus, and I had nothing. They could win, and they knew it or at least thought it possible. If everyone kept quiet, they had me.

I put the papers back down on my desk, looked back at Russell, wondered if I should play the only card I had. Very quietly I said, "Russell . . . what would your dad call this?"

Russell shook his head, closed his eyes, and said, "Aw, man, why'd you have to go there?" He wiped his big hand over his face, closed his eyes again, and looked down in his lap. His massive shoulders slumped, he took a deep breath, his chest expanded and contracted, and he looked me straight in the eye. "He'd call it cheating."

Checkmate.

Marvin and Eugene deflated like balloons. Alan sat quietly.

I nodded. "Thank you. That's what I call it too."

I sat on my desk, my legs dangling off, and they sat slumped in their chairs, looking at me. Long seconds ticked slowly by.

I turned back to Russell. "You need to know before I go any farther that you just showed more honesty and more integrity than I've seen in a long time. I have no respect for what you gave me, but for what you just said, well . . . I thank you."

I slowly turned to Alan. "Alan, what do you call this?"

He sighed, raised his eyebrows, and said in a meek, honest, willing voice, "Cheating."

I turned to Marvin, who had slumped farther in his chair. He could not believe that Russell had just given in. "Marvin?"

"Cheating." His eyes never touched mine.

"Eugene," I said as I turned.

"Cheating." Eugene tossed his head in disbelief. But behind that, his eyes showed relief. He was ready to pay the piper, but I knew he'd still accept a deal.

Going into this, I knew that to have any recourse at all, I had to have a confession. Full and clear. The problem with the game I had just played was that I had no idea what to do with the pieces. School policy is immediate expulsion.

Immediate expulsion. I tossed the idea around in my head. It's not that I thought the policy wasn't fair or just, but it seemed complicated that an adjunct professor should have that much control over one person's future. On the other hand, the only reason I had such control is that the four of them had given it to me. If I did what I was supposed to do, Marvin and Russell would lose their athletic scholarships, Alan would never be the first in his family to get a college degree, and Eugene would always be one class away from graduating.

At that moment, part of me wished I had just given them grades and turned the things back. The other part of me believed that the best I could do for them was march them down to the chair's office. But if I just washed my hands of them, what did that further? Hate? Maybe.

So I turned to them and said, "I'm just curious. If you guys were me, what would you do?"

The deal maker spoke first, before anyone else screwed it up. "I'd just let us rewrite it. I mean, you know." Eugene raised his hands, palms up, and his eyes got real wide.

"Yeah," Marvin chimed in.

"I can do that." I nodded. "Sure. But that sort of washes over the real issue here, which is respect." I waved the papers in front of them. "What you guys gave me disrespected me. You thought you could slip it by me. You also thought you could be lazy and get away with doing nothing. That's dissin' me. And I'm not willing to wash over that. So you're not gonna just 'rewrite it.'"

Marvin, seeing his chance, spoke up with his best display of attitude yet. "Well . . . you always make us feel like we can't write for you. You make us feel like what we write ain't good 'nuff."

Before "nuff" had rolled off his lips, I jerked my head at him and said, "Marvin, don't bring that victim-mentality stuff into my classroom. I've stayed after class, I've helped you rewrite essays, and I've come in here every day and taught you with respect. I'd be willing to stack my class up against any other class you've got. I treat you the way I'd want to be treated, and you know that. So I don't want to hear any lip about how I've made you feel like you can't write for me. You got lazy. That's all there is to it."

"Well, you made fun of me," Marvin said.

"Made fun of you? When?"

"The day I walked in wearing sweatpants, and you made fun of me."

"What'd I say?" I had no idea.

"I don't know. You said that I looked like I just got out of bed or something."

Then I remembered. He was right. I had said it. Although he had looked like he had just gotten out of bed.

I thought for a second. "Marvin, you're right. I did say it, and if it hurt your feelings, I'm sorry, but my insensitivity does not justify this." I held up his paper. "Marvin, I've seen you play football. You take your licks and walk like a man on that field. So start walking like a man in my classroom."

I turned back to Eugene. "I can't just 'let you rewrite it.'"

Eugene knew I was right. He had a good sense of right and wrong. All of them did.

Marvin found his attitude again. "Then you already made up yo' min', haven't ya?"

"No, I haven't. I have no idea what I intend to do."

"You aw'ready decided."

I'm no Freud, but clearly Marvin needed someone to believe in him, and he was testing me.

"Guys, before I go any further, you all need to know what I think about you. Win, lose, or draw, you need to know what I think."

I looked at Eugene. "Eugene, you're smart, people look up to you, they listen to you, and they respect what you have to say. I like having you in my class. You ask good questions."

I turned to Marvin. "Marvin, you've got a great sense of humor. You make me laugh, you're easy to be around, and I enjoy listening to you. I also enjoy watching you play football. You've got real God-given talent. You might even have what it takes."

"Alan, you're always on time, you ask good questions, and you contribute to my class as much as anyone. That's worth a lot. On top of that, folks around here say you can build or fix pretty much anything, and you've already built four cars from the ground up. That's a gift too."

Then I turned to Russell. "Russell, people like you, they look up to you, they listen to you, and they will follow you because you're a born leader. I have a lot of respect for you, not for what you gave me, but what you told me. And you don't need me to tell you this, but any idiot can see that if you stay healthy, your football career will continue long after college."

I waved my hand across all of them. "You guys need to know this. It makes me sick that you'd hand me these papers, expect to slip one past me, and then still expect me to treat you with respect." I got quiet.

After a long moment of silence, I said, "Here's the deal. I really don't know what I'm going to do at this point, but you've got a choice. You can walk down the hall, tell my boss, Mr. Winter, that your professor has wrongly accused you of plagiarism, and bring him to class on Thursday. Or you can write an apology stating that you plagiarized, cheated, and disrespected me and that you're sorry. You've got two ways to get back into my class: bring Mr. Winter or bring a written apology. That's all."

I got up off the desk, turned my back, and put my things together. They slithered off their seats and tiptoed out, never saying a word.

I drove home, my head pounding, wondering what I could have done differently. *Was I too easy on them? Too tough? What will they remember from today?*

At nine-thirty the phone rang. To be honest, I was expecting that. I also needed it. "Hello?"

"Yeah . . . uh . . . Professuh Styles, this is Russell."

"Hello, Russell."

"Uh . . . Professuh . . . I just wanted to call an' tell you that I'm sorry for what I did. I disrespected you, and I'm real sorry." He took a deep breath. "I just wanted to tell you that."

I don't know why, but at that moment I thought of Charlie Bucket returning the Everlasting Gobstopper that he stole from Willy Wonka. As he laid it on the desk, Wonka's hand slipped up, covered it, and he said, "So shines a good deed in a weary world." I've always liked that.

"Thank you, Russell." I tried to sound reserved. "I haven't made up my mind what I'm going to do yet."

"Yessuh, well . . . I just wanted you to know I was sorry."

"I'll see you Thursday."

"Yessuh."

I hung up the phone. I knew that Russell lived in the athletic dorm, and that meant that Marvin couldn't live too far from him. I wondered how long it'd be before I heard from him. The phone rang two minutes later.

"Hello?"

"Um, uh-uh . . . is dis Professuh Styles?"

"Speaking."

"Professuh Styles, this is Marvin."

"Hello, Marvin."

"Yeah . . . um, I just wanted to call and apologize fuh dizre-spekin' you and treating you the way I did." Marvin was scared. He was also sincere. I had not heard this in his voice before.

"I appreciate it, Marvin." I left it at that. I wanted him to sweat, and I wanted him to worry. I wanted them all to worry. To feel the weight of it, right down to the last minute. Is that wrong? What's worse? Causing them to feel the full weight of it, or no weight at all?

"I'll see you Thursday."

"Yessuh."

To be honest, I had hoped that those two would call. Eugene and Alan were good guys, but Marvin and Russell had heart—at least a different heart. Their calling said they knew that they had really screwed up. I needed to know that. It also said they were worried. I needed to know that too.

Thursday came, and my foursome walked in early, more or less together. Each one placed a neatly handwritten note on my desk. I didn't read them but placed them in the cover of my roll book and waited quietly for class to begin.

Judging from their four faces, two days of uncertainty had worked.

Class ended uneventfully, the other students left, and I shut the door. The four of them sat uncomfortably upright in front of me—eager, attentive, and scared. Hands folded in front of them, they looked like the pocket-protector club. I picked up the notes, read each one slowly, and put them next to me when I finished.

"Okay, here's the deal. School policy is that I take this evidence before the dean, at which time he will immediately expel you."

The guys tensed up, and their faces blanched.

"But I'm not going to do that."

Each face relaxed.

"And because I'm not going to do that, here is your option. Each of you is going to write a new essay. The question is simple: What is plagiarism, what is integrity, and can you have the second and do the first? The highest grade you can expect to receive is a C." I raised my eyebrows. "So, if you write an A paper, you get a C. Write a C paper, and you get an F. That's the deal. Take it or leave it."

Eugene was the first to speak up. He nodded and looked to the others. "We made our bed, now we gonna have to lie in it. That's fair."

Marvin said, "Well, I can't write no A paper, so I might as well quit now."

I said, "Marvin, you do what you want to do. But there's one more part to the deal: all of you have to accept. If one says no, then I go to the chair."

Everybody looked at Marvin. Especially Russell.

He ducked his head. "I'll write the essay."

"Alan?" I asked.

"Sounds fair."

"Russell?"

"Yessuh, soun's good to me. Real good."

Marvin spoke up. "How long you want it?"

"Whatever it takes."

"Ooh, dat's the worst kind." He threw up his hands. "When you want it?"

"Well, I know you guys are playing a big game down in Florida this weekend, so I don't imagine you'll have much time between now and Monday." I looked at the calendar on my desk. "Today is Thursday. I want it in a week. If that's not enough time, then bring what you've written, and we'll work on an extension. Believe it or not, I remember what it's like to play football and study."

Russell spoke up. "You played football, Professuh?"

"I did."

"What position?"

"Tailback and"—I looked at Marvin—"corner."

He laughed.

"Marvin, I've seen you play. You've got speed. Good speed. Maybe even good enough speed. But I had one thing you have yet to develop."

"Yeah, I know," he said, holding out his hands. "Thinking. I got to think bettuh."

Russell wasn't done with me. "What happened?"

"Injury."

"Bad?"

"Bad enough," I said. "If I wanted to keep walking, I had to quit playing. That was my choice."

"That's a raw deal," Marvin chimed in.

"That's life, Marvin. It is what it is." I collected the papers. "Guys, you've got a week. And I don't want you getting any help on this one. I want independent thinking."

They grabbed their books and stood, not knowing what to say.

Marvin was the first. He stuck out his hand. "Thanks, Professuh Styles." His hand said thank you twice as hard as his mouth.

"You guys need to know something." I looked at Marvin and Russell. "You two have something I never got. You've got a full ride to do what you do well—play football. I walked on and never made it. You have. If I ever hear of you doing anything like this again, I'll pull this file, walk into the dean's office, and you're gone. And you two, Eugene and Alan, same goes for you. If I ever hear of the two of you getting in any trouble . . . ever . . . this'll be on the dean's desk first thing. It'll be kind of like a criminal record that only I know about, and it'll follow you until you leave this place. You game?"

They all nodded.

Marvin looked toward the door and then shook his head. "That means I got to clean my stuff up."

Eugene stepped up, stuck out his hand, and said, "Thanks, Professuh Styles."

Marvin was next. He stuck out his hand again and smiled

earlobe to earlobe. He would never admit it, but he hated conflict. "Appreciate it, Professuh Styles."

"Thursday, Marvin."

Then Alan. "Yeah, thanks, Professuh Styles."

"Thursday, Alan, and . . . you're welcome."

Finally Russell. He was breathing a lot easier, and his shoulders had relaxed. The thought of not having to tell his mom why he had lost his scholarship and been kicked out of school had hit him square in the chest. His eyes were watery. He looked down on me and said, "Thanks, Professuh Styles. I really appreciate it. Thanks a lot." His big paw wrapped twice around my hand; he could have crushed it if he wanted.

"You're welcome, Russell."

Russell turned to leave.

"And Russell, I meant what I said."

He nodded and left before the tear trickled out of the corner of his eye.

From the hallway, Marvin turned around. "Yo, Professuh Styles. Can I still pass yo' class?"

"That's up to you, Marvin. Mathematically, it's possible. But if I were you, I'd do some thinking on this essay. Think of it this way: you've just picked off a pass, but there's ninety yards between you and the goal line."

"Yessuh." Marvin smiled, performed his best Heisman pose, and skipped down the hall.

They left the building while the faint echo of my different drum resonated off my classroom walls. I had played my best, and Maggie would be proud, but I felt empty, not full. I guess that's because playing your drum only has meaning when you share it with someone else.

It was late when I got home. I walked into our bedroom, slipped off my boots, and left them in the middle of the floor where they didn't belong. Blue hopped up on the bed and shoved his nose under Maggs's pillow while I brushed my teeth.

Turning out the light, I noticed the glisten of Maggs's perfume bottle tucked behind my shaving cream on the sill of the bathroom mirror. I lifted the bottle off the sill as if it were holy water, turned out the light, and walked to my bed. I set the bottle on the bedside table, slipped off the cap, put my head on the pillow, closed my eyes, and breathed.

chapter twenty-one

TUESDAY MORNING THE SUN WOKE ME, AND FOR some reason I did something I had not done since the delivery. I walked into the nursery. I don't know why. Prior to that day, I had no reason, but that morning was different. I walked in and grabbed the baseball glove and football out of the crib. I tucked them both under my arm and walked outside into the field.

The corn was now very much dead, and the weeds had pretty much taken over. It was a couple of weeks to Christmas, and my crop was a long way past hopeless. Midway through the field, I spooked a deer that snorted at me and crashed out through the other side. I made it to the graveside and stood there quietly. A wisteria vine had crept over from Nanny's grave and started growing across my son's granite marker. I have no memory of my dad, but that didn't stop me from wanting to play catch with him most every day of my life. Sometimes, after Maggs would go to sleep, I'd slip out into the stillness of the night with my glove and play by myself.

My favorite movie is *The Natural.* I can't tell you why, there's just something about it. And yes, I've seen it a few times. Maggie makes—or made—fun of me when I'd plug in the VCR and sit down for the umpteenth time to watch the last scene of fireworks, the shower of sparks, and my favorite scene, the last two seconds. Robert Redford and son stand in a wheat field and throw a baseball back and forth while Glenn Close stands stoically to one side. I like that scene because maybe baseball is more than a game. Maybe football is too. Maybe each is a tether that links father to son before puberty and rebellion pry them apart.

Looking down at the grave, I set the football inside the baseball glove and laid them on top of my son. The thermometer at the house had said it was cold, but I never felt it.

LATER THAT AFTERNOON, I DISMISSED CLASS, AND EVERYONE filed out. I turned around, and Koy still sat in her seat. Her glasses covered her eyes and hid her face. She hadn't been in class for two weeks—since the football game—and she knew she owed me some sort of readmit. No readmit and five absences. That's bad. The school requires me to fail anyone who is absent three or more times without a valid readmit. The look on her face said Koy was either scheming or didn't know what to say or where to begin. Probably both.

I broke the silence. "Hello, Koy. You were quiet today."

"Professuh," she started, "I don't have a readmit for missing the last two weeks."

"Koy," I said, coming around my desk and leaning against the front of it, "you know policy." I crossed my arms. "Why not?"

"'Cause they don't give readmits for where I been."

"Why not?"

"'Cause they don't." She looked out the window.

"Koy, that doesn't help me." I leaned forward. "Can you tell me where you've been?"

"Yes."

"Well?" I said quietly.

Koy stood. She was unusually dressed: a long, loose-fitting denim jumper, turtleneck, and boots. She usually wore tight, flashy clothing that revealed more than it concealed. Not hussy stuff, but attractive, revealing clothing, which said maybe more than she intended. She walked to the front of the class and hung her head. That was unlike her too. She stood directly in front of me, her face about a foot from mine. Taking off her glasses with her left hand, she stretched out her right hand and opened it. She uncurled her fingers, and resting in her palm was a crumpled and sweaty piece of paper.

I opened it and read the name of the business silently. *Hillcrest Women's Clinic.* Across the bottom, written in pen, was *$265.00. Paid in Cash.*

I fell back against the desk. The paper was heavy, and I wanted to lay it down. My hand grew hot, and I looked at Koy. Her eyes were red, borderline bloodshot. For a few minutes we stood in the quiet. She offered no excuses, I asked no questions.

After several minutes of silence, I whispered, "Are you okay?"

She nodded, smeared the tears across her cheeks, covered her eyes with her glasses, and walked out of my class. The only sound was the smack and slide of her heels on the old wooden floor.

I walked to the window and watched her open her car door and start the engine. She puttered off, and I sat down next to the window, wrestling with the weight of that receipt.

chapter twenty-two

I WEAR COWBOY BOOTS MOST ALL THE TIME. THEY'RE me. No, they're not the most comfortable shoes ever made, but there's something about them. If you ever start, you'll understand. I grew up watching John Wayne with Papa, so my first pair of shoes was a pair of Dingo boots. Once I outgrew them, Papa had them bronzed and used them for bookends for Nanny's cookbooks. They're in the kitchen now.

Currently I have six pair, seven if you count my barn boots, and Maggie hates every single one. She only tolerates one pair, a pair of black Tony Lamas made out of Brahma bull hide. Good-looking. She bought them for me. The rest are a hodgepodge of whatever I could find on sale. They're old and beat up, and most are in need of new soles. If she could, Maggs would pitch them all—or use them as pots for her plants. She'd prefer that I wear nicer "dress shoes" when I'm out in public, so I compromised and showed her the Tony Lamas that I had been eyeing.

Maggs can flare a temper when she wants. When she gets fed up or frustrated with me, it usually comes back to the boots. "Dylan Styles, you are not John Wayne. This is not a dude ranch, and you are not a cowboy." Then she puts her hand on her hips and mutters to herself, "I married the Marlboro man."

If I came home looking like the cover of *GQ*, or a model for Polo or Johnston Murphy, Maggs would have my head examined. Just 'cause a shoe fits does not mean that you wear it. You have to ask if it's the shoe you want to wear.

The same goes with jeans. I wear Wranglers. The kind with the tab on the right rear pocket. Maggie can't stand them. She likes Levis. I keep telling her that Levis are made for people with low waists and funky-shaped bodies. Wranglers are made for real people with real bodies—people who wear boots.

I bought Maggs a pair one day, rubbed some dirt on them to make them look worn, and then slipped them into her drawer. She was getting ready to go work in the barn and pulled them on without knowing it. She got them buttoned and made it all the way to the coffeepot before she squealed, "Dylan Styles! You sneak. What is this?" Then she tripped over her heel trying to get them off.

I convinced her to wear them, but it wasn't easy. Now she only wears them when she's cleaning out Pinky's stall or working in her garden, but I did catch her going to the store in them one day. I didn't say anything, though, because if I did, that would have been the end of it. She'd have taken them off right there and never worn them again. Sometimes it's best to be quiet when you're right.

That was about two years ago. They look pretty well worn by now, but I think if she was honest, which she'll never be when it comes to those jeans, she likes them. They might even be her favorite pair. In my opinion, they fit her great. Lord, do they fit her. But she'll never give me the satisfaction of admitting it. Funny how that works.

A WEEK HAD PASSED, AND MY FIB-FOUR OWED ME PAPERS. Marvin walked into class first, sat down, and began blowing into his hands. "It's cold as Siberia in here."

He was right. Winter had come on quickly.

Just before the bell, Koy walked in and quietly took her seat. Glasses on.

I lectured on the need to comb one's writing to get rid of filler and get the most out of one's words—to find some happy medium between Hemingway and Faulkner. They were half listening.

Class ended, my foursome dropped their papers on my desk with ear-to-ear smiles, and everybody filed out.

"Koy, may I see you?"

She looked my way, took a few steps, then stood at my desk as the rest of class departed.

"Have you thought about what you'll do when you leave here? Have you thought about getting a four-year degree?"

"Some," she said, offering nothing further.

"Well, in case you do, I took a few of your works, specifically a few assignments and a few journal entries, and sent them to the chair of the English department at Spelman."

"You did what?" she demanded, taking off her glasses.

"Koy, Spelman is a great school. It might be a good fit for you."

"Professuh, that stuff is personal. I thought you said you wouldn't show it to anyone."

"You're right. I did. I broke my word."

"Professuh. Why? I thought I could trust you." Koy put one hand on her hip, and her eyes filled with tears.

"Koy, you can trust me to believe in you. And I believe you have a gift. As it turns out, so does the chair of the English department at Spelman. This envelope explains that. Spelman gives a few writing scholarships every year to promising students. Scripps-Howard gave them a bunch of money, and it seems they want to give you some of it."

She took the envelope from me and read the letter. Twice. "Is this for real?" she asked with disbelieving eyes.

"Every word," I said, smiling.

Koy was silent for several minutes, reading and rereading the letter. Then, as if shot out of a cannon, she jumped up and kissed me square on the lips. "Oops, sorry, Professor. I didn't mean to do that." She kissed me on the cheek, grabbed her backpack, and ran out of class, screaming at the top of her lungs.

Two seconds later she ran back into the classroom, gave me a great big bear hug, kissed me on the cheek again, and disappeared. I heard her run across the lawn beneath my window and up to a group of girls crowding around the soda machines. After a few seconds of hysterical, noisy speech, they started jumping up and down, hugging her, handing the letter back and forth, and dancing as though they'd struck it rich in the Sierra Madre. I stood at the windowsill and wondered how long it'd been since I'd even felt like dancing.

chapter twenty-three

It was Friday, and only one week of class remained. I slipped on my boots and whistled for Blue, who was chasing a jackrabbit down a corn row, and we hopped in the truck. I hadn't been up to see Bryce in a few weeks. I needed to pay him a visit.

Bryce and I don't ever talk about what happened with Mr. Caglestock. We never discuss investments or money or anything of the sort. I just check in on him.

I skirted town, passed the amphitheatre, rambled a few more miles, rounded the corner, and bumped the gate of the Silver Screen, which as usual was locked and chained. I left my truck and picked my way through the trees to the fence just like ten thousand kids before me.

On Friday and Saturday nights, that place used to be the center of the world of Digger. One side was Sodom. The other was Gomorrah. I pulled the fence up, Blue and I slipped under, and we hiked the drive to Bryce's trailer. I'll never understand, and it'll never make sense. Bryce can afford to buy all of Digger, yet he lives in a trailer. At least nobody will ever say that he's reckless with his money.

At the top of the hill, approaching the ticket booth, I heard somebody inside banging on something. After a few more whacks, Bryce appeared with a hammer, a screwdriver, some Liquid-Plumr, and a car battery.

"Howdy, Bryce," I said, backing up.

Bryce took one look at me, said "Dylan," nodded his head, and walked back to the shed next to his trailer. Any greeting other than my name and a nod would be excessive coming from him.

Bryce was actually dressed that day. Which is always nice. Every time I climb that driveway, I prepare myself for the image of his naked frame. Not a pretty sight, but one you'd better be prepared to see if you're going to come up here. Today, he was wearing cut-off fatigue shorts, a T-shirt that used to be white, combat boots, no socks, and apparently no underwear. The hole in the back of his shorts gave that away. But let's praise progress where we see it. Boots were progress. The fact that they were laced up and almost polished was nothing short of miraculous.

"How're you doing?" I asked.

Bryce walked into his shed, dug around for something,

and began throwing odd tools and objects over his head. "Hand me that torch, would you, Doc?"

I handed him the flashlight, and he disappeared deeper into the shed. I don't know how Bryce knows about my education. I've never told him, and we certainly don't travel in the same circles. In the last eight years, I think Bryce has really only spoken to me, Maggie, and Mr. Caglestock. But one thing about Bryce, he may play the ex-marine out-there bagpipes-playing drunk, and he may be, but he knows a heck of a lot more than folks outside of his private hell give him credit for. Sometimes I wonder who's crazy—Bryce or the rest of us?

He came out of the shed holding an enormous fuse and sweating profusely.

"What's that for?" I asked. He had left behind all the other tools except the Liquid-Plumr, which was now looped through his belt and carried like a holster.

"Projector." Bryce stomped past me in a perfect military march toward the projector house.

"Oh, I see." Bryce had something on his mind, and no amount of conversation from me was going to distract him. "Well, then, what's the Liquid-Plumr for?"

Bryce stopped, looked at the bottle hanging from his belt, and appeared to be thinking pretty hard. "Oh, that," he said, and started marching again. "That's gasoline."

"What's the gasoline for?" Sometimes you have to keep at Bryce.

"Well"—Bryce reached the projector house and began

climbing the steps to the projector room—"if this fuse don't work, I thought I'd set it on fire."

"Oh," I said. "Can I help with the fuse?"

"Nope." Sweat was pouring off his forehead. His hands were dripping wet, and the chance of electrocution seemed pretty good. "I got it."

It was apparent that Bryce had not been drinking that day. He was far too lucid. Which was good, but also bad. It made for better conversation but usually ended up in an explosion, a fire, or both. If he didn't get some beer in him quickly, flames were a certainty.

Bryce slapped the fuse into a box on the wall and lifted the breaker switch. The projector reel turned, and Clint Eastwood appeared barely visible on the screen. He was lighting a short cigar and looking at the camera through squinted eyes under the brim of a weathered hat.

"Good, Bad, 'n' Ugly," Bryce said, pointing to the screen. "I was smack in the middle, when the ugly guy death-marches Clint into the desert. Then, whammo, the fuse blows and hacks me off something fierce." Bryce spat. "Took me three days to find the second reel, and then the fuse goes blowing on me. That really chaps my hide." Bryce rubbed his fingers along the handle of the jug hanging from his belt.

"Yeah," I said. "I can tell."

"Well, how 'bout a beer?" he asked.

"No, thanks," I said, holding out my hands. "I'm on my way to town. Just wanted to say hi."

Bryce looked at me out of the corner of his eye. "Well, if you change your mind, *Rio Lobo* is showing tonight."

Rio Lobo is a John Wayne classic and squarely positioned in my top five. Bryce knows this. He must have wanted some company.

"Thanks," I said, nodding my head. "Blue, too?" Never assume anything with Bryce.

Bryce looked at Blue, nodded affirmatively, and marched back toward his shed.

AT THE HOSPITAL, EVERYTHING WAS NORMAL. IF YOU CAN ever call a hospital normal: people walking around in white coats, poking needles in other people, or cutting them open and either putting something in or taking something out. Don't get me wrong. I'm all for hospitals, but think about it. In what other environment do we allow strangers to do the stuff they do to us at hospitals? Where the words "drop your shorts" or "take your clothes off" are not perverted or sexual, but routine? Everything from sawing the top of your head off to checking your prostate to removing a cancerous lump to inserting silicone in a breast. If a Martian came to earth, he'd have a lot of questions about hospitals.

Blue walked with me to Maggie's room and jumped up on the bed with her. He licked her face and hand, then curled up next to her feet. A nurse I did not know walked by, stuck her head in, eyed Blue, and was about to say something, but

I gave her a look, and she quietly disappeared. They had quit bugging me about Blue weeks ago.

Maggs's hair was combed, her sheets and socks were clean, the window shades were pulled to half-light, and Blue's bed was unfolded and spread in the corner. On the table was a cup of crushed ice. Not for Maggie, obviously. For me, the habitual ice chewer.

Amanda again. *Nothing gets past her. How does a girl, almost nine months pregnant, working the night shift, with ankles swollen to the size of grapefruits, do all this? I don't get it.*

I sat next to Maggs for an hour or so and brought her up to date. I told her the latest about Bryce, the farm, and class, and as I did, her breathing sped up. Her lips tightened and then relaxed. It wasn't labored or fretful breathing, but excited breathing. I told her, "Semester's almost over, and DJC hasn't fired me yet. Some of my students are starting to write pretty well." I looked out the door toward the nurses' station. "Amanda has come a long way, and this other girl, Koy, has a real gift. A born writer. My football players? Well, they're just like me when I took that class."

Her breathing skipped, the right corner of her mouth quivered, and her right index finger pointed and then relaxed. Blue laid his head across her leg, and I continued holding her right hand with my left.

"They turned in their term papers almost two weeks ago, so we'll be busy this week. I gave them a few days off to work on their last assignment. Some of them deserve it. Others, well . . . "

Maggs and I sat in the quiet, and I watched her chest rise

and fall with every breath. Her breathing was quiet, but deep, and her nostrils flared with each rise of her chest. She has a beautiful nose. I patted her stomach, which, the doctors say, has healed, and rolled my chair down to the end of the bed to put cream on her feet. Her nails were immaculate. I rubbed her feet, slipped her socks back on, and slid my hand beneath hers. Her right index finger flexed again, and this time it didn't relax. I sat a few minutes watching her finger. Her breathing sped up, and her forehead wrinkled. After a few minutes, her finger went limp and breathing slowed. I looked at her face, and the wrinkle had half disappeared.

I'm a shower person myself, but not Maggs. She has a thing about baths. If we could afford the hot water, she would soak for hours, draining and refilling the tub several times. Maybe it's a woman thing. I went into the bathroom off Maggs's room, shut the door, ran some warm water into the sink, and soaked a washrag until it was just north of lukewarm. Then, careful not to disturb her IV, catheter, or the plethora of electronic nodes, I bathed Maggie. I don't know if that's right or wrong; maybe I just wanted to see and touch my wife. Whatever it was, I know that if the roles were reversed, I'd want her to do the same for me. I'd want my wife's hands on me. I'd want to know she was there, thinking about me, and her hands could tell me that better than anything else she might do.

Every afternoon the physical therapy team, made up of two nurses who look as though they ought to be teaching an aerobics class, spends thirty minutes flexing and stretching Maggs's limbs. Sort of like an involuntary yoga class. Their purpose, while good, is to slow the inevitable atrophying of Maggs's muscles.

My purpose was a bit different. I just wanted her to feel my touch and know I was right there, holding her. "Maggs," I whispered, leaning my nose against her ear, "you can wake up anytime you want. Even if I'm not here. You can wake up anytime."

I toweled her dry and kissed her forehead on the wrinkle, and her finger flexed around mine again, like a promise. I stroked her hand, her finger relaxed, and Blue and I tiptoed out the door.

I SPENT THE AFTERNOON WORKING ON THE TRACTOR, which really needed Bryce's Liquid-Plumr. Not to start it, but to set it on fire. Late in the afternoon, the mailman came and left me a nice present in the form of the property tax bill.

Sundown arrived and found me idling back from the river on the tractor, pulling a trailer full of wood. I had cut a load, not because Jim Biggins had failed to provide his yearly supply, but because the weatherman said we would need all we could find. I stacked it outside, showered, and the moon reminded me of Bryce, so I grabbed my coat and headed out.

Blue and I slipped over and under the fence and found Bryce sitting in a beach chair, watching *Rio Lobo* and surrounded by empty beer cans.

"Hey, Doc. Have a seat." He threw a can of Old Milwaukee at me.

I chuckled. Why in the world a man that rich would buy beer that cheap just killed me.

Bryce stood, stumbled a little, grabbed a rusty beach chair, spread it for me, set it next to his, and then threw me another beer. I had yet to sip the first one.

It was early in the movie, and the Duke was buying a drink for two Confederate soldiers just released from a Union prison. Bryce held his beer high, garbled something inaudible, ended it with, " . . . John!" and chugged whatever was left in the can. He tossed it behind him, popped another top amid foamy spray, and then sat back comfortably.

It was cold, probably thirty-eight degrees, and Bryce had not changed clothes since I left. Or added any, for that matter. From the looks of things, he was working on his second twelve-pack and doing a good job of it too.

The movie reeled on. The Duke made it to Blackthorn, had a barroom brawl, picked up a girl who fainted. After some classic-John conversation, which was short on verbiage and long on body language, the Duke, a French-Mexican called Frenchy, and the girl headed out after the bad guys to Rio Lobo. Along the way, they stopped at an Indian burial ground where they cooked dinner, drank what was left of their Apache herb tonic, and called it a night.

Bryce was right there with them. When it came time to switch the reels, he was in no shape to do it, so I climbed the steps, switched the reels, fed the tape, and sat back down in my chair.

Bryce was out cold. Both literally and figuratively. It would take more muscle than mine to haul him to his bed, so I grabbed a few blankets from the trailer, covered him like a cocoon, and sat back in my chair with my third beer. The temperature had dropped some more.

The movie ended, and the methodical whacking and slapping of the end of the tape in the projector room woke me. I climbed the stairs, cut the machines off, and considered heading to my truck, but instead sat back down in my chair and found the moon. It was moving around in some pretty wide circles but finally stood still when I put one foot on the ground. The night was clear, my breath showed like cigarette smoke, and Blue was curled up next to me to get warm. Surprisingly, Bryce was a quiet sleeper. You'd think a guy like that would snore like a jet engine, but he was quiet as a mouse and sleeping comfortably. Another lesson from Vietnam, I suppose.

"Blue?"

Blue's ears perked up. I scratched his head and neck, and he dug his front paws under my leg.

"What do you think about all this business?"

Blue raised his head, looked at me, then laid his head on my thigh and took a deep breath, putting one leg on top of my thigh as if to hold me down.

"I'm not going anywhere."

He dug his paw back under my leg and nestled his nose in between his front legs.

chapter twenty-four

DECEMBER 23. OUR ANNIVERSARY. THAT SEEMED LIKE another life and two other people. I had split a lot of firewood to buy that diamond for Maggs.

I've never met Maggs's mom, because her parents divorced when she was eight and Maggs hadn't talked to her since she was twelve. Her dad was a hard nut to crack. Loved Maggs, and me, too, I suppose, but he always looked askance at me. I don't think he ever figured me out.

When I went to see him and ask his permission, he sat across from me at his desk in a white shirt and power-red tie and said, "Yes, D.S., you may marry her. Absolutely. But I worry about you guys. It's a tough world out there, and you've never really decided on a career. How will you provide for her? Sometimes . . ." He paused. "I wonder if you have the fire in your belly." Two years later he died.

With the money I saved splitting wood, I bought a diamond, then found an old platinum setting at an estate sale a few weeks later. I had a jeweler put the two together and put it in a little box.

On a late summer night, Maggs and I walked down to the river under the moon. It was hot, but I was cold, and she could tell I was a little tongue-tied. We made small talk, but I was useless. Finally, on the way back through the cornfield, my palms were sweating so badly that I had to do something. I didn't know how to start. Mr. Stupid. I reached in my pocket, grabbed her hand, tried to say something and couldn't. So I just knelt down. Right there in the middle of the cornfield.

She giggled. I opened the box, and she lit up like ten thousand fireflies.

"Dylan Styles!" she screamed. "Where did you get this? Did you pick this out by yourself? What have you been doing?"

I gently took her hand again, as if I could calm her down.

Tears filled her eyes and she nodded. "Yes."

I slipped the ring on her finger, and to my knowledge, the only time it ever came off was on our wedding day. And that was just so I could put it back on her.

We walked back down to the river and sat on the bank, talking about life. Where to live. How many kids we'd have. Their names. What kind of flowers she'd plant in the yard. That was one of the happiest nights of my life. The next morning, as the sun came up over the river, we were still sitting on the bank, talking.

Finally we walked back through the field and called Amos. He said, "Well, it took you long enough."

We married six months later. That was nine years ago today.

MAGGIE WAS SLEEPING WHEN I WALKED IN. BLUE NUDGED her hand and then took his place at the foot of the bed. I wheeled the chair around to the right side of the bed, on Maggie's left. I sat and held her ring hand in my hand. It was the first time I had sat on that side of the bed since the delivery. I don't know why. Never gave it much thought. Just habit, I guess.

I gently slid my hand under hers and began rubbing her hand. Maggie's long, beautiful, slender wrist didn't look right wrapped in a hospital tag. I opened my pocketknife, Papa's yellow-handled Case, and cut the tag off. I stroked her fingers and turned her wedding ring in circles around her finger as we sat in the silence. Turning it, I noticed something wasn't right. The diamond didn't sparkle. I angled it to get it under the light, and still no glisten. It was as though the diamond had gone dead. Looking closely, I saw that a red film covered the top and sides of the diamond. Maybe the back, too.

I slid her wedding ring off her finger and ran it under some hot soapy water. As I washed it, little flakes of blood caked off and splattered the sink below. I grabbed Maggs's toothbrush from the drawer beside her bed, loaded it with toothpaste, and went to work. Then I rinsed the ring under water that was so hot it was painful. Having scrubbed and rinsed, I dried it off. There was no need to hold it under the light now. I sat down next to Maggs, gently held her hand, and slipped it on her finger.

"Maggs." I gently placed my finger on the wrinkle in her forehead. "Maggie." The wrinkle disappeared. "I know you've got a lot going on in there, but I need you to listen for a minute. I need you to wake up. Let's go home. You and me. Let's get up and walk out of this place. Whatever happened is over." I paused.

"It's lonely at home. See . . ." I rolled up my sleeve, tore off the bandage, and placed her hand on my arm. Her fingers rested on the scab and scar of my left forearm. The wrinkle returned. "Honey, I need you . . . I need us."

I laid my head next to her hand, kissed her finger, and closed my eyes. "Baby, I can't get to where you are. So you're going to have to get to me."

chapter twenty-five

Christmas Eve day was cold and overcast and looked like snow. It was probably just one or two degrees below thirty, but who was counting? I think the wind chill was a good bit lower.

Maggie loves Christmas. Our house always showed it too: wreaths, candles, stockings, the smell of evergreen. And she never let us get away with a fake tree. Last year we put so many strands of lights on the tree that when it came time to undecorate it, we couldn't. We ended up taking off all the ornaments, leaving seventeen strands of lights on a six-foot tree, and hauling the whole thing out to the hard road for pickup. A thirty-four-dollar tree and fifty-four dollars' worth of lights. Maggie saw it no other way.

"You can't have a tree if you're not going to put lights on it."

"Yes," I said, "but honey, we don't have a Christmas tree. We've got a fire hazard at the cost of about five dollars a night. Between now and the time we take it down is about $150."

She laughed, batted her eyelashes, and said, "I know it, but it's Christmas."

The "but it's Christmas" statement really cost us. And shopping? I swear, if the Taj Mahal were on sale and Maggie knew of someone who really wanted it, she'd figure a way to get it. I can hear her now, "But it was only $90 million. That's half off!"

Our house was always neat, but I did my best to dirty it up. I'd leave underwear on the floor, the toilet seat up, the toothpaste cap off, books right where I left them, shoes where I took them off, pantry door open. Not Maggie. We'd cook dinner, and she'd have all the dishes cleaned and put up before we ate. The kitchen looked as if we were never there. Sometimes at night, I'd get out of the bed to go to the bathroom, and I'd be gone maybe thirty seconds. When I got back, the bed would be made up.

Papa and Nanny's house isn't much. Take away my romantic descriptions, and it's basically an old farmhouse with creaky floors, a built-in draft, bowed ceilings, a rusted roof, and forty layers of cracked and peeling paint. But that didn't stop Maggie.

Our front lawn looked like Martha Stewart stopped by on

her way south. Plants everywhere. Colors? Honey, we got colors. And smells? If you get downwind, you almost can't smell Pinky. Maggie's thumb is so green you can take dead branches, give her half a cup of water, some mystery juice that she cooks up out in the barn, three days, and whammo! Blooms. I have seen that woman take dead fern, I'm talking crunchy-in-your-hand dead, and in a week's time it needs splitting and transplanting.

Maggie's absence from our home was more evident than ever on Christmas. I had built no fire, and I didn't intend to. No need to accentuate the obvious. The yard was in disarray. Weeds were rampant. The house was a mess. Laundry was, well, like the weeds. If I didn't know any better, I'd say a bachelor lived in my house.

The wind beat against the tin roof, and somewhere outside Pinky was making noises. Blue was curled up by the fireplace, whimpering.

"If you're gonna keep that up, you can go outside," I said.

He placed his front paw over his nose and looked at me out of the corner of his eye. His tail was still.

I needed to go to the hospital, but this day was harder than others. I showered, dressed in clothes I had worn several times, and headed out. Blue met me at the door and waited while I pushed against the screen. He knows better. Blue and I got into a cold truck and headed for town. Driving past the Silver Screen, I naturally thought of Bryce. I needed to stop in. "After Maggie," I muttered to myself.

We parked at the hospital, which was more or less deserted,

and headed in. Maggie was in her room, right where I left her. In the air I smelled Amanda's perfume. What was she doing, working on Christmas Eve?

I stood next to Maggs's bed and held her warm, beautiful, elegant hand. Lately, I've sat less and paced more. Or stared out the window talking over my shoulder. Maggie understands. I couldn't sit still at home. What makes me any different here?

Standing at the window, I heard footsteps behind me. Amanda was getting pretty big, and her walk had turned into a distinct shuffle. She was well into the full-blown pregnant-woman waddle. Which is beautiful.

I have experience with only one pregnant woman. I mean, experience that really counts. And I couldn't say this before, but few things are more beautiful than my pregnant wife was as she stepped out of the shower or stood in front of the mirror and asked me if I thought she was fat. Nothing was ever more alluring to me than the sight of my wife carrying my son. If you've never loved a pregnant woman, then you can't understand, but if you have, then you do, and you know I'm right.

I didn't turn around. "Good morning, Amanda."

"Good morning, Professor. Merry Christmas to you."

I turned and looked at her. "You look nice. New dress code for working holidays?"

She was wearing casual clothes, not the hospital issue I had grown accustomed to.

"Oh, I'm not working. Just stopped in on the way to my Mammy's." She paused. "My grandmother's."

"I got it," I said, turning back to the window.

"Professor, you got any plans for today?"

"Now, Amanda." I held out my hand. "Don't you start scheming. Blue and I are spending Christmas Eve right here with Maggie. The last time you schemed, I ended up embarrassing myself in front of your dad and his entire church. Not today. I'm parking it right here. But thank you for whatever you were scheming." I smiled.

"Professor," she retorted, "you didn't embarrass yourself." Her eyes showed excitement. "Daddy's been asking me to invite you to church. He said he wishes you'd come back."

"Yeah, so he could preach that fire and brimstone right down on me rather than just let it filter through the windows and drift a few miles down the road? No thanks. Your dad's a good preacher and a good man, but I'll pass."

My voice grew soft, and I turned back to look at Maggs. "Your father doesn't need my doubt in his church. Neither does your church."

Amanda's face said she realized she was getting nowhere. She opened Maggie's bedside drawer and took out a brush. She gently stroked and brushed Maggie's hair. As she did, it struck me how much Maggie's hair had grown. Maybe an inch or two.

"Where'd the brush come from?"

"Oh, I bought it. Got it at the dollar store." Amanda didn't look up.

I fumbled in my pockets and pulled out a handful of loose bills and change. "How much was it?"

"Professor." Amanda looked straight up at me and put her

hands on her hips. "It's Christmas Eve. You don't pay people for the gifts they give you." She dropped her head and continued tending to Maggie.

I sat down next to the bed and slipped my hand under Maggie's. Amanda eyed my Bible.

"I see you brought along something to read. Kind of dusty, isn't it?"

"Yeah, that's what happens when you don't read it," I said, looking at the drab cover.

"Umm-hmmm," she said, as if she had a follow-up statement but decided to keep it to herself. She finished her brushing as snow began to fall outside. Heavy, thick flakes started sticking to the windowpane.

We sat in the quiet for a few minutes. "How you doing?" I asked. "I mean, with the baby and all. What do the doctors say?"

"They say he's big, and I'm little. Say I ought to think about a C-section. So I'm thinking about it. I'm not opposed to the idea. I'm just not sure I want a zipper on my stomach." Amanda made a motion across her stomach and smiled.

I laughed. It was the first time I had laughed in Maggie's room. Amanda too. We actually giggled. It reminded me of Maggie.

Outside, the snow fell more heavily. Inside, the silence hung warm and easy. Not talking was just fine with all three of us. After a while, Amanda stood up from her chair and quietly slid it back against the wall.

"Professor, you take care of Miss Maggie." Standing in the

doorway, she turned to me. "And Professor?" Amanda's eyes searched my face and bored into the back of my head. "You don't have to be celebrating Christmas to talk with God."

I nodded. Amanda left, and Blue and I continued to sit with Maggie. After an hour or so, I rang for the nurse.

"Yes," she barked over the intercom, as if I had interrupted her nap.

"Umm, do you know where the Bible talks about the birth of Jesus? You know, Mary, Joseph, 'no room in the inn,' the wise men?"

"Luke 2," she said promptly.

"Thank you," I said, wondering how in the world she knew that. I thumbed for Luke, skipping over it twice, and turned to the second chapter.

Maggie had told me that her dad read the Nativity story to her when he tucked her into bed on Christmas Eve. Holding up the thin pages to the light, I read the whole thing aloud to her. When I finished, the corner of Maggie's closed right eye was wet, but her breathing was slow and easy.

Maggie was at peace. I placed my palm on her flushed cheek and felt the warmth of her face. For another hour, Blue and I sat quietly with her, watching snow fall on oaks and old magnolias. When I stood up at last to look out the window, snow covered everything in sight.

It was ten o'clock when I left. I squeezed her hand and kissed her gently. Her lips were warm and soft. One orange light lit the parking lot and cast an odd glow into the room.

"Maggie," I whispered. "All this . . . it's nobody's fault. It just is." I brushed her nose with mine. "I love you, Maggs . . . with all of me."

Blue and I walked down the quiet hallway. A light shone from the nurses' station, but that was about it. The night nurse was reading the *Enquirer* and munching on a bag of cheese puffs.

While I was walking down the hallway, it struck me for the second time that I had actually laughed in Maggs's room. Amanda and I both had laughed. It felt good too. Maybe, under all that haze of sleep and heavy eyelids, Maggs just needed to hear me laugh. The last time I had really laughed was a few hours before we went to the delivery room—just moments before the bottom fell out of my life.

As I was walking out through the emergency room, I passed the counter where they kept the scanner crackling with police and ambulance activity. It served as mission control for the emergency room. For the waiting room, it provided some sort of entertainment. Over the static, I heard Amos's calm voice saying he was just west of Johnson's Pasture and headed to the hospital with somebody.

That was nothing unusual. During the week, Amos made almost as many trips to the hospital as he did to the jail. I used to tell him, "You know, Ebony, if things don't work out with the sheriff's department, you'd make one jam-up ambulance driver. You already know the entire lingo."

He never thought that was too funny. There it was, Christmas Eve, and he was probably transporting some drunk who had had one too many at a Christmas party, gotten in a fight, and needed a few stitches. Put me in Amos's place, and I'd have thrown the sucker in jail, slapped a Band-Aid on his face, and let him sleep it off. Not Amos.

If he was west of Johnson's Pasture, that meant he was eastbound on 27 and would be at the ER in about ten minutes. I didn't feel like answering any of his questions tonight, so Blue and I walked through the electric doors and onto the sidewalk. As I did, my feet flew out from under me, I went down, and I almost cracked my tailbone. A solid sheet of ice covered the pavement. Pulling myself up by the flagpole, I cussed, rubbed my butt, and hoped nobody had seen my tumble. Especially not Miss Cheese-puff. Blue stood a few feet away, watching me with suspicion.

The parking lot was empty when I started my truck. Even in this cold, the old girl cranked without a hitch. The older she gets, the more oil she burns, but Chevy made a good truck in this one. The fuel gauge was bumping on E, but I had enough to get home.

We pulled out of the hospital, I touched the gas, and the rear end of the truck slid out from underneath me, spinning us around 180 degrees. "That's twice," I whispered to myself. "Better take it slow."

Three miles out of town, I plowed slowly west on County Road 27. Several inches of snow blanketed the blacktop, and the temperature had dropped to twenty-eight degrees. With both hands on the wheel, and keeping an eye out for hazards, I let my thoughts wander. In front of me awaited an empty and cold house on what would have been our first white Christmas. Behind me lay Maggie. And in between, there was me.

A lonely place.

I wasn't in any hurry, so I dropped the stick into low gear and spun up Johnson's snow-covered pasture. Cresting the hill, I coasted down the other side, letting the engine RPMs act as my brake. About midway down the hill, I approached the railroad crossing, where eighty years before Chinese immigrants had laid railroad track for the Union Pacific.

The snow was spreading over the windshield like a blanket. I flipped the wipers to "high" but still couldn't see anything. As I bumped over the tracks, a light caught the corner of my eye. I was only going about five miles an hour, so I slowed to a stop on the other side of the tracks and rolled down my window. Looking down the hill in the direction of the light, I strained my eyes against the cold sheet of white that was biting into my face. The flash looked like a taillight, but down there was no place for a taillight, much less a car. I guess that's why it caught my attention.

I started rolling up the window when the wind swirled, and I caught a break in the snow. This time there was no mistake. It was a taillight, at the bottom of the ditch about five feet off the ground. That meant the car, or truck, or whatever was connected to it, was upside down with its nose in the ditch. I pulled to the side and left the truck running. Blue's eyes followed me out, but he kept his nose muzzled under his forearm and didn't budge from the passenger's side floorboard.

Stepping into the snow, I pulled the collar up on my jean

jacket, crossed back over the tracks, and stood in the emergency lane of the eastbound traffic. The taillights were sticking up in the air, creating a small red halo effect around the car. On the snow beneath it were the scattered remains of what looked like blue plastic police lights that were once strapped atop the car. Leaning sideways, I read the upside-down reflective letters on the back of the car: Colleton County Sheriff's Department.

I hit my butt and started sliding down the bank. I had intended to scoot down to the car, using my heels as a brake, but the cold and wind had turned the snow-covered bank into a sheet of ice.

My descent was fast and painful. I couldn't stop, slow down, or veer to the left or the right. Midway down, I hit a small embankment that tossed me head over heels and sent me tumbling like a human snowball. Gaining speed, I passed Amos's car and shot headfirst into the ditch. The splash surprised me, but not as much as the cold water. After a millisecond, the only thing I wanted was out.

I planted my boots in the muck below and reached for the bank. Pulling at snow and frozen grass, I kicked my toes into the bank, pushed up, and reached for the window frame of the car. The car was resting on the edge of the ditch, and every window was shattered. A few more inches, and water would have been pouring in. Dragging myself up on the bank, I didn't have time to think about being cold because I bumped the body of what appeared to be a big, limp man lying in the snow. When I found the face, it shocked me.

"Amos!"

His glassy eyes were looking at me. He was wet, and his face was a blood-soaked mess. Surprisingly, he was not shivering. Without saying a word, he slowly lifted his left hand, clicked on his flashlight, and pointed it through the driver's window. The light was swaying back and forth, and I could tell he was having a hard time staying conscious. Hanging upside down in the passenger seat was a mangled mess of long, black, wet hair. Amos's drunk party-goer, no doubt.

"All this for some drunk . . . " I grabbed the flashlight and scrambled around to the other side. As I did, the car slid an inch or two further into the ditch, and water started seeping in, filling what used to be the top of the car. I shined the light into the bloody and swollen face of the passenger. Her eyes were closed, and her arms were hanging limp down below her head. Brushing away the hair, I slowly tilted myself sideways, trying to see who I was looking at.

Amanda.

"Amos! What the . . ."

I don't know how long she had been hanging there, but her face looked blue and puffy in the light. The passenger's window was also blown out, and little pieces had cut her face. Glass was everywhere.

If she wasn't dead already, Amanda needed to get out of that car, because in a few minutes her head would be underwater. I reached up, put my hand around her throat, and felt for a pulse. It was slow and weak.

"Amos?" I said, scampering back around the car.

His eyes were still closed, and he hadn't moved. His breathing was slow, shallow, and apparently painful, 'cause he winced every time he tried to breathe too deeply. If I had to guess, I'd say he had two or three broken ribs.

Looking inside the car, I saw that the air bag hung deflated, and the steering wheel was bent where both his hands had been. In the back, Amos's workout bag was sitting on the ceiling-cum-floor in an inch of water. I pulled it out and looked inside, where I found a set of gray sweats. I wrapped the sweatshirt around his head and propped it up with some snow.

Amos looked at me through two glassy eyes that kept rolling back behind his eyelids.

"Hey, buddy," I said, tapping his face, "stay with me."

Like his face, Amos's uniform was splattered with blood, and the gray sweatshirt had begun to spot red. To make matters worse, I was starting to notice the cold, and my fingers were getting pretty numb and close to useless.

I grabbed the radio off Amos's shoulder and punched the talk button. "Anybody . . . HQ . . . anybody . . . this is Dylan Styles." I closed my eyes to think. "I'm at the railroad tracks at Johnson's Pasture. Amos had a wreck."

What road is this? Come on, Dylan, think.

"County Road 27. We need an ambulance! Now." I dropped the radio and grabbed Amos's head with my left hand. "Come on, buddy, focus."

The dispatch crackled. "Come again, Dylan. This is Shireen. Come back, Dylan."

I grabbed the mike again and mashed the transmit button.

This time I shouted, "Shireen, send an ambulance. Amos is hurt bad. So is Amanda Lovett. Railroad tracks on 27. Shireen, get an ambulance."

Shireen said something, but I couldn't hear it because I was too busy pulling on the passenger door. It was jammed. I gently patted Amanda's cheek. "Amanda." I patted harder this time. "Amanda, help's coming. Hang in there. Help's coming."

There was no response. Reaching for her throat again, I felt for a pulse. Still there, but no improvement.

The snow was still falling heavily. By the looks of the car, they had flipped over several times. I needed leverage to get Amanda out, so I checked the trunk, which was dangling open. I yanked out the tire tool, shoved it into the door crack, and leaned hard against it. The door still wouldn't budge, but the car did. It slid another inch or two into the water. I leaned harder and Amanda rocked in her seat belt, waving her hands back and forth in the air below her head.

"Come on! Open!" I leaned into it with everything I had. "Please don't do this to me." The door creaked and moved another inch and stopped. As I pushed, the car slid a foot farther downhill, pulling me down into the water with it, where once again the cold took my breath away. When I stood, water was covering Amanda's hands and was mid-thigh on me. I dropped the crowbar on the bank, placed one foot on the side of the car, and pulled against the door handle.

Nothing.

Growing frantic, I started banging on the door with Amos's crowbar. My fingers were frozen, my footing was bad, and I was running low on options and time. I began swinging the tire tool as hard as I could. On about the sixth whack, it slipped out of my hands, ricocheted off the frame, and spun through the darkness. Splashing in the water a few feet away, it was gone. I was now almost waist-deep in water with nothing to pull on, no footing, and I was losing control over my muscles.

Looking back inside the car, I could see Amanda's hands covered in water that was bubbling up against the top of her head. I don't know if it was the sight of Amos, cut and bloody; the sight of Amanda, blue, limp and unconscious; the thought of my wife, lying in that bed for four months; the thought of my son, lying in a cold, dark box; or the thought of me living in the middle of it all, but somewhere in there, I came apart.

It began low and guttural. Pretty soon it was angry, violent, and all I had. The snow had been beating against my back, so I turned to face it.

"Where are You?" Swinging at the snow, I fell chest-deep into the ice and water. "Huh? Where? You may be in that river watching over a baptism, and You may be hanging on the wall and watching when those numb people walk down and eat and drink You in every steeple-topped, vine-encrusted, pigeon-drop palace around here, but where are You now? For six days You left Amanda stripped and tied to a tree, You left me alone in a puddle on the delivery room floor, and You aren't here now!"

I kicked the water and screamed as loudly as I could. "Why won't You answer me?"

The wind picked up, and the snow fell harder. "Don't You

hang up on me! Nuh-huh. Not now, when I've got Your attention. You want my attention? You want my belief? Is that what You want? Not until You get in this ditch!"

I stood up in the water. My clothes were stiff, wet, and covered in ice. I leaned my head against the car, breathing heavily, and closed my eyes. The snowfall had stopped and the moon appeared over my shoulder, casting my shadow on the water below me. Listening to my own wheezing, I stood weakly, close to broken, and hanging by a thread. "Lord," I whispered, "I need You in this ditch."

The car gave way, slid another foot, and partially submerged Amanda's head. I opened my eyes. "That's not helping me."

I lifted her head forward and gently pulled her shoulders toward me. Her eyes flickered. I pulled on her arms, but she didn't move, and I couldn't reach up across her stomach to unbuckle the seat belt. I reached into my back pocket, pulled out Papa's knife, fumbled to open the blade, and then cut the seat belt across her chest. The lap belt held, so I reached up, hooked under it, and pulled. I knew I was taking a chance, but I didn't have many others. Amanda's limp body fell forward, and she groaned. I pulled her arms and head out the driver's side window, but her stomach was too big. I cradled her in my arms and rested my face against hers.

"Amanda? Help's coming. Help's coming."

Her eyes opened and closed.

"Amanda? Amanda?" I gently slapped her face, and her eyes opened, but her pupils were everywhere. "I can't pull on you. You got to kick yourself out of this car. Move your legs. Come on. Help me get you out." I cradled her tighter and tugged until she groaned. "Help me, Amanda. Please help me."

I slapped her face again. Harder this time. She groaned, tried to move her legs, groaned again, and then her eyes closed and she let out a deep breath.

"Nuh-huh. Not you too! Don't you breathe out on me like that's your last breath." I dug my feet into the muck below and pulled as hard as I could. I placed my mouth against her ear. "Amanda, you do not have my permission to die in this ditch. You hear me? I know you're in there. You do not have my permission."

I pulled again.

"Amanda, open your eyes. D'you hear me? Talk to me. Please don't let this happen."

Amanda hung limp in my arms. Losing my grip, and slipping further in the ditch, I bear-hugged her head and shoulders and rocked her back and forth in the car. Her hips slid, and something gave way.

"That's right. That's right."

Amanda's petite frame slid through the window up to her stomach. She groaned, and it was then that I realized that her stomach was rock hard.

"Amanda," I whispered in her ear again, "I'm going to turn you and slide you out this window."

She groaned, but I turned her anyway. Her sweater caught on some glass, ripped, and exposed her stomach. I dipped down into the water and lifted her shoulders and head up.

Her eyes flickered again. I lifted, pushed, pulled one more time, and she slipped out of the car and into the water.

Sliding out, all of Amanda's weight drove me down into the water. My feet lost their grip, and the water rose around my shoulders and my neck and then wrapped its cold fingers around my face and head. Pulling at me, it swallowed my head and ears. My head submerged, and I shouted under water. It was an eerie, muted explosion of anguish. I heard the swish of the water above me, felt the weight of Amanda's limp body on my outstretched arms, but my left hand told me that Amanda's head was out of the water. For an eternity, I fought the ice and water to hold her above my head, while struggling to get my feet under me. In fear, and involuntarily, I sucked in a lungful of water.

I kicked my feet into the muck below and caught something solid. Maybe a rock or a root. My legs shot us out of the water, and we landed on the bank. I was coughing, gasping, screaming for air, and Amanda lay on the ground, limp, lifeless, and without expression.

I tried to drag her up the ditch, but she was too heavy. I took off my coat and feebly wrapped it around her, but she wasn't shivering.

Resting my arm underneath her head, I leaned down and placed my face close to hers. Through the moonlight, I saw that she was open-eyed and crystal-clear focused on me. Her eyes startled me.

"Professor?" she whispered.

"Yeah . . . yeah. Hey, I'm here. Right here."

"My son."

"Don't talk. We got to get you to the hospital. The ambulance is coming." I looked back up the bank for those headlights.

"Professor . . . my son." Amanda gritted her teeth. "He's coming."

I looked down, placed my hand on Amanda's stomach, and felt the contraction hit. She groaned.

"What, right here?"

Above me, coming around the back of the car, I heard movement. Expecting Blue, I looked up, but it was Amos crawling to me with the sweatshirt still wrapped around his head. "Amos! Get to the road! Stop the ambulance!"

"Not coming," Amos whispered. "Road's too iced over. Sending a four-wheel drive, but it'll be twenty minutes 'fore he gets here."

"But she's having this baby now!"

Amos looked at me, leaning against the bank and breathing heavily, and said, "I know." He had regained his focus. "We were sitting in church when her water broke. We were on our way to the hospital when we hit the tracks." He tossed his head in the direction of the road. "Guess we're delivering that boy right here."

Amos closed his eyes and breathed as Amanda's stomach went soft again. She opened her eyes, they rolled back, and her head fell limp to one side. The left side of her head was cut, swelling, and bleeding a lot.

Amos grabbed my arm with his right hand and jerked me

down on top of him. His eyes were three inches from mine. Through clenched and bloody teeth he said, "Dylan, you got to deliver that boy right here." He winced. "D.S., this is your time, your minute. You hear me? I can't help you, but I can talk you through it."

He opened his arm toward Amanda and slid down next to her. "D.S., place her head on my chest."

I did what he said.

"In my trunk is a wool blanket. Wrap it around her."

I reached into the open trunk and grabbed the blanket. Then I slid off Amanda's underwear, the middle of which was soaked a deep red, and wrapped her, as best I could, in the blanket.

"Can you see the head?"

I shined the light. "No, not yet."

"How far apart are the contractions?"

"I don't know . . . a minute. Two at the most."

Just then Amanda's stomach tightened, she grunted, and her limp legs stiffened.

Opening his eyes, Amos asked, "That one?"

"Yes."

"How 'bout now? Can you see the head?"

I looked again. "Sort of. I can see something." I shined the light again. "Yeah, I can see the top of his head."

"All right." Amos wrapped his right arm over Amanda's chest and cradled her to him. Talking in her ear, he said, "Amanda, baby, I know you can hear me. I know it hurts. I know everything in you hurts, but you the only one can do this. Can't Amos or Dylan do this for you. You got it?"

Amanda made no response.

"Good, don't talk. But when it hurts . . . you push."

Amanda's stomach tightened, she groaned louder, her legs tightened, and the baby's head came through the canal.

"Head's out, Amos." I caught Amanda's son's head in my fingers, and a warm, slippery, sticky liquid coated my hands.

It was no longer cold. The moon broke through from behind a single cloud, cast a shadow on the three of us, and glistened off the snow. I didn't need the flashlight to notice the blood.

"Make sure the cord isn't wrapped around his head."

"How? What am I looking for?"

"Just run your finger around his neck and tell me if you feel a cord."

Shoving the flashlight in my mouth, I looked for a cord. I held the baby's head with my left hand and felt for the cord with my right.

"No cord," I said around the flashlight.

"Good," Amos said. "All right, Amanda, one more. This boy's coming right here. This is it."

Amanda's stomach tightened, she groan-coughed, and the baby's right shoulder slipped out.

"Amos, I got a shoulder."

"Gently, Doc."

Amanda's breathing was labored, and she was moaning.

"Make room for the other shoulder. Don't be afraid to use your hand. Make room. Pull if you have to, but not on the baby. You know what I mean. You've seen this done before."

I nodded. I ran my finger along the baby's back, slid my fingers in between Amanda and the baby, pulled gently outward, and the baby slid out. A wet, gooey, warm baby landed in my hands. Pulling him to me, I saw that he was blue, limp, and silent.

"He's out."

Amanda let out a long, deep breath.

"Is he breathing?"

I stuck my ear against his face.

"No."

Amanda whimpered.

"D.S." Amos raised his head, and the veins in his neck showed in the moonlight. "Get him breathing." His tone was urgent. "Put your mouth over his nose and mouth, and breathe into him. Breathe a full breath, but don't force it."

I cradled Amanda's son in my arms, placed his mouth and nose in my mouth, and breathed.

"What's happening?" Amos asked.

Again I pulled the baby's mouth to my cheek. "Nothing."

"Do it again."

I did. "No good."

"Take three fingers and compress his chest. Think of it like you're pushing on a roll of bread and you don't want to push through. Just mash it down."

I did.

"Anything?"

"Nothing."

Amos's eyes showed fear, and he kicked the ground beneath him. "Slap him."

"What do you mean, 'Slap him'? Where?"

"Slap the kid, Doc! Just slap him!"

I smacked Amanda's son on the bottom. He jerked, sucked in a deep, gargled breath, and screamed at the top of his lungs.

Bathed in the moonlight, we sat listening to Amanda's newborn son. It was, quite possibly, the most beautiful sound I had ever heard.

Amos nodded, "Nice job, Doc. Nice job." His head fell back against the bank, his eyes closed, and there, in the middle of all that, Amos smiled.

I grabbed the sweatshirt off his head and placed the baby on Amos's chest. Shining the light on the bank, I found my knife, cut the cord midway between Amanda and the baby, tied a knot, and wrapped the baby tight inside the sweats. Amos's big hand cradled the child while his right arm covered Amanda.

"Amanda, honey," Amos assured her, "this boy's fine."

Kneeling in the snow between Amanda's legs, I looked down and noticed the dark, sticky flow. "Amos, I got a lot of blood."

"How much?" Amos asked.

I shined the light. "It looks like Maggie."

His brow wrinkled. "Can you get us to the hospital in your truck?"

"Maybe, I'll check." Scrambling to the top of the hill, I found my truck quiet. No exhaust was coming from the pipe. It was dead as a doornail. I turned the ignition and mashed the accelerator to the floor, but she had seized up and wouldn't turn over.

Sliding back down, I whispered, "It's dead."

"Dylan, you got to get us to the top of this hill. That truck'll be here soon."

I carefully took Amanda under the arms and pulled her toward the top of the hill. Beneath her, the snow trailed red. Digging in his heels, Amos inched upward with his right arm and held the baby with his left. His head was bleeding again. As Amanda and I reached the road, I heard the low whine of gears and saw headlights climbing toward us. As I lay there in the road, in a pool of blood, holding Amanda's head in my arms, two men jumped out of the truck and ran toward us.

They quickly placed Amanda on a stretcher, wrapped two blankets over her, and slid her under the topper of the pickup. One of the men took the baby from Amos and then helped him to his feet, holding him steady. I crawled into the truck next to Amanda, and one of the medics handed me the baby. The other man grunted, lifted Amos into the truck, and laid him down on the other side of Amanda.

The first man looked at me and said, "Do you know her name?"

I nodded and said through my chattering teeth, "Amanda Lovett."

Just before the driver shut the tailgate, Blue jumped in with us. The man ran around to the front of the truck and jumped into the cab. We could hear the radio exchange through the open window between the cab and the back.

"HQ, this is 716."

"Go ahead, 716."

"Shireen, we're inbound with four. I need a blood type check on Amanda Lovett."

"Did you say Amanda Lovett?"

"That's affirmative." The driver paused. "And Shireen, tell 'em we need lots of it."

As our speed increased, I realized that the driver, whoever he was, was pushing the limits of what the snow and ice would allow. A dim light inside the topper shone on Amos's eyes. He was looking at me. He didn't say a word, but his eyes flashed to Amanda and back to me. She was entirely limp.

I shook my head. Amos's right hand came up and grabbed hold of Amanda's. The baby was quiet and still in my arms. His face was shiny and puffy, and his eyes blinked open and shut in the dim light. He appeared to be comfortable, and thanks to Amos's sweatshirt, mostly dry. A whitish paste covered him, and he was sticking long fingers in his mouth. The little guy was as bald as a cue ball.

In a few minutes we reached the hospital. The truck stopped; somebody raised the window, lowered the tailgate, and a woman in a white uniform appeared. She reached for the baby, I extended the boy to her, and she disappeared behind two sliding doors and into a host of people.

Two men pulled Amanda from the truck. They placed her stretcher onto a gurney with wheels and disappeared between the two electric doors. Pastor John and Mrs. Lovett met them at the door and ran along behind them.

The doors to the emergency room were crowded with people. Two large men dressed in blue smocks jumped into the truck, grunted "One, two, three," and lifted Amos onto a stretcher, then briskly rolled him through the sliding double doors while holding a towel on his head and shouting his vitals as they ran.

Back in the truck, I was shivering so hard that my head was bobbing back and forth, and I could not stop my teeth from chattering. Two more nurses climbed into the back of the truck, grabbed me under each arm, and lifted me onto a stretcher. They rolled me inside, down a hall, past a room with a lot of shouting and bright lights, and into a tile-covered room under a stream of a warm shower.

"Can you stand?" one of them asked.

I nodded.

They lifted me off the stretcher and set me on my feet. I was bent half over, my head hanging and my arms pressed against my chest. Warm steam filled my lungs, and warm water crawled down my back.

I stood.

One nurse worked to cut off my clothes while the other prepared some sort of IV and a breathing mask. "What hurts?" the first nurse said.

"N-n-n-nothing."

After five minutes in the warm water, he looked up from his cutting and asked again, "What else hurts?"

"E-e-e-everything."

He nodded. "Good. That's good."

chapter twenty-six

I WOKE UP AND TRIED TO MOVE, BUT DOING SO WAS strangely painful. I ached everywhere, and a hundred nicks and cuts stung most every inch of my body. Clarity came easy in the morning light. I was in the room with Maggie, a patient now myself. Lying there, I remembered Papa kneeling next to Nanny. One strap of his overalls had slid off his shoulders, pushed down by the weight of a broken heart. His big, callused hands were holding hers—tenderness cradled in the palm of might.

I looked over at Maggs, closed my eyes, and said, "Lord, I'm begging You. Please don't take her away from me."

"Merry Christmas," I heard from the foot of my bed. I

looked up and saw a nurse dressed in white. She was not the answer I was looking for.

"How do you feel?"

I had forgotten it was Christmas morning. "Poorly."

"That's to be expected."

"How's everybody else?"

"The baby is fine. Deputy Carter is pretty banged up. A few head lacerations, but he says he'll live. Amanda Lovett is in ICU."

"Will she live?"

"We've given her six units of blood. But whatever you two did out there is the reason she's still here."

The nurse left, and I pried myself off the sheets. My boots lay on the floor, but the paramedics had cut them off last night, so they were useless. Maggie would have liked the sight of that. I unhooked my IV, grabbed another hospital gown from the shelf next to the closet, and threw it over my shoulders. I still felt cold, so I pulled another blanket out of the closet and wrapped it around myself. I took three steps and knew immediately that I needed some pain medication, quick. Hunched over, I walked down the hall, and a nurse behind the counter ran around to stop me.

"Sir, you really need to get back in bed. What happened to your IV?"

She put her arm around me, trying to guide me back to my room. I stopped and looked at her. "Amos Carter. Where is Deputy Amos Carter?"

She pointed. "He's at the end of the hall."

I aimed my face in that direction and said, "Let's go see him."

"But sir, he's sleeping."

"Then I'll just have to wake his lazy butt up."

She shadowed me to Amos's room, supporting me the few times I stumbled, and told another nurse to page the doctor. When I walked in, Amos was lying in his bed with an IV similar to mine. I pulled the metal stool on casters next to his bed and eased down on it. Thinking she had me cornered until the doctor arrived, the nurse left me alone with Amos. His room was lit only by a single dim fluorescent tube on the ceiling. His bald head was covered in a patchwork of stitches. It looked as though someone had played tic-tac-toe on his forehead.

"Amos?" I whispered. "Amos."

His mouth opened. "Hey, buddy."

"You okay?"

"Feel like I been rode hard and put up wet."

"What hurts?"

"Nothing right now." His eyes darted over his shoulder. "Thanks to that bag."

"You gonna be all right?" I asked.

"I'll walk out of here." Amos paused. "Dylan?"

"Yeah."

"You did good last night. Real good." Amos coughed and closed his eyes. "You hear what I'm saying?"

The doctor snapped his heels together and entered the room. I slid the stool back and stood to meet him.

"Mr. Styles, you really need to get back to your room. You are in no condi—"

"Amanda Lovett," I interrupted him.

"What?" he said.

"Amanda Lovett. Where is she?"

He frowned and put one hand in his pocket. "I don't suppose you're going to listen to me, are you?"

"Please, I just want to see Amanda Lovett." I wrapped my blanket tighter around me and raised my eyebrows. "Three minutes is all I want."

"Dylan, when you came in here, your body temperature was eight-six. Do you know how close . . . ?"

I straightened, which was painful, and for the first time I looked him squarely in the eyes.

He thought for a moment. "And after Amanda, it's back to bed?"

I nodded.

"I have your word?"

"You do."

"Come with me, please." He led me down the hall to a wheelchair. "Will you at least sit?"

"Thanks," I said and gingerly sat in the wheelchair.

Heels clicking on the sterile floor, he wheeled me down the hall, around a corner, and down another long hallway. After he punched in his code on the keypad, he steered me through two doors marked with lots of red reflective tape and ICU on the door. I have to admit, I was thankful for the ride. Outside of Amanda's room, Mrs. Lovett sat on a bench, her eyes closed and head resting against the wall. Inside, Pastor John knelt next to Amanda's bed, holding her hand with both of his and resting his head on the mattress. He looked asleep, but I knew better. This was a vigil.

The doctor checked my pulse and then left me at the foot of Amanda's bed. The tiny red flashing lights from Amanda's heart monitor bounced against the walls of the room. The continually expanding and contracting blood-pressure cuff around her right arm breathed in and out audibly, almost like an invisible presence. Amanda's eyes were shut, and she looked blanched and exhausted.

Pastor John spoke first. "It was a few hours last night before they could stop the bleeding." He lifted his head and looked at Amanda. "It seems my grandson's shoulders were larger than the space God gave him to come into this world. Soon after you arrived, half your class lined up to give blood. The other half arrived an hour or so ago."

He wiped away tears. "They gave her six units last night and two more this morning. She hasn't been awake since she's been here." He looked at me. His eyes were bloodshot and sunk deep in his head. He looked as if he could crack at any minute.

I shuffled to the opposite side of the bed, where I pulled up a chair, sat carefully, slid my hand under Amanda's, and rested it in my lap. This was the same hand that had brushed my wife's hair, slipped clean socks on her feet, painted her fingernails, changed her IV, bathed her, and checked her pulse. For a few minutes, we just sat there in the quiet.

I had done the same thing with Maggie a thousand times.

But Amanda's hand came alive, gripped mine, and held the grip. Behind her eyelids, she knew I was holding her hand, and in return she held mine.

Pastor John raised his head, and his eyes grew large and round. Tears filled the corners. When I looked up, Amanda was looking at me. Seeing his daughter's eyes open, and a faint smile bending her lips, Pastor John dropped his head, and his shoulders quivered.

"Professor?" Amanda whispered.

"Yes, Amanda."

"I heard you talking to God last night."

"Is that what you call it?"

"I do." She nodded slightly. "You sounded like Job."

Mrs. Lovett tiptoed into the room and stood beside her husband.

"I'm not sure Job used that kind of language," I said.

"From where I was sitting," Amanda continued, half-laughing, "I heard the whole thing." She closed her eyes again. "And I got to be honest."

"What's that?" I asked, knowing she had baited me and was about to tell me what she really had in mind.

"You were wrong about one thing." She pulled my hand to her chest, bringing my face just inches away from hers. "He was in that ditch with us last night. Just like He spent six days tied to a tree with me." She tilted her head and whispered, "How do you think I made it through?"

I shrugged.

"Professor, I'm not that strong."

I dropped my head and looked at the white in the palm of her hand. "Maybe."

"Professor?"

I looked up as a tear dropped off my lip and landed on my hand. "Yes, Amanda."

"You weren't alone in that delivery-room puddle of blood. He was there. Covered up with it, just like you. You were never alone."

I wrapped my hospital gown tightly around me and shuffled down the hall to the sobbing and grateful hysterics of Pastor and Mrs. Lovett. A nurse informed the ICU waiting room that Amanda Lovett was awake, and it erupted in a chaos of hugging parishioners and friends. Most of my students were there. Marvin and Russell stood next to the waiting room door, drinking Coca-Cola and looking at me. The tape across the insides of their elbows almost made me laugh. The blood of two athletes, flowing through Amanda's veins, would speed her recovery.

A hush came over the room as I walked through the sliding doors. Russell stood first. He met me at the door, opened his arms, and bear-hugged me, lifting my feet off the ground. Marvin raised his Coke can, nodded, and said, "Morning, Doc." His wide grin told me he was having fun.

When I arrived on Maggie's floor, my faithful nurse was waiting for me, and the doctor was on the phone. I entered Maggie's room and found Blue curled up in a ball, sleeping peacefully on his blanket. Beneath the window, Maggie lay angelic and perfectly still. I dropped my blanket and lay down next to her.

"Sir, you really shouldn't do that," the nurse said hastily.

"Lady," I said gently, my wife in my arms, "go away."

She left, and for the first time in four months and thirteen days, I slid beneath the covers and fell asleep next to my wife. Drifting off, holding back the sleep and fighting the medication, I felt Maggie's warm breath on my nose.

A few hours later I woke up to a clear, dark night. No snow falling. I don't know how long I had been asleep, but they hadn't moved me. And more importantly, they hadn't moved Maggie. They had replaced my IV and pumped me with some more fluids.

I lifted my head and looked at Maggie. I admit it, I expected her to be looking back at me. To be honest, I expected to wake up and see her eyes wide open and as crystal clear as the moment they wheeled her down to delivery.

They were not. She was sleeping quietly, and beneath her eyelids, her eyes were moving back and forth.

Maggs was dreaming.

I'm not quite sure where, but from someplace deep within, where the scabs are hidden, where the doubt can't go and the scars don't show, I began to cry. I couldn't hold it anymore, so I buried my head against Maggie's chest and cried harder than I have ever cried in my life. My sobbing brought the nurse running. She stood by the bed a few seconds, covered me with a second blanket, and left.

chapter twenty-seven

THE NEXT MORNING, MAGGIE AND I WOKE IN EACH other's arms. Or rather, I woke up holding her in mine. For a while, I just lay there with my arm across her tummy. She had no choice, so I extended the moment as long as possible. I took her socks off and felt her cold feet rest on my legs. It was the first time I had ever willingly let her do that. After a while I sat up, covered her with my blanket, opened the closet, and rummaged through the clothes that I had left over the last four months. Dressing in the early morning light, I noticed that my hands were cut, scabbed, and sore up to my shoulders. I guessed the medication had worn off. I pulled out the IV and walked to the side of the bed.

"Maggs," I whispered. "I've got something to do. Don't go anywhere." Blue got up off his towel, stretched, and looked at me with a where're-we-going look on his face. I told him to sit, which he did. Then I held my hand out and whispered, "Stay." He lay back down, rested his head on his foreleg, and cocked his ears toward me. "Take care of Maggs. I'll be back." He stood up and looked at Maggs. I said, "Okay," and he hopped up on the bed and curled into a ball by her feet.

Pulling on a jacket, I walked out of Maggs's room and down the quiet hallway. A light shone from the nurses' station, but that was about it. The nurse was reading the *Enquirer* and munching on a new bag of cheese puffs.

"Merry Christmas," I said, realizing I was a day late.

She turned the page and never looked up. "It is? What's so merry about it?"

At the end of the hall, they had admitted an elderly lady with pneumonia. She'd been there two days and they said she'd make it, but her lungs were pretty full, so she would stay awhile. Anyway, her room looked like a floral shop. She must have been one of the pillars of some community, because her room was a blooming jungle. They brought in tables from the cafeteria just to give her more shelf space. Her door was cracked open, so I walked down the hall and silently entered. She was sound asleep.

I grabbed the biggest bunch of flowers I could find. It was a tropical arrangement at odds with the snow outside. In the greenhouse her room had become, she'd never miss it. I set the attached card inside another arrangement, whispered, "Thank you," and pulled the door closed behind me. Walking back down the hall, I set the flowers gently on top of the *Enquirer.*

The nurse put down her bag of puffs, licked the orange cheese off her lips, and studied the bouquet. Cocking one eye, she looked up at me over the top of her glasses. I just stood there, smiling, with my hands in my pockets. Careful not to disturb her lipstick, she dabbed the corners of her mouth with a napkin, moved the flowers to the corner of her desk, and kept reading.

"Hope you have a nice day," I said, rocking on my toes and heels and running my fingers through the change in my pocket like an old man in church.

"Umm, hum."

I leaned over the counter and tried again. "Hope those cheese puffs don't instep-clog your arteries, causing a massive heart attack right here when you're working so hard."

She took a deep breath, folded her flabby arms on the table, and slowly looked me up and down, this time through her glasses. Leaning back in her creaking chair, she folded her hands and considered whether to call security or just give me what I wanted. Finally, she relented. "Merry Christmas, Mr. Styles."

I turned to walk away, but she stopped me. "You going home?" she asked. I nodded, wondering where this was going. "Well, you can walk if you want to, but I'm headed that way. You might as well come along." I stared at her, hands in my pockets, remembering the sight of my truck stranded on the roadside. "Well, don't just stand there," she said. "Let's get going."

I followed her downstairs and out into the parking lot. At

the curb, her Buick Century idled up alongside me. She leaned over and unlocked the passenger side door. Between us sat the half-eaten bag of cheese puffs.

We pulled out of town, retracing the same route I had driven the night before. The air in the car was warm and easy.

Little snow had melted, but the roads were clearer and everything had a wet, glistening look to it. We made it to the railroad tracks, pulled off on the shoulder, and saw where the tow truck had fetched Amos's car and my truck. Only drag marks remained.

Pastor John's church was bathed in white, and in spite of what I had said, the blanket of snow really was a beautiful sight. Another mile and we drove into my drive and around the back of the house.

I opened the door and squatted down, resting one hand on the seat and one on the door. "What's your name?"

She smiled, tapped the name tag pinned to her shirt, and raised her eyebrows. It read, *Alice May Newsome. RN. Serving for 38 years.* She looped her finger beneath her seat belt and readjusted it. "My friends call me Allie."

"Thank you, Allie."

She nodded, rolled up my window, and quietly drove away.

I WALKED THE TREE LINE AROUND TO MY SON'S GRAVE AND down to the riverbank where the sunshine shone warm on my back. When I got to the sandy bank of the river, I stripped down to my birthday suit.

There I stood—a part-time teacher and sometime farmer, showing the first signs of weather and wrinkles, married to a woman who might never wake up, teaching dropouts, wrestling my pride, and looking into a future in question. I couldn't see beyond that second. But for the first time in a long while, I felt a smile on my face. I was standing on that bank like an idiot, smiling. Smiling! Yeah, it was cold, but I wasn't too worried about it. I had been colder.

The flow of the current was about normal when I stepped in. And the water was warmer than I thought it would be. I waded down to waist level and let my toes hang off the lip of the swimming hole where Maggs had taken her swan dive. Down there, the depth dropped to about twelve feet. I looked up at the bluff to my left and thought about our waking up in the middle of the late-summer night and walking hand in hand to the edge. About her stripping down, about her slender calves, graceful arms, the small of her back, about her soaring through the moonlight like Tinkerbell. Arms wide, feet together, her skin like porcelain. Then splashing into the black water, only to surface and let the water drip off the sneaky smile that spread across her face.

I saw us lying on the bank, watching the stars, while the warm, wet water pooled around us. I saw us walking back to the house, her shoulder tucked under mine. Swinging my cold hands, gently skimming the top of the water with my fingertips, I thought about that a lot.

Then I thought about my son, not too far from here, and

how the wisteria had grown across his grave. How the blooms were dead and gone but would be back.

Then I thought about the ditch and the night before. Deep down I was conflicted—an even mixture of fear and peace. Fearful, because maybe Amanda was right. And at peace because I hoped she was. If He had been there all along, then my doubt had no home and would be turned out. I realized that was what took me there, to that place, and it was the reason I was standing in the water.

I stepped off the ledge, took a deep breath, and buried myself in black water. The current swirled around me and pushed me to the bottom, where it held me while small bubbles rose from my nose and mouth, tickling my closed eyes. I saw Maggie, bright lights, the delivery-room floor, my son's face, doctors screaming, and Maggie crying. I hovered above my son's tombstone and the tops of the cornfields. Blue licked my face; Pinky grunted; the tractor idled; the river slid by, bubbling with yellow urine; Pastor John wiped sweat off his face; the railing creaked; Amos's bald head shone; the church bell rang; and Mr. Smiles beckoned.

Trembling, I rose, fell forward, and bit the bitter bread. I stood sweating in my classroom beneath the fans. Koy stared blankly through dark sunglasses, Russell and Marvin danced at football practice. Mr. Carter held forth atop his dog box, I walked the Salk, smiled at moonlight shining through silver hair, sat with Jim Biggins, rocked on the front porch, put my hand in the buzzard hole, saw a man in a dirty kilt with a chestful of medals, felt condensation running down a cold beer, stood in a deserted parking lot, laughed at Mr. Caglestock's bow tie, and heard the echo of John Wayne's voice.

I was in the library studying, writing my dissertation, eating take-out, selling my guitar, and wearing cowboy boots and faded jeans. I was on the front row of the amphitheatre, sitting in moonlight and listening to the wind filter through the pine trees.

Back at the splintery railing, Pastor John offered the cup to Amanda. "Baby, this is . . . " and then he offered it to me.

I sipped, and it stung my throat.

Standing next to Maggie's bedside, I heard her laughter, dialed voice mail, saw Blue lick her feet, slipped socks over her cold toes, saw Amos standing in the hall, touched the wrinkle on Maggie's forehead, sat with Amanda while she cleaned and dressed my arm, and felt Maggie's fingers gently touch my scar.

I swallowed.

It was dark and black on the bottom of that river, but above me light cut through the water like sunshine after the rain. That's when I knew. He was there. He was there all along. I pushed off that sandy bottom. Breaking the surface, I opened my eyes, looked downriver, and as far as I could see, the bank was white. On it, the sun shone brilliantly.

Standing in shoulder-deep water, I stopped to look at myself. I mean, really look. I studied my water-logged hands and the red scar on my arm. I marveled at my pale skin mottled with blue veins and goose bumps from the cold. And for the first time in a long time, I was clean. No blood. No blood anywhere.

chapter twenty-eight

On Sunday morning Pastor John's church was alive and kicking when I drove by. To say it was loud would be an understatement. Blue and I were headed home, which was a mess, so I spent the day cleaning the house. Blue passed most of the afternoon staring at me as if I had lost my mind. Next I moved on to the barn, where he trailed behind me in disbelief.

Pinky was as protective and mean as ever. I threw some corn to her, and she grunted, crapped, and kicked the door of the stall. At the end of the day, Blue and I hopped on the tractor and idled under the oaks and along the river. Blue loved the tractor. We drove to the edge of the river, cut the engine, listened to the wood ducks fly overhead, and watched the sun disappear.

Back at the house, I cooked a dinner that looked a lot like breakfast. I'm not much good at anything else; Maggie could tell you that. Six eggs, an entire package of bacon, and some toast. I devoured it and then washed it down with percolated Maxwell House. The front porch was quiet except for the creaking of my rocker—a sound Maggie loved. Before me, moonlight bathed the cornfield, and a silent breeze waved through the rows of dry cornstalks.

I was starting to heal. A lot of the nicks and cuts were closing up, and the soreness was mostly gone. I guess people are like that. We scar, but in the end, we heal.

Amos didn't know it, but I had borrowed his Ford Expedition. I had my truck, along with Amos's squad car, towed to Jake's Jalopy Auto Center, one of those places where you can get most anything done. He'll fix your car, or better yet, sell you another if he can't. Consequently, he sells a lot of cars. I finished my coffee, slipped on my running shoes, and figured it was time to go get Amos. He'd probably had just about enough of that hospital.

I crossed the dirt road and pulled into Amos's drive, grabbed a duffel from his bedroom, packed him some clothes, and turned on a few lights to make it look welcoming. I would have cleaned up, but unlike the bachelor across the street, Amos kept a pretty tidy house.

The hospital was relatively quiet when I arrived. Maggs was asleep, as was Amanda, and the baby was sucking the nipple off a bottle held by Mrs. Lovett. The doctor, standing at the nurses' station, looked up from a clipboard and waited.

I waved. "Evening, Doc."

"You here for him?" he asked, pointing to Amos's room.

I nodded.

He considered that for a moment, then whispered something to a nurse. Looking back at me, he said, "Drive slowly. He'll be sore for a few days."

Amos was waking up when I walked into his room. I sat down and propped my feet up on his bed. "How's the head?" I asked.

"What happened to your boots?"

"They ended up on the emergency-room floor. A nurse cut them off me when we came in." I looked back toward the nurses' station. "So, what does the doc say?"

Amos shifted under the sheets. "He says I'm lucky to have been wearing my seat belt and even luckier the air bag inflated when it did. A couple more days in here, a week or so at home, and I should be up and about."

I threw his duffel on the bed, and his clothes spilled out.

"I was hoping you'd bring that," he said.

Amos stood gingerly, gained his balance, and said, "Man, this room is spinning." He leaned on me, I helped him dress, and we walked out of his room.

Amos looked at me. "I want to see Amanda before we go."

We exited the elevator onto the recovery floor where they brought people from ICU. Amanda was horizontal, but her head was propped up, and her eyes met ours when we walked into the dim room, empty except for thirty or forty flower arrangements.

"Hey." Amos sat down and gently took her hand.

"How you feeling?" Amanda whispered. "They say your head really put a dent in the steering wheel."

"Yeah, that's what happens when you have a hard head." Amos held his rib cage and tried not to laugh. "I'm okay," he said, "but I'm still taking a few days' vacation."

"You've earned it."

"What do they say about you, baby?" Amos asked.

"Well, I broke a few ribs, cracked my pelvis, suffered a concussion, and lost a lot, if not most, of my blood, but I'll mend. I'll probably spend a few weeks in here. The folks in Daddy's church and my classmates who gave blood have been just great. I don't think I can breast-feed, but we'll see." She smiled and looked out into the hall. "If I can get him away from Momma for two seconds, I might give it a try."

Amanda turned to me, careful not to move too quickly. "Hey, Professor."

"Hey there. How's your boy?"

"He's been here most of the day. Momma just took him down the hall to give him a bottle and walk him around a bit. She thinks he doesn't like being cooped up in this room." Amanda laughed. "I keep telling her that it's a lot bigger than where he's been the last nine months."

"You given him a name?" I asked.

"Yup," Amanda said, proudly raising her chin. "His name is John Amos Dylan Lovett. We're not sure yet what we're going to call him, but Daddy's already calling him 'Little Dylan.' Momma said that's all Daddy could talk about this morning in church. 'Little Dylan this,' and 'Little Dylan that.' "

Amos and I looked at each other and then back at Amanda.

"Are you sure you want to name a child that? I mean, he's liable to get in a good bit of trouble with a name like that." I paused and nodded. "I did."

Amos chipped in, "Still do."

Amanda pointed at the bedside table. "See for yourself. Even says it on his papers."

"Sure enough," Amos said, smiling. He read the photocopy and then handed it to me.

"Professor." Amanda looked up at me. "I asked Miss Maggie, and she didn't seem to mind. I hope it's okay with you."

I nodded and smirked. "It's okay with me. You name that boy anything you want."

Amos squeezed Amanda's hand. "Amanda, honey, I've got to get home, get in my own bed, stop the world from spinning, and get some sleep. I'll check in on you in a day or so. Soon as the world settles down."

Amos and I walked through the door and toward the exit. "That is one tough girl, Amos."

He nodded. "Woman. Tough woman. And I hope that kid never gets in trouble in school. 'Cause he'll have one heck of a time spelling his name on the chalkboard."

We walked out into the parking lot, and Amos noticed his Expedition. "Nice truck," he said.

"Yeah, well, the current owner is laid up and won't need it for a few days."

"How bad is yours?"

"Jake said I burned up the engine. When I get time, I'll go down and talk with him."

I dropped Amos off under a full, clear moon that cast long, beautiful shadows over the trees and his house. I went home wrapped in a warm, peaceful cloud of relief and reflection. So much had happened, I needed to kick back and absorb for a while. I sipped Maxwell House on the front porch, and Blue lay on the floor next to me, listening to the rocker. About midnight, I grabbed my coat and walked out into the cornfield.

Walking through the rows, I held out my hand and tapped each dry stalk as if I were numbering the posts on a picket fence. Papa would have plowed it under by now. After ten minutes, Blue and I walked out the other side, wandered down the side of the pasture, and paused underneath the big overhanging oak, where I sat down quietly with my son. His grave was covered with acorns and snaking wisteria, so I lifted a vine, brushed off the acorns with the palm of my hand, and blew the dirt off the tombstone.

The breeze filtered through the leaves above, bounced off the river, and swirled around my collar and back through the corn. It was gentle, cold, and quiet. And that was good.

chapter twenty-nine

ON DECEMBER 30, THE WEATHER WAS BITTERLY cold and overcast as I walked down the drive to check the mail. It had been unusually cold in Digger this year, but this was getting ridiculous. Amos had borrowed his Expedition from me and driven to town to get some groceries. Since the accident, a bunch of women from his church had cooked him casseroles, pies, meatloaf, roasts, and more pies, but he had eaten all that already, and Amos wasn't one to let himself go hungry. I decided to spend the morning by myself, but when Amos got back with his truck I'd drive in and check on Maggs.

The chill wind whipped around my boxer shorts, dropping the temperature from real cold to even colder and persuading me to move quickly. I was standing by my mailbox, freezing and stuffing mail under my arms, when a Chevrolet Lumina with the words *Mike's Courier Service* on the side screeched to a halt behind me. I dropped the mail and turned to see who had just scared three years off my life. A sixteen-year-old kid, with more zits than cream could cure, hopped out.

"You Dylan Styles?" He was holding an envelope and waving it in my direction.

"I'm Dylan," I said, jogging in place and wondering if the hole in my boxers was open.

"You're hard to find. I been driving around these dang boondocks for an hour and a half. How do you live out here? This is Egypt." He shook his head and threw the envelope at me. Without another word he hopped back into the car, gunned the engine, spun the tires, fishtailed, and disappeared.

I jogged back to the house, dropped the mail on the floor, and took the letter over to the sofa by the fireplace to open it. It was printed on watermarked paper, embossed at the top, and signed by my boss at the college, Mr. Winter.

December 27
Dear Dr. Styles,

Your teaching performance and student evaluations are exemplary. As a result, the DJC Board and I are pleased to offer you a one-year contract extension for this coming school year. We would be delighted to have you join our staff on a more permanent basis. If you so desire, please sign the attached, keep a copy for yourself, and return the other to me at your earliest convenience. I am available at any time if you wish to call.

Happy New Year.

Sincerely,
William T. Winter
Chair, English Department
Digger Junior College

I scratched my head and looked down at Blue, who was studying me and pointing his nose toward the wind.

"Well, I'll be." I pointed to the letter. "Looks like I might get to teach after all. Go figure."

Blue hopped up on the sofa, put his head in my lap, and rolled over, sticking his stomach in the air. I leaned back, propped my sockless feet on the coffee table, and thought how much I liked the sight of my drum perched atop the mantel. I thought Maggie would like it too.

chapter thirty

BY MIDAFTERNOON, AMOS HADN'T SHOWED, SO I thumbed a ride to town with the contract in my pocket. I wanted to show it to Maggie. I stood in the cold for forty-five minutes before anyone passed me, but an hour later, the second car stopped. The driver was a young guy making his way to a party. He was eighteen and driving a 1979 Pontiac Trans Am. The same thing Burt Reynolds drove in *Smokey and the Bandit,* although my new friend had made a few alterations to the engine.

"Yup," he said, stroking the gearshift, "this one here's got the small block fo'hundr'd. So I bored it, stroked it, polished it, threw in some angle plug heads, a solid lift cam, couple of eight-sixties, and then I run the exhaust out through some three-inch headers and a couple of glass-packs. She's loud, but she'll dang near fly. I figure I'm pushing a little over fo'hundr'd hos'pow'r. On top of that, I took the rear end out of a seventy-two 'Vette and locked her down pretty tight. Lowered my gears to around fo'eleven."

I could barely hear him, but I believed him. He hit the accelerator and pinned me so hard against the seat that we were going eighty before I could lift my head up. It was the loudest, fastest car I had ever ridden in. He could burn rubber in all four gears, and he was all too happy to show me. The dashboard was a cockpit of gauges, switches, and flashing lights. I don't know how he saw the road over the thing sticking out of the hood.

We drove the remaining twelve miles to town in about seven minutes. We were going so fast at one point that when I opened my eyes, the dotted yellow line in the middle of the road looked solid. I tried to thank him when he dropped me off, but he couldn't hear me over the exhaust. He said he was on his way to the gas station, so I gave him the three dollars I had been saving to buy my dinner. I would have given him more, but the only other thing in my pocket was the next year's contract, and I didn't know how that could help him.

Maggs was serenely beautiful when I walked in. I married above myself. *Lord, that is one good-looking woman.* I sat down next to the bed and held her hand in mine. A familiar feel. Her fingers had been more active since Christmas. I even think she squeezed me once, but it was hard to tell. Maybe it was only more of that involuntary spinal activity that the doctor told me not to get too excited over.

I squeezed her hand anyway. Every time I sat down in that chair, I squeezed her hand three times. That meant "I love you." Maggs knew that. Throughout our dating and married life, three squeezes of any kind always meant "I love you." And the person getting squeezed squeezed back either two or four times. Two squeezes meant "Me too" and four, "I love you too."

When I squeezed her hand that day, Maggs squeezed me once. No, it wasn't two, three, or four squeezes, but it was a squeeze. And don't tell me that was some spinal reaction. That was a soul thing. I told her about the contract, and her eyeballs began rolling back and forth behind her eyelids, and her breathing picked up. I sat there laughing. Laughing at the thought of a college hiring me to teach on a regular basis.

As I was sitting in Maggs's room, somebody knocked on the door. I kissed Maggie and cracked the door. It was Koy.

"Hello, Professor. Sorry to bother you, but I wonder if I could talk with you."

"Sure," I said. "Give me a minute." I covered Maggie's shoulders with the blanket, made sure her socks were pulled up on her feet, turned out the lights, and closed the door behind me. Koy and I walked down to the coffee machine; I poured myself a cup and offered one to her. She shook her head.

"Um, Professor." She took off her glasses and looked around behind me to see if anyone else was listening. "Do you still have the, um . . . the readmit I gave you?"

"I think so. I think it's in my roll book at home. Why?"

"Well," she said, fumbling with her glasses. "I was wondering if I could have it back." She looked at the ground and waited for my response.

"Sure, you can have it back." I paused and looked closer. She looked as though she hadn't slept in a few days. "Koy, are you all right?"

"Yeah, I was just wondering if I could have it back. That's all."

"I'll bring it to school next week. I've got to turn in grades."

"Well," she stuttered, "I-I was wondering if I could have it sooner."

"Only if you don't mind coming to get it."

"I don't mind," she said quickly.

"I won't be home until late tonight, but if you come by tomorrow, I'll be there most of the day."

"Thanks, Professor. See you tomorrow."

Koy left, and after a minute I slipped out a side exit. I didn't want her to see me walking home, and I sure didn't want her to offer me a ride. The sight of a teacher and a student alone in a car has led to more than one accusation. Home wasn't that far away. I'd walked it before.

I was about three miles from the hospital when Amos came flying up behind me. He pulled alongside. "Thought that was you."

I climbed in. "Man, am I glad to see you. It's getting cold again."

"Amanda's going home tomorrow," he said. "Pastor John stopped me in the grocery store and said they were releasing her in the morning."

He dropped me off at the end of the drive, so I turned up my collar and walked through the pitch black with my hands in my coat pockets. When I got to the porch, somebody with sunglasses was sitting on the front steps, resting her head in her hands. Like the courier service guy, she scared another three years off my life.

"Koy?"

"Sorry, Professor. I couldn't find a light switch."

"Well, the sun will be up in about eight hours."

"Yeah. I thought maybe I could get that readmit tonight."

She looked cold, but not from the temperature, and she sounded as though she'd been crying.

"I'll get it." I walked inside, turned on the porch light, got the receipt, and walked back out on the porch. I handed it to her, and this time she did not take her glasses off.

"Thanks, Professor."

"Koy?" I said. "You don't have to answer me, but why do you want it?"

"I j-just want to keep it," she stammered and walked backwards to her car. "Thank you, Professor." She closed her door and slowly drove out of the driveway. It was eleven when she left.

I went inside, rubbed Blue between the ears, and poured myself a cup of milk. Standing on the porch, stargazing and sipping some sweet, creamy milk, I watched as a northwest breeze picked up and flapped through my corn.

My dry and very dead corn.

I polished off the milk and grabbed a match from the mantel. At the edge of the cornfield, with the wind blowing behind me, I struck the match and lit the stalk in front of me. It sputtered as the wind caught it and almost went out. I cupped my hands around the dead leaf and gave it another chance. In under two minutes, the fire was raging. I stepped back, crossed my arms, and watched it spread across twenty acres, quickly turning the field into a single, huge, roaring blaze.

Amos saw the flames and came running out of his house. He ran up my drive in his socks and grippers, dodging sparks and flames and breathing hard. He shouted above the crackle and roar, "Ivory, have you lost your mind?"

I stood there watching the glow and lost in the flames.

"No," I said, as the fire reached the road and began to die. "Actually, I'm just starting to get it back."

Amos shook his head and started jogging back to his house. I heard him mutter to himself, "Blasted idiot. All that education and he's still dumb as a brick. Burn my house down . . ."

I stood there long enough to watch the fire die and feel the cold return. Then I skipped back inside, lay down on the couch, and for the first time in several months, slept peacefully in my own house.

chapter thirty-one

Jake Powers owns Jake's Jalopy. Aside from being the only auto repair shop in town, it's also the only car dealership in Digger. You might say he's got a monopoly on a very small market. His selection is a hodgepodge of nearly new and very used cars and trucks . . . mostly very used. Not a single car on the lot is still under extended warranty, much less factory warranty.

The place reminds me of the Island of Misfit Toys. How Jake has managed to stay in business this long is the Eighth Wonder of the World. And it's not as if he can sell. I think people go there because they feel sorry for him, his mealy-mouthed wife, and his four pitiful-looking kids. Actually, the whole pitiful thing is probably a marketing ploy. He's probably a mastermind when it comes to yanking a customer's chain.

I was a perfect case in point. I had made up my mind that I was going to Walterboro to buy a real car, the kind with zero miles, when I remembered the billboard that showed the happy Powers children sitting on Mom and Dad's lap. Underneath, the caption read, *Come to Jake's Jalopy. Your purchase will help me feed my kids.*

It's pretty well known that if you want something reliable, something with a warranty, something that won't leave you stranded, you better get to Walterboro. But if you're in a fix, and you're a sucker, a Jake's jalopy will do. I wasn't really in a fix, but I didn't feel like haggling with a Walterboro car salesman, and besides, Jake had my truck. Maybe I could interest him in a trade. To be honest, I had an idea of my own. I also remembered that Jake worked holidays and would be open on New Year's Eve. So I headed out the drive and began walking to Jake's.

After a seven-mile jog-walk with Blue at my side, I turned in the lot.

"Hey, Jake."

Jake stepped between me and the gate before I could change my mind and leave.

"Hey, Dylan, how are you doing?"

Jake and I graduated high school together, and he's always been a little slow on the uptake. Truth is, he does have a child with some special needs, and he's good to his family. He works all the time, and the lot is always open. During Christmas, many people get their trees there. He'll hold as many trees as your wife wants to look at without batting an eye. Then he'll give you a fresh cut, load it on top of your car, tie it down, and wish you a Merry Christmas, which he genuinely hopes you have.

"I'm fine," I lied. The truth would take too long. "How's my truck?" I asked.

He shook his head. "Cooked. Engine's burnt slap up. It'd cost you more to put a new engine in it than what the truck is worth."

This was where Jake usually started trying to sell you something on his lot. But I knew this going in, so I just listened. Besides, he wasn't the only one scheming.

He continued, cocking his head as if he were doing me a favor. "I might could give you more in trade than you'd ever sell it for."

"Well, what do you have?"

Jake smiled, and behind his eyes I could tell he was doing the math. Old Jake thought he had me. But months ago I had seen a truck in the back of his lot that had piqued my interest. When mine burned up, I had the excuse I was looking for.

He slid a tattered three-by-five card from his shirt pocket and looked through the bottom of his glasses. "Let's see . . . " He scanned his card. "With a family and all, you probably need something like . . . " He squeezed his chin between his fingers. "Like this van here." He pointed to a Chrysler van at the front of the lot, parked beneath the row of flapping red, white, and blue flags.

It would take a bigger sucker than I was to leave there with that thing. I pointed to the back of the lot and said, "Uh, Jake, what about that truck?"

Jake looked up from his card and said, "Oh yeah. *That* truck."

We both gazed at the faded orange Ford pickup, covered in leaves and parked against the rear fence.

"Wow. You know how to pick 'em, Dylan." He slapped me on the shoulder as we walked to the back of the lot. "That's a '76 Ford F-150, four-wheel drive, no doubt. It's got about 140,000 miles on it, but the engine was just rebuilt and it's only got eight hundred miles on the new one, transmission, and rear-end."

Jake took off his glasses and kind of looked around before he continued. "Dylan, I know I sometimes sell some less-than-stellar stuff, but to the right owner, this is some decent transportation. I mean, the bed is rusted and duct tape covers some of the tears in the seats, but as for reliability?" Jake quietly patted the hood of the Ford. "I think this may be one of the more reliable units on the lot."

In this particular instance, Jake was probably telling the truth.

"It's got a four-sixty with a couple of small modifications. I think it dynos at about four hundred horsepower." He squinted his eyes in the sun. "Is that too much for your needs?"

"No." I tried not to smile. "I can probably make do."

"Okay, um . . . The gauges work pretty well, and the tires . . . " Jake kicked the tires. "They look pretty good. They're a little big for my taste, but you own a farm, so they might come in handy." He rested his hand on the top of the tire that came to the middle of his thigh. "How 'bout twenty-five hundred?"

Jake was reaching. He must have been having a tough month. The thing wasn't worth fifteen hundred. Not to anybody.

Except me.

He interrupted me before I could reply. "Nope, I tell you what, I'll give you five hundred for your trade and take fifteen hundred, but that's just 'cause you and me got some history."

I shook my head. "Jake, you're too good to me." I rubbed my hands together, as though I were doing the figuring in my head. Good thing Jake couldn't read my mind. I'd have paid ten.

"Will you take three?"

"Well, all right, I can cut it to a thousand, but . . ." Jake scratched his head. "What did you say?"

"I said I'd feel bad if I took her for less than three thousand. This is a classic, and you and I both know it. You're just doing me a favor 'cause we've known each other so long." I slapped Jake on the back and handed him my driver's license.

His eyes doubled in size, and he looked at me as though I had lost my mind.

"Dylan?" He collected himself. "Umm, yeah, let's go inside and get started on the paperwork."

While he was sitting at his desk, Jake's smile grew. The smile alone was worth three grand. The truck was just the icing on the cake. Or at least that's what I was going to tell Amos when he gave me a hard time about buying this truck from Jake.

I reassured him. "Yeah, Jake, I really do appreciate your kindness. I know you're an old pro, and you know cars. I also know that you've always been good to the people who come in here. You've done a lot of good in Digger. 'Specially come Christmas, or when folks just need some help."

Jake squinted again as if he wasn't quite sure what was coming next. "I have?" he asked. "I mean . . ." He cleared his throat. "I have. Thanks for noticing."

"Listen, we all do," I lied again.

Jake handed me the key and said, "I'll hold the title, of course, and send it to you in about twenty-four months. If that's okay with you."

"Sounds good. Hey, tell Liza and the kids I said hello."

Jake looked as though he'd just seen Elvis. He nodded, and I climbed up in the truck.

Finally, a four-wheel drive. I hit the starter, and it rumbled into a slow idle. Ahhh. It's a truck thing. If you don't understand by now, you might as well quit, because you never will.

As I was putting the stick into first, an older, hunchbacked, black woman pulled into the lot. She opened her squeaky door, climbed out of her car, walked over to Jake, and pulled out a neatly folded wad of bills. I overheard her say, "Mr. Jake, that's my ninth payment. I've got six more to go before it's paid for."

I waved at Jake. "Hey, good to see you, pal," I said. "And thanks for taking such good care of all us Digger folks. This beats Walterboro any day."

Jake scratched his head and turned his attention to the lady. "Miz Parker, you're real good about paying me. You're here every month just as soon as your Social Security check comes in. Let's just call it even. I've earned my money on that car."

"But Jake," she protested, bobbing her head, "I still owe you close to three hundred dollars."

"Yes, ma'am. Two hundred and forty-seven, to be exact." Jake put his arm around her and led her back to her car. "And maybe you know of some people who might need a car one day." He smiled. "Don't you have a bunch of kids?"

"Honey." Mrs. Parker put her hand on her hip. "I've got nine of 'em, and if any of them buys a car anyplace but here, I'll beat them like a redheaded stepchild." She reached up, clutched Jake to her big sagging bosom, and kissed him square on the mouth.

I pulled out of the lot with Blue sticking his head out the passenger's window to catch the breeze. I switched on the broken, scratchy radio, and Blue and I hummed down the highway to the sound of mud tires in need of alignment. I was in love.

I probably should have driven straight home, but I didn't. Instead, we filled up, something that, were it not for dual fuel tanks, we would have to do often. Then I eased her into first. Jake was right, that vehicle was not underpowered. Someone had modified that thing at some point. We left Digger with the windows down, and I pointed the hood toward Wherever, which is just south of Whocares. Blue and I wanted the wind in our faces. Maggs wouldn't have minded. If she'd been able, she'd have told me to get out of the hospital anyway. The sun disappeared around Charleston, so we turned south and headed down low country roads around Walterboro.

In need of some new boots, I stopped by the Western World in Walterboro and browsed the aisles. It didn't take long.

They were on the top shelf and just about jumped off at me when I walked by: Olathe Mule Skinners. Tough brown leather, medium toe, double welt, double-thick leather sole, medium heel, eleven-inch shank. They looked like the boots that Dean Martin wore in *Rio Bravo*, and when I slipped them on my feet, my search was over. I loved them. Maggie would not.

I turned to the attendant. "I'll take them . . . And yes, I'd like to wear them out."

He picked up my running shoes with two fingers, wrinkling his nose, dropped them into the box, and closed the lid. I paid the cashier, but not before buying two new pairs of Wranglers. Something Maggie would never let me get away with.

I walked out smiling like a cross between an artificial redneck and a wannabe ranch hand. But I was smiling, and that was not something I had done a lot of those last few months. Crossing the parking lot, I stepped in a puddle on purpose, and then Blue and I loaded up and I backed out of the parking lot.

My smile stopped me when I looked in the rearview mirror. I pushed in the clutch and sat there looking in the mirror at my face. After I recognized myself, we headed northwest up toward Columbia, and then south along a bunch of back country roads and some small towns that had grown up around cotton, peanuts, and tobacco.

Blue fluctuated between sticking his nose out the window and curling up in a ball on the seat next to me. He sniffed everything between the two locations. His nervousness told me he wasn't quite sure what to make of me or this truck. I rubbed his ears and he settled down, finally putting his head on my lap. I sat with one hand on the wheel and the other on the windowsill. Occasionally I'd look in the rearview mirror just to see my smile, trying to get used to it. If Maggie were here, she'd have been smiling, too, and it was that thought that kept the guilt away and the food down. Without Maggie's smile, I'd have never made it out of Jake's parking lot.

Just before dark, we were rumbling along some back road that was an irregular patchwork of dirt, hardtop, and potholes when something caught my eye. A side road with my name on it. Blue and I slipped off the hardtop and down the wet, grassy, low road with cypress trees so large that Maggie, Amos, and I all together couldn't reach our arms around them.

We idled for maybe a mile or so and then pulled up onto a sandy riverbank. I parked and let Blue smell the bushes. Hopping up on the hood, I crossed my legs in front of me, took another look at my boots, then tilted my head back and watched the sun go down over some no-name creek in some forgotten part of South Carolina through the limbs of a cypress tree that few humans had probably ever taken time to notice. I lay there for quite a while, humming a Randy Travis song.

The sun disappeared, and the cypress limbs took on a shape and character of their own in the dark. Blue whined. I turned the truck around, and we pulled back out on the hardtop. I don't know how many miles we drove that night. Maybe three hundred. We were gone five or six hours, but it sure didn't feel that way. Time is like that in Digger. It stands still for some people.

We pulled back into town about nine o'clock. It was dark,

cool, and clear, and I could have driven for three more days. I still had five or six good songs in my head that could have kept me busy all night. Turning onto the drive, I laughed because it occurred to me then how much Maggie would have hated this truck. If you looked up the word "redneck" in the dictionary, you might see a picture of my truck. But she'd love that I love it.

I rounded the house and parked it next to the barn, then placed a pan beneath the engine so that tomorrow morning it could tell me if it was leaking oil. New engine or not, it was an old truck, and old trucks burn oil. It's just part of their language. You drive one long enough, and you begin to speak it. I lifted the tailgate and heard light footsteps on the gravel behind me.

"What is that?" Amos asked, pointing at my faded orange beauty.

"This," I said, still smiling with my hand affectionately resting on the tailgate, "is heaven."

Amos pushed his baseball cap back on his head and looked at me skeptically. "Please don't tell me you bought that thing at Jake's."

"Yup," I said, rubbing my hand over the rusted tailgate.

"What'd it cost you?" Amos said with his hands on his hips.

"I'm not saying. All I'll say is that Jake cut me a fair deal, and I agreed to pay him every month for the next two years."

"Dylan." Amos tilted his head sideways. "Did you pay that boy more than his asking price?"

"Now, Amos, what makes you think I'd do a fool thing like that?"

"Just answer my question."

I looked into the bed of the truck. "The purchase of this vehicle was a private financial transaction between Mr. Powers and me . . . "

Blue lay in the back with his paws covering up his eyes.

". . . the details of which I am not at liberty to discuss."

"Dylan, you are dumb as dirt!" Amos turned and walked down my drive, shaking his head.

I walked inside, grabbed the jar of peanut butter and a bagel, and then walked back outside, where I put down the tailgate and sat in the bed of the truck with Blue.

After Blue and I finished off the jar of peanut butter, I went back inside and put on my PJs. Which meant taking off my new jeans and leaving my boxer shorts on. I built a fire and sat down, flame-watching with Blue. An activity he was fond of and something we had done a lot lately. While I was mesmerized by the flames, it dawned on me that I needed to get the mail. I walked down the driveway to the mailbox in my boxers. It was cold, but who was gonna see me? This is the boondocks. You heard the man: "Egypt"!

I opened the box, fished around in the dark, and pulled out two envelopes. I walked back up the drive, and by the porch light I saw that the return address on the first read *Thentwhistle.* As I ran my finger beneath the tab and tore open the letter, the hair stood up on the back of my neck and sent chill bumps down my arms. I'd been expecting it, and no, I had no way of paying Maggie's bills other than mortgaging the farm. I opened the letter, prepared for the worst.

Dear Mr. Styles,

It is my duty to inform you that the current bill for your wife's complete and ongoing care since her admission is $227,753.87.

The size of the number took a few minutes to register. I looked across the farm, Nanny's house, Papa's fields, and I knew I had to let it go. I could never make payments on that type of mortgage. Life was about to become real different. I read on:

Secondly, and it truly is with great pleasure that I inform you: Hospital administration has just notified me that an anonymous donor has unexpectedly paid your bill in full and requested that all future bills be forwarded to an address other than yours for the duration of Maggie's stay with us. If you have any further questions, or I can be of any help at all, please call.

Respectfully,
Jason Thentwhistle

P.S. Dylan, I sincerely regret the timing of our previous conversation and wish you and Maggie all the best.

It took me about a half a second to determine the identity of the anonymous donor. That was just like Bryce; his actions always spoke louder than his words. And get a load of old Thentwhistle. Maybe he wasn't as smug as I'd accused him of being.

The second letter was less formal and addressed to *Professor.* I recognized Koy's handwriting.

Dear Professor,

I leave tomorrow for Spelman. I can start classes in the spring semester. I never thought I'd get out of this cesspool. Now that I'm leaving, it ain't all that bad. I did a lot of dying in Digger. Lately, I've done some living too. Living and dying—it's just a choice.

One thing I do know is that death is wrapped all around you like a blanket. You've been dealt a terrible hand, and in spite of it—or because of it—you live. You're the livingest person I ever met. When you walk around, something inside you seeps out of your pores and screams, "I'm alive!" and "I'm not dying today!" It's electric, and people feel it. They know you're coming around the corner because something in them rises up to meet whatever it is that you got.

I can't quite put my finger on it. Maybe it's hope, maybe it's love, but those words fall down. They don't describe that thing that is you. I wish I could talk with your wife, because I think maybe she knows. Maybe she's got the secret—the key—and then maybe I'd know.

I hope you don't mind, but I went to see your wife last night. I walked into her room with the lights off—the light of her heartbeat bouncing off the wall—sat down next to her bed, held her hand, and let my tears fall into her fingers.

Professor, I swear, so help me God, if I could I would walk into that hospital room, take off my skin, and give her me, I would. I'd strip before the devil himself, but life doesn't work that way.

My insides hurt pretty bad when I think about that clinic, what I did to my little girl, and what fate did to your son. That won't ever go away. There will always be two tombstones. But here today, right now, I'm living, and you did that. I was carrying a whole bottle full of pills, and I didn't eat them because you turned the corner, walked up to me, and breathed life into me when I didn't want any air. All I wanted to do was swallow.

Professor, you don't know it, but you introduced me to me. This life needs people who stand in the ditch and argue with God because the rest of us are either too scared or too proud. I don't really like all I see in the mirror, but I'm beginning to think that the girl behind the glasses is worth digging into. Maybe I'll take them off one day.

Koy

I folded the letter and placed it back in the envelope, and I realized that I was still standing on the porch in my boxers. I went back inside and sat by the fire with Blue, where I reread the letter five times. When the coals grew powdery white, I slipped on my new boots, grabbed my sleeping bag, and walked out to the truck. I cranked it, left the lights off, and idled down to the river. After parking on the bluff, Blue and I hopped in the back and curled up in my sleeping bag. I couldn't count the stars. My eyes wouldn't let me.

chapter thirty-two

I SHOWERED AND SPENT MOST OF NEW YEAR'S DAY on the porch. Thinking. Sleeping some. Rocking some. I missed Maggie's black-eyed peas. I don't know if I missed the peas themselves, the smell, the anticipation and taste of the peas, or the sight of Maggie wrapped in an apron, covered in flour and messing up the kitchen. Anyway, something was missing.

It may seem odd, and it was, but all day I had been thinking about Pinky. Once I got my nerve up, I got off my rocker, jumped down from the porch, and figured it was time to fish or cut bait.

I grabbed my bucket, filled it full of corn, and stepped into the stall. Pinky immediately grunted and banged against the opposite side.

"All right, girl," I said, teasing her with the bucket, "isn't it about time you and I got to know one another?"

Pinky snorted, crapped, smeared it across her buttocks with her tail, and kicked her stall.

I closed the gate, put the corn bucket down next to me, and squatted some fifteen feet in front of her. "I mean, think about it. How long have I been feeding you? Three years? Maybe four? Haven't I always taken care of you? Look around you." I pointed to her latest litter of twelve little pigs, only two weeks old and all vying for a chance to suckle. "Look at all that I've let you do. This place is full of pigs, and that's all because I feed you. You're a sow-shaped Hoover. All you do is eat."

I patted the bucket and sprinkled two or three kernels of corn in front of me. "Today is a new day. You and me, we're getting friendly." I patted the bucket again. "So come over here, and let's shake ears, or snouts, or whatever it is that people and pigs shake when they're getting friendly. I'll rub you 'tween the ears."

Pinky grunted and blew snot out her nose.

"Nope, that's not good enough," I said, wiping my face with my shirtsleeve. "That will not do. I'm talking about a full down-the-back-of-the-head-and-ear-rub. Snorting won't get it. Now get your big self busy, and come on over here."

Pinky swaggered back and forth and desuckled a couple of little ones. They were as filthy as she was. I needed a pressure washer. And the smell? Horrible.

"All right, you can swagger all you want, but you are not getting one kernel of this corn until you come over here and apologize for being so dang mean and ugly to me." I twisted a kernel of corn back and forth between my thumb and index finger. "And don't think grunting and blowing your nose in my face is going to get it, 'cause it ain't, as my students say. I ain't meeting you halfway. You got to come all the way, and I got all day. So, when you get hungry, I'll be squatting right here. It's your call."

Pinky banged her shoulders against the side of the stall, and her nose got wide and showed wet.

"Come on." I held the corn in the palm of my hand.

That pig then lowered her head and charged at me full speed, detaching six piglets from their faucets and flinging dirt everywhere as she charged. A half second later, all three-hundred-plus pounds of Pinky, led by her snout, hit me in the abdomen and rocketed me against the side of the stall. My head hit the top beam of the gate, the room blurred, and I found myself lying flat on my back, looking up at the rafters.

When my eyes opened, I was shoulder deep in pig crap. It was in my hair, and I think, in the cracks of my ears. Sitting up, I heard somebody outside the stall. I lifted my head, looked through the boards, and saw Amos rolling on the barn floor, holding his stomach.

"Oh, stop! Don't make me laugh!" Amos's black face looked almost red, and tears were streaming out the corners of his eyes.

I sat up in the middle of Pinky's stall and flung my fingers to get the clumps of manure and hay off them, and then cleaned out my ears. Inside the stall, Pinky finished her triumphant, tail-up victory parade, then walked over and began sniffing and licking my face. Looking at me eye-level, she nudged my leg with her nose, dug a little hole with her hoof next to my leg, and lay down in the hole. With a loud sigh, she laid her head on top of my thigh and released a deep, snot-blowing breath. Twelve little pigs then surrounded her, and consequently me, and began fighting for a teat.

Amos pulled himself off the ground and lifted himself up by the rungs of Pinky's stall. Wiping his eyes and catching his breath, he said, "D.S., you know . . . " He began laughing again. "You know you're covered in pig crap?"

I looked down, patted Pinky on the head, picked up one of her little ones, and held it like a kitten. "Yeah, well . . . clean don't always look it."

Amos rubbed his eyes again, still chuckling, and said, "Well, Mr. Greenjeans, when you get cleaned up, and I think that's probably a good idea, maybe even a priority, there's somebody at the hospital who wants to see you."

Accountants, doctors, and other constipated pains-in-the-butt came to mind. "Who?" I said, wrinkling my brow. "If they want to talk about the bill, I just got a letter from Jason Thentwhistle . . . "

Amos held his chin in his hands. His eyes looked down on me, and his teeth showed pearly white. Then his bottom lip quivered, and he broke into a smile.

MY SPEEDOMETER WAS PEGGED AT JUST OVER ONE HUNDRED miles an hour as I jumped the railroad tracks on my way to the hospital. The engine was whining as all four tires came off the ground on the other side of the tracks.

Amos followed in his Crown Vic, flashing blue lights, tooting his horn, and shouting over his PA system, "Slow down, you fool!"

Blue lay sprawled and whining on the floorboard, covering one eye with his paw. When I turned the corner and crested the hill that led up to Bryce's trailer, Bryce stood piping at his gate in full regalia, decked out with all his ribbons. He stood, feet together, red-faced, and blowing for all he was worth, but I was going too fast to hear what he was playing.

The hospital was a zoo when I arrived. I bounded up the stairs, tripped on the top step, and slid three rooms down on the janitor's nicely waxed floor. Blue jumped over me, disappearing down the hall and into Maggie's room, where a crowd stood looking in. I began to raise myself off the floor, but the sound stopped me—a sound that I had heard only once in almost five months.

The last time I had heard Maggs's voice, she was crying and screaming, "No, God! Please, no," as the doctor pulled the sheet over my son. Now I sprawled paralyzed on the floor, listening. The voice that had said "I love you" ten thousand times, the voice that said "Dylan Styles!" the voice that whispered "Let's go swimming" had cracked back into the world and filled my empty soul.

Moments before, I lived in a world where wisteria snaked across my son's grave as he rotted beneath a cement slab; where Vietnam Vets inhaled beer to help them forget the day they wiped Vicks salve in their noses so they wouldn't have to smell the bodies as they zipped up the bags; where a no-good farmer bathed in a cornfield but couldn't wash the blood clean; where snow fell on iced-over railroad tracks; where used-car salesmen robbed old women with inflated prices and double-digit interest rates; where little boys peed in the baptistry and pastors strutted like roosters; where evil men tied innocent girls to trees, stripped them, raped them, and left to them die; where students cheated and burnt-out professors scribbled useless information on sweat-stained chalkboards and couldn't care less; where not-so-innocent girls paid $265 for scar tissue; where the most precious thing I had ever known lay listless, scarred, childless, and dying in a nondescript hospital room in the armpit of South Carolina.

But then came Maggie's voice.

I looked around and found myself in a world where wisteria blooms in December; where a Scottish piper sings through his pipes; where used-car salesmen open car doors for little old ladies; where pastors dunk themselves with scared children who emerge clean and hungry; where students say, "He'd call it cheating"; where not-so-innocent girls carry receipts in their pockets and write books that will be read by Oprah; where a no-good professor bathes in the river, burns dead cornfields, and basks in moonlight and flames; and where my wife speaks.

I now lived in a world where the dead danced.

I walked into my wife's room, and there, under the window and glowing like the sun, lay Maggie—her big brown eyes meeting mine for the first time in so many months.

Breathing heavily and fumbling with my hands, I didn't know what to say. *Where do I start? Am I the same Dylan that she fell in love with, and is she the same Maggie? How deep are the scars? Are we the same us?* Standing there in my new boots and covered in pig smear, I didn't know who to be until I knew where she was. I needed Maggs to tell me who to be—because that would tell me where she was, and most importantly, who we were.

I closed the door, knelt down next to Maggs's bed, and watched her cracked lips quiver. I slid my hand beneath hers and searched her eyes, aching to know and be known. She blinked a lazy blink, tilted her head, and smiled.

afterward

It was midnight when we heard the pipes. We crawled out of bed, slipped on some jeans, and walked hand in hand along the tree line. Standing under the overhang of oaks, next to my son's grave, was Bryce, decked out in full military regalia, ruddy-cheeked and blowing so hard the veins on his neck stood out like rose vines. He was somewhere in the middle of "It Is Well with My Soul" when we walked up. A gentle breeze skirted along the bank and fanned over us as we stood facing the river. Our long shadows ran down to the river and disappeared into the water.

Without a pause, Bryce slipped into "Amazing Grace." The music went through us like the morning sun, warm and glowing. As the last hollow note of his pipes echoed off the river and faded into the distance, Maggs walked over and kissed him on the cheek. Bryce stood rigid, heels together, at attention, his eyes fixed on the horizon. He was wearing a green beret, his military dress shirt, and a chest spangled and twinkling with medals. Everything, from his hat to shirt to kilt to socks, was clean, pressed, and worn for the first time in a long time. Without saying a word he turned, began blowing, and disappeared like an angel into the darkness. As we stood underneath the canopy of oaks, the pipes faded away downriver.

Maggie slid her hand under mine and tugged on my arm. The air was cool, but nothing compared to the previous year. I stood on the bank while she ran in front of me and climbed the sandy bluff. In the moonlight, she stripped off her jeans and stood silhouetted against the moon, which formed a halo around her body and threaded her hair with silver. I watched, waist deep in the water, mesmerized. Enchanted. The slender calves, the small curve of her lower back, the graceful shoulders. She skipped to the edge and took a swan dive off the bluff, splashing into the water a few feet away from me. The ripples lapped against my stomach and brought chill bumps to my skin. When she broke the surface, and that black water dripped off her nose and ears, a sweet and sneaky smile creased her face.

Half a dozen wood ducks soared overhead, brushing the tops of the cypress trees with their wing tips. An owl hooted low and hauntingly; farther north along the river, a lone bluetick hound sounded a single lonely ping somewhere in the Salk. A mile south of us, the sound of singing, pungent with joy and ripe with smiles, rose like a flume of steam from Pastor John's church steeple. Maggie and I swam close together, swaying with the slow rhythm of the river while the echoes of voices showered down on us like a warm summer rain. Beneath it all I had only one thought, one need.

Lord, I'm begging You. Please give me sixty-two more years with this woman.

acknowledgments

SOMEWHERE IN DECEMBER OF 1995, I BEGAN THINKING about this story. I was driving through one of the bridge tunnels in Hampton Roads on my way to UPS, where I worked in the early morning preload. It being the Christmas season, I think we had to clock in before 3 A.M. It may have been earlier, but I've tried to block that out. I had been in graduate school at Regent University, and in order to remain focused on school, I had suppressed my stories for so long that they had begun to rebel and bubble their way to the surface. Cream does that.

Let me interject one thing—my graduate school experience was phenomenal. One lightbulb after another clicked on and lit my path. I wouldn't trade it for the world. Three men in particular contributed to this, and I am greatly indebted to each—Doug Tarpley, Michael Graves, and Bob Schihl. Guys, thanks for a seat at the table. My hat's off to you.

At any rate, I remember driving through the tunnel and could hold it back no longer. Remember the grammar school project where the kid pours the vinegar over the baking soda in the papier-mâché volcano? As I was nearing the bottom of the tunnel, one scene erupted and flashed across the screen on the back of my eyelids: a man standing in a ditch, screaming at God. I knew he was cold, alone, and at the end of himself. Much like Crusoe, he was shipwrecked, a castaway in need of Friday to rescue him off the island. *The Dead Don't Dance* grew from that early-morning flash, or hallucination, as the case may have been. In later drives, mostly through the back roads of South Carolina, I saw a beautiful girl and somehow knew her name was Maggie, a handsome black man who looked like Mr. Clean with a badge, and a farmhouse with a rusted tin roof—one I knew well.

The path from idea to trade paper has been, as with other first novels, a graveled road marred with washouts, blind corners, stop-and-go traffic, and U-turns. Yes, I've worked hard, early mornings, late nights, stoplights, but that is the least of it. Many writers work hard. I, and this book, are in large part a product of other people's unselfishness. People who gave me a chance. Who believed in me. Without them, I'd not be here, and you'd not be reading this book.

I won't backtrack to my youth, but I need to start by thanking one of the finest writers I've ever met: John Dyson. John worked for *Reader's Digest,* writing some 160-plus articles and more than twenty-three books over a three-decade career. He's a writer's writer, a true craftsman and wordsmith. Not to mention a pretty good sailor. I won't bore you with the story, but John was instrumental in my first work as a writer. You know that process of smelting, where the silversmith heats the silver and removes the dross? John did that to me. Painful too. Somewhere in that furnace, he taught me what good writing looks like, and maybe more importantly, sounds like. Somewhere early in our work together, he told me "Charles, an editor is one who walks back through the battlefield and shoots the wounded." He was right, and true to form, came with both barrels blazing—though, in my case, that's not always bad. As a dwarf running among giants, I stand with one foot squarely atop John's broad shoulder. John, thanks for allowing me the view, for letting me whisper in your ear and ask the same irritating questions over and over, and for not brushing me off your lapel.

While one foot is resting on John's shoulder, the other is balancing on the tall shoulders of Davis Bunn. About two years ago, I had come close to my wits' end. I had finished the book, bought the *Writer's Guide* like all writers are supposed to, and sent out a couple hundred dollars' worth of manuscripts and postage to as many agents and publishers as I could find. Soon my mailbox began filling up with some of the nicest letters of rejection I've ever received. Each one was so kind and so completely rejecting that for about eight months, I quit going to the mailbox. During that time, Christy would walk in, drop the letter on my desk, kiss me on the cheek, and say, "You're not a reject to me." It was little consolation.

At any rate, Davis—who's written some sixty-plus novels—attended a party in D.C. and got cornered by my well-meaning but not-to-be-refused grandfather. Looking for an exit but hounded by my mercilessly pestering grandparents, Davis relented and broke his never-read-a-first-novel rule. A few days later, he invited me to lunch, where he fed me a sandwich, made two quick phone calls, and befriended me. Something I was in need of. When I got home, I had received two e-mails and one voice-mail asking to see this manuscript. A week later, I had an agent. And six weeks later, a publisher.

Granted, I'd not have had those if the work couldn't stand on its own, but Davis helped open the door. One I'd been bashing my head against. Maybe he recognized the flat spot on my forehead, and it reminded him of his own. Davis is a true professional who's taught me much about this business, how to navigate it, and what to do when the storms come—because they will. Davis, thank you for the view, the conversation, the friendship, and for relenting.

Davis led me to the office of a true statesman, one of the real patriarchs in this business, Sealy Yates. Sealy introduced me to a young bulldog in his office named Chris Ferebee. Chris read my novel over the weekend and called me on Monday night. "Charles, I'd like to help you get this book published."

It took me a few minutes to recover from that phone call. I'm not sure my neighbors ever have. Chris made a few suggestions,

I made a few corrections, and six weeks later, Thomas Nelson offered to publish my work. Chris, you're a true counselor, sounding board, ally, and friend.

Chris sent my work to an editor at Nelson named Jenny Baumgartner. Jenny read it and offered to buy me breakfast at this pancake restaurant in Nashville where they serve these fantastic buckwheat pancakes. We struck up a conversation, and not long after, Nelson bought this book, and Jenny became my editor, and maybe more importantly, my advocate at Nelson. Jenny has a great eye for fiction, a remarkable ability to take something good and make it better, and a unique talent to communicate all that into a form that even a writer can understand. I am also indebted to the team around her: Jonathan Merkh, Mike Hyatt, and Allen Arnold. To the rest of the team at Nelson and the many people that I've never met who have worked so selflessly, from designers to salespeople, please accept my sincere thanks.

Throughout this eight-year roller-coaster ride, my family and friends at home have helped me maintain my perspective and keep me off medication, and out of a room with padded walls.

Without getting too sappy, I'd like to thank: Johnny and Dave. True brothers. When I scraped my knees, you guys—at different times and in differing ways—picked me up, brushed me off, and helped me strap my helmet back on. My in-laws, Alice and O'Neal. Thank you for your encouragement and for not disowning me when I said, "I'm working on a book." My sisters, Grace, Annie, and Berry. You all read my stuff and told me it was good even when it wasn't. Thanks for lying to me. Keep it up. My grandparents, T.C. and Granny. When you asked to read my work, I was a bit worried that you'd find it foolish. "All that education and he's doing what?" You didn't, and what's more, you became two of my best cheerleaders. Thanks for cornering Davis. Mom and Dad. Thanks for your sacrifices, for loving each other, and for teaching me to run with reckless abandon and then letting me do it.

Our boys—Charlie, John T., and Rives. Thanks for running in here and hugging my legs or asking me to play catch or go fishing or build Legos or wrestle at regular intervals. I needed it. Still do. Always will. Most importantly, thank you for praying for my books. This is proof the Lord really does answer us, and I think you three had a lot to do with it.

Christy. Phew! I'm worn out. How about you? Ready for a vacation? You've earned it. Anywhere you want to go, just as soon as we pay off the credit card. How you kept your sanity through ten years of marriage, graduate school, three boys, and my dreams is a mystery. You amaze me. People ask me how I created Maggie, but I didn't have to look very far. She was walking around my house, digging in the yard, tucking in my boys, whispering in my ear, holding my hand, and sticking her foot in my back. Thank you for believing in me and hoping with me, because I know there were many days in this process when I was less than lovable.

Lord. What can I say that You haven't already heard? Thank You for this, for the people I've listed, and for hanging in there with a guy like me. My cup runs over.

about the author

CHARLES MARTIN earned his B.A. in English from Florida State University, and his M.A. in journalism and Ph.D. in communication from Regent University. He served one year at Hampton University as an adjunct professor in the English department and as a doctoral fellow at Regent. In 1999, he left a career in business to pursue his writing. He and his wife, Christy, live a stone's throw from the St. John's River in Jacksonville, Florida, with their three boys: Charlie, John T., and Rives. When he's not writing, Charles fishes with his boys, works in the yard with Christy, coaches T-ball, and kneels by his boys' beds at night. Right now, the boys are praying for two things: a boat "with space for a cooler, three or four people, and five or six rods" because they're not catching any fish off the neighbor's dock, and "Daddy's book." Charles is currently working on his second novel, which will be published by WestBow Press in March 2005.

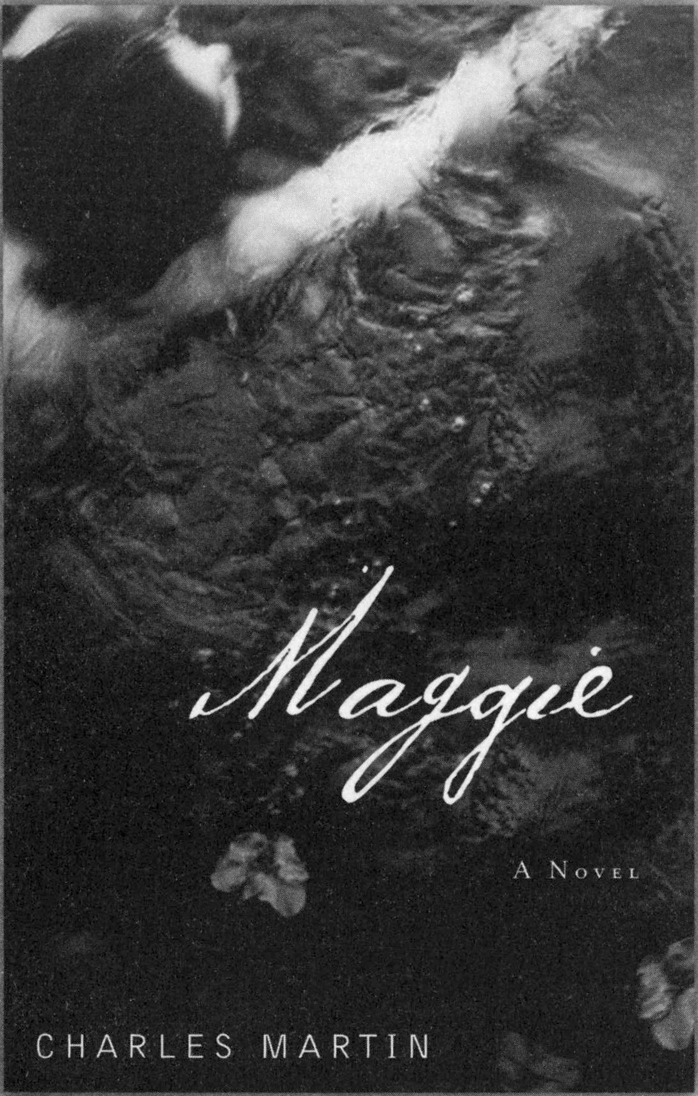

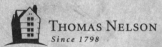